Contents

Languages and Their Speakers

Languages and Their Speakers

Timothy Shopen

Australian National University

under the auspices of the Center for Applied Linguistics

University of Pennsylvania Press
Philadelphia

Originally published 1979 by Winthrop Publishers
Copyright © 1979 Winthrop Publishers
Paperback edition published 1987 by the University of Pennsylvania Press by
arrangement with the Center for Applied Linguistics
All rights reserved
Printed in the United States of America on acid-free paper

10 9 8 7 6 5

Published by
University of Pennsylvania Press
Philadelphia, Pennsylvania 19104-4011

Library of Congress Cataloging-in-Publication Data

Languages and their speakers
    Reprint. Originally published: Cambridge, Mass.: Winthrop Publishers, © 1979
    Includes bibliographies.
    ISBN 0-8122-1250-9 (pbk, alk. paper)
    1. Language and languages. 2. Language and culture. I. Shopen, Timothy
[P106.L318   1987]
401'.9   87-6014

Photo credits: p. 11, Jane R. Wattenberg; p. 58, Scott Jackson; p. 240, John Dominis,
Life Magazine, © 1958 Time Inc.; p. 245, *Japan* 1971 (no. 2); 279, Qantas

Illustrations

Introduction

Languages and Their Speakers is complemented by a second volume entitled *Languages and Their Status*. Both volumes are written for a general audience, and the readers are led to become involved in learning some linguistics as well as something about languages and their cultures. Each chapter is an essay on what it means to be a speaker of a particular language, in this volume Jacaltec, Maninka, Malagasy, Guugu Yimidhirr, and Japanese, and in the companion volume Mohawk, Hua, Russian, Cape York Creole, Swahili, and Chinese. For each language the basic question we pose is "What kind of language is it among the languages of the world?" At the same time we look at speakers and examine the way languages gain their use and subsistence among them. In this volume the essays show how people know their languages; in the companion volume the essays present the social forces that influence the ways the languages develop and indeed determine their very survival.

If we abstract languages from historical process to look at them in a single instant in time, and if we look only at the languages and not at the speakers, then much of the internal structure of each language can be viewed as an autonomous system, independent of anything outside. Important symmetries emerge and meaningful comparisons can be made in these terms between distant and unrelated languages. But when we take an interest in how language behavior varies and changes and what its meaning, value, and function are in a cultural scheme, we have to see a language both as a structural system and as a functional tool. The pure grammatical studies are an input to the broader inquiry.

In this volume we consider how speakers know their languages—know them as grammatical systems and know them as part of a cultural fabric. In the first chapter, Colette Grinevald Craig discusses the nature of linguistic field work as she narrates her experience doing field work on Jacaltec, a Mayan language spoken in Guatemala. She describes some of the outstanding characteristics of Jacaltec and illuminates the way in which a speaker views a language as opposed to the way a linguist views it when working out an analysis of its grammatical structure.

The remaining four chapters all discuss what one has to know to be a good speaker of a language. They all demonstrate that to become a good speaker of a particular language, one has to know not only its grammar but also the principles that determine the appropriate use of the language in various cultural contexts.

Charles Bird and Timothy Shopen describe Maninka, a Niger-Congo language spoken widely in West Africa. They assume the role of a newcomer to a Maninka village and tell what that person will have to learn to become a good speaker of the language; they discuss this in terms of grammar and in terms of aspects of style and verbal art that affect everyday communication.

Edward Keenan and Elinor Ochs write about Malagasy, an Austronesian language and the language of Madagascar. They explore in some detail the highly developed system in Malagasy for making the information content of sentences clear; at the same time they describe the constraints that the culture places on the communication of information with illustrations drawn from their experience living in a Malagasy village.

John Haviland presents a chapter on Guugu Yimidhirr, an Australian language. He gives a grammatical sketch of the language, placing emphasis on the large amount of meaning packed into Guugu Yimidhirr words. He then proceeds to show how the grammatical devices of the language are used in a remarkable system of deferential speech registers, where for different kinship relationships between speaker and listener almost every word in a sentence can change. More than that, he demonstrates that not only do social relationships influence language use, but also that the use of language very often determines the social relationships.

The final chapter is by Kyoko Inoue on Japanese, the only language in the volume with a long-standing tradition of literacy. Consequently, this chapter tells much more about the cultural history of the language than do the other chapters, and one sees that the experiences of the past generations contribute to what one has to know to be a good speaker of a language. The author explains the writing system, grammatical characteristics involved in conveying truth value meaning, and then principles of structure and language use concerned with the speaker's perspective and with social relationships.

ACKNOWLEDGMENTS

I wish to acknowledge the generous support of the National Endowment for the Humanities, the Center for Applied Linguistics, and the Australian National University for the development of *Languages and Their Speakers* and *Languages and Their Status*. Peggy Good and Peg Griffin, formerly of the Center for Applied Linguistics, were unfailing sources of help and encouragement. The conception of these two volumes would not have been possible without my partnership with Charles Bird when we wrote what was to be the prototypic chapter for the two volumes, "*Maninka*." When we had written the chapter, I circulated it and proposed a series organized around the notion of what it means to be a speaker of a language. The response from the people who have contributed chapters has surpassed my best expectations, and I am grateful to them for all I have learned while working with their manuscripts.

My colleagues Peter Austin, Bob Dixon, and Mary Haas, and my wife Agnes Shopen have been my best critics, but others have made important input to this volume as well, including Anthony Alfonso, Cynthia Allen, David Bradley, Rosemary Cameron, Terry Crowley, Tamsin Donaldson, Bill Foley, John Harris, John Penhallurick, Michael Ryan, and Leoni Strickland. Paul O'Connell of Winthrop Publishers has given valuable editorial advice and support; Pat Torelli has done excellent work as production editor. Val Lyon of the Geography Department of the School of General Studies at the Australian National University has provided expert and artistic help in the preparation of maps. My thanks to all.

Timothy Shopen
Canberra, Australia

Preface to the 1987 Edition

When the Center for Applied Linguistics asked Timothy Shopen to edit a set of books on language for students with widely varying backgrounds, our goal was to help teachers introduce their students to the diversity of language and to the intimate and complex relationship between language and society. *Languages and Their Speakers* was one result of that request and, judging by the enthusiastic response from teachers of anthropology, English, and linguistics all over the United States, the book has succeeded beyond our most optimistic expectations. When the volume went out of print, the steady stream of requests for it and the pressure from teachers to reissue it convinced us of its continuing value. We are, therefore, delighted to be able to make this book available again, through the University of Pennsylvania Press, in a paperback edition. We hope that, through *Languages and Their Speakers* and its companion volume, *Languages and Their Status* which is also being reissued in paperback, new generations of students will experience the fascination of the study of one of man's most unique and important behaviors.   -

The Center for Applied Linguistics

I

Jacaltec
Field Work in Guatemala

Colette Grinevald Craig

INTRODUCTION

Jacaltec is one of the twenty-five languages of the Mayan family still spoken today. Its speakers number approximately 20,000, and they live in the northwest corner of Guatemala. Guatemalan society, in general, is divided into two separate groups, the Ladinos and the Indians. The Ladinos are for the most part descendants of the Spaniards; they speak Spanish and rule the country. More than half the country's population of five million are Indians, which is the largest proportion of Indian population in all the Latin American countries. They are descendants of the Maya civilization, essentially an agricultural society. They speak Mayan languages and to some extent Spanish when in contact with Ladinos.

In this presentation, the Jacaltec language will be considered from three different viewpoints: that of a field worker, that of a general linguist, and that of the native Jacaltec speakers. The nature of field work is the topic of the first part, including a discussion of the methods involved in investigating languages through native informants. The second part is a grammatical sketch of Jacaltec. It is focused on three features of the language that may be unfamiliar to speakers of English and other European languages but that are common to many languages

Colette Grinevald Craig, a French citizen, has lived in Algeria, France, the United States, and Guatemala. She has taught Spanish in France, has studied and teaches linguistics in the United States, and has been taking field trips to Guatemala since 1969. She teaches at the University of Oregon, Eugene, while continuing her research on the structure of Mayan languages.

of the world, occurring in African and Asian languages as well as in other Native American languages. The three characteristics of Jacaltec are its systems of case marking, directionals, and noun classification. The third part is a discussion of what it means to be a speaker of Jacaltec and deals with the attitudes and beliefs that Jacaltec people have toward their own and other peoples' languages.

1 FIELD METHODS

1.1 **Field Work**

The expression "field work" refers to scientific investigations carried out at the primary source of information. It is a term that has particular prominence in studies of human behavior and the artifacts of human cultures: for an anthropologist and a sociologist it means an investigation among the populations they are studying; for an archeologist it means an investigation of archeological sites. For a linguist it means the investigation of a language directly from its native speakers.

In order to carry out this type of research, the investigator must "go to the field" to be in direct contact with the source of information. In this context, the word "field" has the general meaning of "natural setting." It designates any type of location ranging from an urban center to a desert, from lush jungle to arid mountains. For example, anthropologists can do field work in lush rural Samoa or cold inhospitable Arctic land, archeologists in a desert of the Middle East or in the heart of an Italian city, and sociologists in the overcrowded suburbs of Rio de Janeiro, the ghettos of Chicago, or the suburbs of New York City. Going to the field usually implies an expedition of some importance, settling somewhere for a stay of a few weeks to a few years, although one can do field work only a few blocks away in the same city, a few hours at a time.

Linguistic field work consists of collecting material on a language directly from the native speakers. The language itself may be written or unwritten, partly described, or still unknown. It may be a thriving language or a language close to extinction. Although the expression "field work" traditionally evokes exotic and faraway scenery, it can also be used to refer to the investigation of very familiar languages such as French or Spanish, whenever this is done through the interviewing of native speakers.

What all linguistic field work situations have in common is that the information is provided by native speakers, generally referred to as "informants." Depending upon the circumstances, informants may be young adults or very old people, literate or illiterate, monolingual or fluent in a second language also known to the linguist. As for working conditions, they may easily be imagined as ranging from comfortable to precarious indigenous habitats.

There are some good reasons for people to go into other cultures to do field work, and in particular to study their languages. Although particular cultures and languages vary in many details, there is a unity to human behavior that field workers aim at uncovering. Finding out what all languages have in common, as well as how they can vary, will give us insight into an important aspect of human nature.

What follows is an account of the field work experience of the author, an American-trained linguist who set out to write a grammar of Jacaltec. We will retrace her steps from her preparatives before leaving for the field to her settling to work in a highland village of Guatemala where she spent over a year. The native informants with whom she worked were bilingual young adults who spoke Jacaltec and Spanish, a language in which she herself was fluent. Jacaltec, the language she investigated, had been partially described several years earlier by another linguistic field worker. As with all the other Mayan languages of the country, Jacaltec could be characterized as a thriving spoken language. Although it had been reduced to writing in recent years by missionaries, only a handful of native speakers were literate in it. In the sense that native speakers did not write it for their own purposes, it was an 'unwritten' language.

1.1.1 *Preparation for the Field* The goal of this field work expedition was to gather material for a descriptive grammar of Jacaltec that would be of interest both to the specialists of Mayan languages for comparative studies of Mayan languages and to general linguists for a better understanding of the nature of language.

The preparatory work before leaving for the field consists of establishing in as particular a way as possible the goals of the research and learning as much as one can about the language to be studied. One sets up hypotheses about what one can expect to find, hypotheses that will be modified and augmented as the investigation proceeds. All of one's past experience as a linguist will play a role in this process, but now one concentrates on learning in detail about the language and the family of languages to which it belongs.

Important perspective can be gained from information about other languages in the same family. To say that a set of languages belongs to the same family is to say that each was originally a single language, the way we know that French, Spanish, Portuguese, Italian, etc. were originally variants of a single Latin language. The more similar they are, the more recently one can assume that they split apart, and the more likely it is that insight into one of them will suggest something about the structure of the others.

There was more material available for the investigation of the

Jacaltec language than is often the case for field work on 'unwritten' languages. There was a grammatical sketch written by anthropologists in the twenties; a recent study of the sound system, word formation, and basic syntax written by a linguist; a didactic (teach-yourself–type) grammar written by a native speaker who had been the informant of the priest and the linguist; and texts produced by missionaries—translations of the New Testament and health pamphlets.

In view of the scant information available until recently on most of the languages of the western corner of Guatemala where Jacaltec is located, the exact relationship of Jacaltec to the neighboring languages is today still a matter of discussion. The discussion evolves around the task of determining the boundaries between independent languages and their dialects within the Kanjobalan branch of the family.

Figure 1.1 shows the position of Jacaltec within the family of Mayan languages.

Some of the better known languages are Yucatec Maya, Cakchiquel, and Quiché, for which we possess documents dating back to the early period of the Colonization in the form of treatises, vocabularies, and sermons written by missionaries. Of great importance are the three collections of the *Books of Chilam Balam* for Yucatec Maya, the *Popol Vuh* for Quiché, and the *Annals of the Cakchiquels* for Cakchiquel. These writings were compiled in the sixteenth century by native speakers who recorded the beliefs, legends, and history of their people.

Partly because of the existence of such old documentation, most of the modern literature available on Mayan languages deals with questions of historical linguistics—such as the genetic classification of the languages and the reconstruction of Proto-languages—rather than with descriptive linguistics.

1.1.2 *Final Preparatives and Worries* As time of departure nears, however, the most overwhelming concerns are nonlinguistic. Suddenly the investigation of the grammar of Jacaltec sounds like an easier task than it did before. Anxiety centers now on final decisions and guesses about the nature and the amount of equipment necessary and questions about the weather and living conditions. Generally there are no answers to be found for these questions in a big North American city.

It is only reasonable to anticipate moments of discomfort and distress for which there is probably no better preparation than the will to keep happy and working. In a country like Guatemala, one has to be ready to work in the dampness of the rainy season on a steady diet of black beans, tortillas and coffee, sitting all day on hard straight chairs and spending part of the night working in the solitude of a hissing gas lamp. Together with the anxiety produced by the linguistic work itself, one will also have to deal from time to time with obsessive dreams of

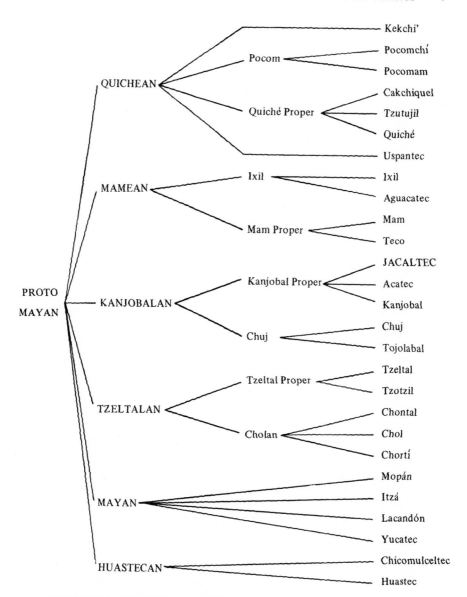

FIGURE 1.1 The Mayan Languages

being "back home," or taking a hot shower, or eating a huge green salad, or rambling on with a friend in one's own language.

But in field work, there is also the peace and beauty of the mountains, the slowing down to a more human pace of life, the encounters with new people, new smells, new tastes, and old forgotten values. One can also anticipate the rewarding moments to come—going to the market and understanding the chit-chat of the women, dropping in on a Jacaltec conversation in the bus to the amazement and delight of the travelers, and maybe even, some day, making a Jacaltec pun. Going to the field often means for the field worker finding a new home and making new friends, and later, back in a North American city, feeling homesick for that home and those friends, for the noise of the rain on a tin roof, for the smell of tortillas, and for the sounds of a language that has become familiar to the ear.

1.1.3   *Off to the Field*   Our destination is Jacaltenango, an important town in the northwest corner of the Guatemalan highlands, on the border of Mexico. After landing in Guatemala City, the first day is spent taking a bus ride to the town of Huehuetenango, at the foot of the Cuchumatanes mountains. From the city, the road winds through the highlands where the Mayan population is concentrated and crosses the lands of the Cakchiquels, the Quichés, and the Mams. The second part of the trip, from Huehuetenango to Jacaltenango, is becoming easier every year as the construction of roads continues. Over the last decade, the stretch from where the road ended to Jacaltenango has shortened from a long day's horse ride to a pleasant walk. Now in the dry season when the road is not washed out by the rains, the bus goes all the way to Jacaltenango. It takes about five hours on good runs to cover the distance from Huehuetenango to Jacaltenango, thirty miles as the crow flies. One dirt road circles west through lush coffee plantations and climbs the west slope of the mountain. The other one heads north from Huehuetenango to climb up to a moonlike plateau of inhospitable cold lands. Then suddenly, it dives down toward Jacaltenango at the edge of the flat from where the surrounding mountain ranges look like foothills. After hours of bad trail either way, one always experiences the same amazement upon reaching Jacaltenango and its white adobe buildings clustered at the edge of a formidable cliff.

The town is a very important center in the life of the Cuchumatanes mountains. Its market, hospital, and schools draw crowds from far away. The urban population is close to 5,000 and that of its *municipio* (township) nears 12,000. The population is composed mostly of Jacaltec Indians. A few Ladino families have come to work as schoolteachers, postmaster, or as other public officials; and families of Mam Indians from the cold and harsh lands of Todos Santos have settled at the edge of town.

The official language of the country, and the language of the school, is Spanish. Spanish is spoken around the school and on the main street where most Ladino families live and is now spreading to Indian households downtown. Jacaltec is the prominent language heard as one walks through the market, the hospital, the church, and as one wanders away from the main street. As is characteristic of bilingual situations, men are

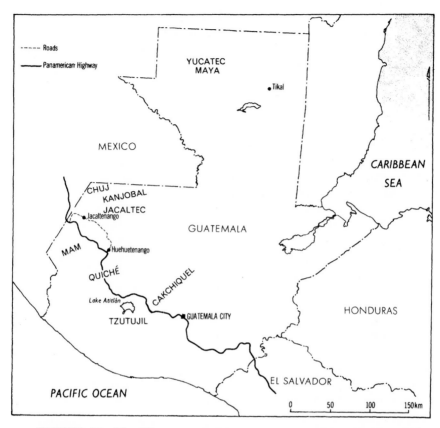

FIGURE 1.2 **The Way to Jacaltenango (with the location of some Mayan languages)**

more familiar than women with the dominant language, and the rate of bilingualism is rising through increased schooling, the use of radio, and army training.

1.1.4 *Settling Down* Upon arriving, the first task is to find lodging. In this particular case, the director of the school offered a room in his house—a rather big compound set on the main street and built around a courtyard. In this compound that year lived a family of eight, two Ladino schoolteachers from Huehuetenango, and the "gringa" linguist. Arrangements were made with the owner of the local "comedor" for meals to be shared with the single schoolteachers from out of town. Once desk, chairs, and filing boxes were ordered from a local carpenter, it was time to think about getting to work.

1.1.5 *Hiring Informants* The first essential step in the study of a language in the field is to locate and hire informants. When one is a new arrival and does not know anyone in the town, a good place to go and ask for names of possible informants is either a mission or a Peace Corp office, if there is either of these nearby. Most of the time, both missionaries and Peace Corps volunteers have themselves attempted to learn the language of the local population. They are aware, therefore, of the skills required of an informant and can suggest literate and bilingual individuals who may have worked for them. Somehow, field workers have to move with more caution when asking local people for suggestions as to who would be a good informant. The advice and suggestions they give may often reflect personal preferences, a desire of having a relative hired, or a common belief that people with more formal education and more prestige in the town are better candidates. Unfortunate ill-advised decisions may later cause strain in the relationship between the foreign linguist and the community.

What makes a good informant? The basic prerequisite is that the informant be an intelligent person with a good linguistic intuition. This means someone who is sensitive to the workings of language and who can convey to the linguist what nuances of meaning are, someone who likes his/her language and is proud of it, and someone who enjoys discovering together with the field worker its mechanisms, laws, and exceptions. In all cultures and societies, some people are good with language while other people have little curiosity about it or feel for it. Ideally, linguistic field workers look for undiscovered or ignored native linguists—people with whom they will share their interest in language and from whom they will slowly learn the secrets and beauties of the language.

In addition to being linguistically qualified, these informants must be available for reasonable periods of time, at best several hours a day. Whenever possible, they should be bilingual, conversant in a language also known to the linguist. Formal education is not an absolute criterion when choosing informants. Although literate persons may learn how to read and write their native language faster than illiterate ones, linguists must also consider the effect of a rigid, traditional, and often dogmatic education that may turn native speakers with longer schooling into inhibited or doctrinaire informants.

In this particular case, the two main informants hired to work on Jacaltec were a woman in her late thirties and a man in his early thirties. They were complementary informants. María Trinidad Montejo (hereafter referred to as T.M.) was a seamstress with no formal education but possessing intelligence and a striking independence of mind. Unmarried and very outspoken, she was considered by the community to be a strong character. She was hired full time, at first mainly to be a language teacher and guide around the community, and later, as she acquired typing and reading skills, as a linguistic informant.

Antonio Feliciano Mendez (hereafter referred to as A.M.) had many years of formal education and a long experience as a specialist of the Jacaltec language, being one of the main translators for the parish. He was also the informant of Christopher Day, the first linguist to work on the language. He was hired part time while working for the parish and full time when not employed elsewhere. He was very skilled at handling data.

Three men in their late twenties and early thirties were hired part time. They had all worked for either the hospital, the parish, or a Peace Corps volunteer and were literate in Jacaltec. They came a few hours each afternoon, during which time they wrote and translated texts and occasionally answered questions on the language.

All the informants were hired for pay. Another aspect of field work is having to assume a role of employer and finding out what wages are currently being paid in town. Informants hired full time were paid wages comparable to the incomes of skilled workers such as carpenters and tailors. Part-time informants were paid hourly wages comparable to those of the employees of the parish or the hospital. Because of this position of new employer in the town, a field worker always attracts the attention of the community. He/she is often not only solicited by people looking for work, but also generally considered as a potential lending institution. Being solicited, watched, and gossiped about is also a part of field work.

FIGURE 1.3   Colette Grinevald Craig and María Trinidad Montejo (T.M.) in the Main Street of Jacaltenango, November 1976

Hiring informants is hiring members of a community who have to answer to that community for their behavior. As in all small towns, gossip is rampant. In the case of Jacaltenango, one also had to deal with the gap of very different cultures—the always present confrontation of the Indian and the Ladino societies—and in these particular circumstances in which the field worker was a woman, with the status of women, both foreign and native.

T.M., the only regular female informant, was paid wages comparable to those of the male informants, an uncommon practice in the town. Interestingly, she did not want other people to know it in order to protect herself from more gossip than she already had to endure for being an independent self-supporting woman working with men. She did not want to have people asking her to lend them money, so she pretended that she was paid only half of what she was receiving. She was also afraid of robbers. This fear generated a reasonable protective behavior on her part, although it was the source of unpleasant confrontations for the gringa employer, who was accused by some of exploiting her, by others of lying, and by T.M. herself of exposing her to gossip. One man quit working because of pressure from his peers who were making fun of him for working for a woman and with a female co-worker.

Being a temporary employer also calls for some reflection in a situation where cash employment is very scarce and wages usually low. The work is temporary, field workers always leave after a few months, but the informants remain in the community. They have to adjust to the departure of the linguist on whom they have come to depend not only for income but also for a job that they might prefer over others, for company, and sometimes for close friendship. This also has to be considered when hiring and working with informants. Working for the field workers should not result in the informants' losing their regular incomes on which they will again have to depend for a living. This means giving time off to the informants whenever they need it to carry out their usual work and in general adjusting to their schedule.

Ideally, good informants should be considered and treated as potential linguists; they should be taught linguistics and encouraged to investigate their own languages, for they have the native intuition on which all good linguistic analysis must rely. However, the question of training informants to become linguists themselves is a delicate one. Before the linguist does this, he/she must think about the job market available for the native speakers and help them look for possible jobs. The traditional channels of college education and teaching are often closed to the informants whose only formal education is a few years of elementary schooling. More likely, the opportunities will be to become literacy teachers working for private institutions such as parishes or for language institutes. It is a part of the field worker's responsibility to consider all these aspects of the impact of his/her temporary presence in the life of the informants. Making the results of the investigation available to the community should also be a part of the field worker's responsibility.

1.2 Getting to Work

The study of any language starts with the study of its sound system. The first task of the linguist in the field is to get used to hearing all the sounds and to reproduce them as accurately as possible. It is important at this initial stage to work with informants who have a clear articulation and who know how to slow down their speech and to isolate words. In the process of learning how to articulate words, the linguist listens for which details of pronunciation are important. Informants will demand the exact pronunciation of some particular phonetic features while not appearing very concerned with variation in that of another.

For example, there are two series of consonants in Jacaltec which are distinguished by the feature of *glottalization*, a popping sound effect produced by the closure of the glottis. One must pay close attention to this glottalization feature since it can make the only difference between two words as between *caj* "red" and *c'aj* "flea," or *ac* "turtle" and *ac'* "new." However, the informant will seem to alternate sometimes between the nonglottalized and the glottalized back velars *k/k'* within the same word and will accept the same variation from the linguist. The linguist studies all the sounds looking for the distinction between contrasting sounds, called *phonemes*, and noncontrasting sounds, called *allophones*. *c/c'/k'* are phonemes while *k'/k* are allophones, that is to say, two possible realizations of the phoneme *k'*.

Native speakers are conscious of the contrastive sounds of their language but they are often unaware of the noncontrastive ones. They know when a slight change of pronunciation is important because it might result in a change of meaning, while they hardly notice the changes that are not meaningful. Take as an example of this the fact that many English speakers are unaware of the aspiration that accompanies the pronounciation of an initial *p* as in *p^{h}en*. Aspiration is distinctive in various other languages but not in English. It helps to distinguish *p* from *b* at the beginning of words, but leaving it out does not change the meaning. Whether or not *p* is aspirated depends on the position in which that sound occurs: for example, that puff of breath is normally absent from *p* at the end of a word, as in *tap*. The *p* sound with aspiration and the *p* without it are different allophones of the same phoneme. Putting a detail like aspiration in the right places is important to sounding like a native speaker of English, but there is never a contrast, e.g., no *p^{h}en* vs. *pen*, or *tap^h* vs. *tap* meaning different things. This is why an English speaker is much more likely to notice someone saying *ben* in place of

$p^h en$, substituting one phoneme for another, than to notice someone saying *pen* with the wrong allophone for *p*.

Field workers have to listen carefully to the informants because the same sounds found in two languages might be contrastive in one but not in the other. For example, Jacaltec has two contrastive *sh* sounds, one similar to the English *sh* of *shoe* and the other pronounced with a curled-up tongue, similar to the way people with a lisp might pronounce *sh*. This second sound therefore is not unknown to the linguist, but while it is a peculiarity of some individuals in one language, it is now a very important distinctive feature of the sound system of the other. In Jacaltec it happens to mark the difference between the present and the past tense:

šal naj   he says (*š* is the same as *sh*)

xal naj   he said (*x* is the retroflexed sound, like a curled-up *sh*)

Field workers who work on languages never described before start with a detailed phonetic transcription in which they reproduce exactly what they hear. Then they determine which sounds are contrastive in order to devise a simplified writing system called a *phonemic writing system*.

1.2.1   *Writing Mayan Languages*   It is interesting to note that the Mayan family of languages is famous for its ancient hieroglyphic writing system, which was lost with the fall of the brilliant Maya civilization. Experts are still trying to decipher this writing in which, unlike the one discussed in the previous paragraphs, the symbols represent words and ideas rather than sounds. The next period in history when Mayan languages were reduced to writing was at the time of the conquest and colonization, when the Spanish missionaries started studying them and devised alphabets for them. These alphabets were based on the Latin one, with the addition of a few symbols that they invented to transcribe the unfamiliar glottalized sounds. They transcribed *c'* as 𝟺 and *k'* as ₵ for instance.

In recent times, Mayan languages have been written mostly by missionaries and linguists. There are two traditions of writing systems in use nowadays—a Guatemalan tradition based on the Spanish alphabet and a phonetic alphabet in use among North American anthropologists and linguists.

1.2.2   *Writing Jacaltec*   In order to do field work on Jacaltec, it was not necessary to go through the initial stage of studying the sound system and devising an alphabet. A Spanish-based alphabet was already in use in Jacaltenango and a modern study of the sound system had been done in recent years by another field worker. The Spanish-based alphabet had been devised by a missionary in the fifties and was known to a handful of Jacaltecs who had worked for the parish. Although the language was, technically speaking, already written, the use of writing was limited to translations of sermons done for the priest and stories collected by the linguist. There was no spontaneous use of written Jacaltec among the native speakers. Spanish was the only written language used for official and private matters.

The Jacaltec alphabet is a combination of letters that have the same sound value as in Spanish and letters not used in Spanish that are given arbitrarily a specific Jacaltec sound value, and special marks on letters called *diacritics*.

The letters that represent the same sounds in Spanish and in Jacaltec are:

a c ch e f i j l m n o p r s t u y

The letters that are not used in Spanish and are given special value in Jacaltec are:

k w x tz tx

The diacritics added to letters are ' and " as in:

b' t' c' ch' tx' k' and *ñ* and *ƚ*

This alphabet has two advantages for the Jacaltec native speakers over the one used by linguists and anthropologists: first, it is easy to type on any typewriter and second, it is easier for people who already know the Spanish alphabet to learn. For those who become literate in Jacaltec first, it will facilitate learning the Spanish alphabet.

There are five vowels, which correspond to the Spanish vocalic system:

$$i \qquad u$$
$$e \quad o$$
$$a$$

There are twenty-seven consonants: Table 1.1 shows their sound value. The characteristics of the Jacaltec sound system are:

1. the absence of voiced stop or fricative sounds (the traditional spellings *b' tz tz'* do not refer to voiced sounds). Jacaltec has no b, d, or g except in Spanish borrowing as in *seboya*: Spanish *cebolla* "onion"
2. the glottalized consonants *b' t' c' k' tz' ch' tx'*, which are typical of all

TABLE 1.1 *The Sound Values for Consonants in the Jacaltec Alphabet*

	bi-labial	labio-dental	dental	alveolar	palatal	retroflexed	velar	back velar	glottal
stops	p		t				c		'
glottalized stops	b'		t'				c'	k'	
affricates				tz	ch	tx			
glottalized affricates				tz'	ch'	tx'			
fricatives		f		s	x̂	x		j	h
nasals	m			n			ñ		
liquids				l					
				r					
glides	w						y		

the languages of the Mayan family. These sounds are recognizable by the pop-like noise that accompanies them.

3. the retroflexed sounds *tx tx' x*, which are sounds made with a curled-up tongue.
4. the velar nasal *ħ*, which sounds like the single sound represented by the letters *ng* in English *song, wing,* etc., but can occur in Jacaltec in any position as in *ħah* "house," *toħe* "only," and *maħ* "without."

EXERCISE 1

The following paragraph is a short text transcribed in the Jacaltec alphabet on the top line and in a phonetic alphabet widely used in America on the second line. Try to read it. Remember that every letter must be pronounced, that the diacritic ' means a glottalized sound like a pop, and that the *x, tx,* and *tx'* are retroflexed sounds. The most difficult sounds for English speakers are the glottalized ones, and especially the *k'* sound, which is difficult not only for being glottalized, but for being a back velar pronounced very far back in the mouth (still further back from where the German "ch" sound of *Bach* is pronounced).

Text

(1) *tzet   chu   swatx'i   no'   xotx*
      ȼet   ču   swač'i   no'   šoč̣
      how   is   made   animal snail
            how to cook snails

(2) *b'ab'el   ɫchac'laxiloj   syutz   no'*
      p'ap'el   ščak'lašilox   syuȼ   no'
      first   are cut out   its tail of it (animal)
            first you cut out their tails

(3) *lahwitu'   xin   ɫtx'ahlaxiloj   no'*
      lahwitu'   šin   šč̣'ahlašilox   no'
      after that then   are washed   they
            after that then you wash them

(4) *tato   sxolħe   ha'   ɫtxiclax   no'*
      tato   sšolŋe   ha'   šč̣iklaš   no'
      if   in only   water are cooked they
            if you cook them just in water

(5) *cat   yaytoj   ixpix   b'oj   seboya   sxol   no'*
      kat   yaytox   išpiš   p'ox   seboya   sšol   no'
      so then goes down   tomato   with   onion   in   them
            then you throw in with them tomato and onion

(6) hun   hunjuyħe   cha'   no'
     hun   hunxuyŋe   ča'   no
     one   boiling only give   they
           when they start boiling

(7) cat   xin   jinihay   no'   yib'aħ   k'a
     kat   šin   xinihay   no'   yip'aŋ   q'a
     and   then   we take down   them on its top   fire
           we take them down from the fire

Notice how capital letters are not used in transcription in either writing system and how the punctuation at this stage is limited. Were more Jacaltec speakers to use writing for their language, they would no doubt develop a punctuation system. It is easy enough to take 'standard' punctuation such as we are used to in English and apply it to Jacaltec or any other language, but in fact there are differences between languages (even ones as close historically as English and French) that make it important for the native speakers themselves to work out the conventions for written texts.

Any language can be reduced to writing by linguists who study their sound system and devise an appropriate alphabet for it. Since letters are symbolic representations of sounds, many variations of writing systems may be used, depending on the purpose of the transcription. Two variations were shown in this sample. The Guatemalan variation was said to be the most appropriate for the native speakers of Guatemala who are familiar with Spanish. The North American variation is more appropriate in communications among linguists, particularly for linguists who are not specialists of Mayan languages, although the transfer from one system to the other requires only a small adjustment for them.

1.2.3 *T.M. Writes Jacaltec* What was meant earlier by "good informant" may be illustrated by the story of how T.M. taught herself to read and write Jacaltec. She had been skeptical of her ability to be a linguistic informant, considering her illiteracy as a serious handicap, as did the community in general. She had made it very clear that she could neither read nor write because she had never finished first grade. However, she kept close watch on how I transcribed texts that she had recorded and she started making remarks such as "I did not say [čitam]—I said [ȼitam]," after noticing a wrong nonretroflexed transcription *chitam* instead of *txitam*. Convinced as she was that only people who had gone to school could ever read or write, it took her a long time to accept the fact that she had discovered what reading and transcribing were about. At her age (late thirties) learning to hold a pen in her hand turned out to be the greatest obstacle. This was solved directly by her teaching herself to use the typewriter. She seemed to know instinctively how to write Jacaltec. She understood the relation of letters to sounds and never misspelled a word. She also knew when to type a final -*j*, even if it had not been pronounced, similar to the way we write "see him" in standard English, even if all that was said was "see 'm." She knew when words started and when they ended. As a matter of fact, informants were always the final judges as to which particles and words were independent words and which were part of a word as suffix or clitics. This is similar to the way an English speaker will know to spell "nowhere" and "nobody" as one word but "no money" and "no way" as two.

Once T.M. could write Jacaltec, she still had to be convinced that she could also write Spanish. She was even more self-conscious about writing Spanish, which was strongly associated in her mind with schooling, education, foreign language, and literary tradition. She finally began writing Spanish, at first with predictable misspellings such as *rrojo* for *rojo* (red), *grasias* for *gracias* (thank you), and *jues* for *juez* (judge), transcribing Spanish the way she spoke it in a strictly phonemic system.

1.3 Gathering Linguistic Material

Studying the grammar of a language is a very different exercise from learning how to speak a language. One of the differences in approach is that in order to learn how to use a language, one must acquire an active knowledge of as much vocabulary as possible. Emphasis is given to the communication aspect of the language where what is important is to understand and to be understood. In the learning process, there is a fair amount of guessing, of approximation, and of putting meaningful words together without much regard for their grammatical arrangement.

On the other hand, a linguist working on a language will pay particular attention to its grammatical structure. The emphasis is then on the organization of the elements of the language more than on active communication. Very often linguists do not even attempt to become very fluent in the language they are investigating—an endeavor that would take years if not decades—but an elementary level of fluency is always desirable. This fluency, from a human point of view, is important in relating to the community and in communicating with the people who know only that one language. Generally these are the older people and the women. It is also important from a linguistic point of view to acquire some feeling for the language in order to be able to manipulate at least simple sentences when working with informants on particular grammatical points. It is common for field workers to acquire vocabularies dealing with some particular semantic domain in order to be able to construct numerous sentences on the same topic. When the field worker is a man, he is more likely to learn the vocabulary pertaining to men's activities, such as agriculture, carpentry, construction work, mythology or politics. A female field worker is more likely to become fluent conversing about household chores and child care.

Linguists need to know enough words to have a large sample that is representative of all grammatical categories—nouns, verbs, adjectives—and within each category, words of all different semantic structure—animate and inanimate nouns, concrete and abstract nouns, transitive and intransitive verbs, etc. Together with this sample lexicon, the important tools of linguists are the grammatical words that are of a limited number in every language and of which a linguist makes a complete inventory. Such grammatical words are the tense markers, the plural markers, the prepositions, the conjunctions, the personal pronouns. With the sample of vocabulary representative of all grammatical categories and the grammatical words at hand, linguists study how they function together to produce meaningful and grammatical sentences.

1.3.1 *Collecting Texts*   Working on a language with no written tradition means that there are no bookstores in which to buy reading material in the language, no teach-yourself book or tourist phrase book, no novels, no newspaper, no comic books or children's books. In this situation, the field worker is totally dependent on the informants for language material. The task of collecting written linguistic data for analysis consists of two different activities. One is to collect texts that will provide samples of written material produced spontaneously by native speakers; the other is to conduct with the informants sessions of elicitation that are similar to grammatical interviews.

The texts collected in the field are a substitute for the novels, newspapers, fiction and nonfiction books that one cannot buy in a store. These texts are usually recorded on tape. Once recorded, they need to be written down and translated, and the linguistic information they contain must be further filed in proper fashion for grammatical analysis. With modern recording equipment, tape recording is technically relatively easy. The main problems encountered are usually nontechnical, such as the pouring rain on a tin roof, or chickens, pigs, and children screaming, and neighbors and passers-by laughing or commenting. All these produce a noisy background usually difficult to eliminate or control in places where isolation and privacy are difficult to obtain. As a rule, people are less afraid of tape recorders than they are of cameras, although Jacaltecs used to refer to the tape recorder as "the machine that steals your voice." Most often, however, people are fascinated and amused by the immediate playback.

Tape recording is but the first step in the time-consuming process of collecting texts. Transcribing the recorded texts will take many times as long as the actual recording session. Twenty minutes of a story turns into hours of phrase-by-phrase playback and transcription. At some point during the field work, all linguists must have visions in their dreams of hundreds of hours' worth of recorded tapes, all transcribed and indexed in thick volumes bound and handy on a shelf, ready to be thumbed through in search of a good example. The reality of the situation is that while time in the field is usually limited, once back from the field, time is often just as limited; one realizes that there is no use recording hours of text that will never be transcribed, translated, or filed away. Other limiting factors to be considered include both the high price and the bulk of high-quality tapes, and, where electricity is not available, of good batteries. But these realistic limitations have to be reconsidered in the special situation where the language being investigated is spoken by fewer and fewer persons—maybe by even just one or two very old people. In such cases, material consideration should not hamper the efforts to collect as many texts as possible of what will be the last samples of a language soon to be added to the long list of extinct languages.

The main purpose of tape recording is to obtain spontaneous material from informants who can speak naturally at their own speed of speech. Tape recording also allows for a varied collection of texts, which are provided by people who would not be chosen for informants either because they are very old, because they are not bilingual, or because they are too busy and unavailable for more than a casual visit and a few minutes' recording on an occasional basis.

The topics of the texts collected may vary from traditional or mythological tales retold, most often, by older people to narratives recounting remarkable events in the life of the community—weddings, fiestas, and accidents—or routine activities such as how to grow corn, make tortillas, make soap, or build a house.

Another way of collecting texts, besides recording them, is to have the informants directly write down texts of their own with a translation. This method obviously saves the field worker a great deal of time. It is a particularly advantageous method when the informant is a good writer who can manipulate written language with ease. It is important to take advantage of the personal skills of native speakers and occasional or full-time informants. Speakers have many ways of being artful at handling language—some may be good storytellers, others may be inspired writers, others may be perceptive critics. In this phase of field work, native speakers have the initiative. Informants and storytellers are asked to write or talk about topics of their choice, in the style of their choice. The objective is to obtain samples of natural language, the language as it is used among native speakers. The role of the linguist is that of an attentive observer.

1.3.2 *Text Analysis*   Once the first text is collected and transcribed, the linguist analyzes it with the informant in order to gain an overview of the grammatical categories and grammatical structures of the language. The analysis consists of establishing an exact word-by-word translation followed by an investigation of the grammatical structure and function of each word. Let us consider, for example, the Jacaltec sentence:

> *xb'ey   heb'   naj*
> went   Pl   man
>   they went

From a cursory analysis of this simple sentence, we can already learn the following about Jacaltec grammar:

1. Verbs appear in initial position.
2. *xb'ey* is a verb in the past tense. There is also a present tense which, for this verb, would give the form *x̃b'ey*.
3. *heb'* is a plural marker for humans. There is another marker for nonhumans as in **hej** *no' txitam* "the pigs."
4. *naj* is a classifier, a word that signals one of the many noun classes of the language. *naj* marks the male human class and means "man," although in this sentence it carries the pronoun meaning "he."

The information is generally gathered by asking the informant to translate expressions. Since most informants have never had any linguistic training, it would be pointless to ask direct questions such as: Is there a present tense? Is this a plural marking? The same information can be obtained by asking for the translation of the same noun in the singular and in the plural (how do you say man/men?) or the same verb in different tenses (how do you say they go/they went?). As one advances through the text, the cursory analysis of the first sentences is refined in the light of the new data. For example, what was first labelled present/past tenses will later be described as a contrast of incompletive and completive aspects.

The analysis of the first text is always very time consuming and that of the first sentences the slowest. But as grammatical forms and constructions start repeating themselves, less and less inquiry is necessary. By the time one reaches the end of a sizable text, one has usually gathered enough information to be able to draw a sketch of the grammar of the language with careful notes on the topics that require more scrutiny. After working on a few texts, linguists can begin to proceed swiftly through the others by only asking questions about the new forms encountered.

      1.3.3 *Direct Elicitation*   The method of collecting and analyzing texts, however, is not sufficient for the gathering of linguistic data. It must be complemented with a methodical inquiry by linguists in a phase of what is commonly referred to as "direct elicitation." In this phase of field work, the linguist takes the initiative and asks direct questions of the informants about a specific grammatical point under investigation. The goal of such grammatical interviews is to obtain as systematic a check as possible on a specific topic, including information on both what is and what is not grammatical.

The role of the linguist is first to choose a topic and to prepare a session. The preparation consists of organizing questions to ask the informants. These questions are not random questions, but rather they are formulated on the basis of a set of assumptions and expectations. As the elicitation advances, preliminary analysis is done, and decisions are made at each step as to what should be asked next. The best preparation is to have anticipated the likely links and to be ready to follow leads when the answer to one question seems to uncover new facts worthy of exploration.

The role of the informants is to answer accurately the questions of the linguist and to take as much of an active part in the investigation as possible by volunteering comments and by pointing out to the linguist other facts that may be related to the problem being studied. Informants are asked to translate sentences from the working language into their native language, to substitute one particular element of a sentence with some other possible one in a given context, or to complete sentences.

1.3.4 *A Session of Direct Elicitation*   One of the first sessions of direct elicitation might be on word order, for example. Word order is one of the basic characteristics of a language, and studies have shown that the place of the verb, in particular, will determine several other facts of grammar. The first task is to determine what is the unmarked word order—that is to say, the word order of a simple declarative sentence. Once the unmarked word order is established, the second task is to determine how free the constituents are to move and under what circumstances they move. We would expect to be able to say by the end of the session what the basic word order of the language is, whether it is a rigid word order or whether it is relatively free, and what meanings accompany changes in the basic word order.

A guideline of the session is prepared to ensure that no important question is left out. Running a session requires so much concentration, immediate analysis of the data being collected, and quick decisions about what to do with unexpected information that it is best to have an outline of all the questions that must be gone over. The first set of questions will check the word order of all types of simple clauses:

(a) John is rich (stative verb)   (b) John came (intransitive verb)
(c) John saw Mary (transitive verb)

Notice how the sentences are kept very simple. There would be no point in asking the informant to translate a sentence like "my cousin John came yesterday after lunch" instead of the simple sentence "John came" if all we are considering at first is the position of the verb. Making up sentences is not always as easy as it seems; the linguist must strike a balance between a very simple sentence that isolates the point of grammar under investigation but sounds unnatural to the informant and a sentence more likely to be used by the informant, with more explicit context, but longer and more cumbersome to transcribe and use many times. One must also be careful to make up sentences that are culturally meaningful, and in Jacaltenango, to avoid sentences like "it snowed," "I ate a pork chop," "he is frustrated," etc., since snow, pork chop, and frustrations are not part of the experience of a native Jacaltec and would unnecessarily puzzle the informants.

The session begins then with the informant translating the first sentence as:

> *k'alom   naj   łuwan*
> rich   man John
>   John is rich

and the second sentence as:

> *xul   naj   łuwan*
> came   man John
>   John came

In both sentences, the predicate (adjectival predicate and verbal predicate) comes first. On the basis of these data, the following hypothesis of word order may be formulated: Jacaltec is a verb-initial language. However, when asked to translate the third sentence, the informant says:

> *naj   łuwan   x'ilni   ix   malin*
> man John   saw   woman Mary
>   John saw Mary

This time the word order subject–verb–object does not conform to the verb-initial hypothesis. There are two alternative interpretations of this third sentence; either the word order of transitive clauses is different from the word order of intransitive clauses, or the informant did not give the unmarked word order for this sentence. The latter sounds more probable for two reasons: first, because languages usually do not exhibit different word orders in their transitive and intransitive constructions and second, because the text analysis that preceded the phase of direct elicitation provided examples of transitive sentences with verbs in initial position. So the informant is asked if there is another word order for this sentence, although not with a direct question. The linguist can either ask if there is another way of saying the same sentence, or try to make up the Jacaltec sentence and ask the informant if it is a good sentence, usually a more efficient method. However, when asked to judge the sentence *x'ilni naj łuwan ix malin*, which shows the verb in initial position, the informant answers a flat "no," leaving the linguist somewhat confused. Luckily the informant is very helpful and adds "but you could say *xil naj łuwan ix malin*" and even adds "that is how we would actually say that sentence." After a few minutes of probing with other transitive constructions and discussing with the informant the notion of natural or unmarked word order, the following analysis emerges: the word order in transitive sentences is also verb–subject–object, but the informant had given the word order that followed the word order of the Spanish sentence, thinking that it was what the linguist wanted. Furthermore the ungrammatical sentence made up by the linguist uncovered the fact that the verb takes a special marking whenever the subject of a transitive verb is preposed for emphasis. The translation given initially by the informant was an emphatic sentence, while the linguist expected the nonemphatic one:

Nonemphatic:

xil	naj	łuwan	ix	malin
saw	man	John	woman	Mary
V	S		O	

John saw Mary

Emphatic:

naj	łuwan	x'ilni	ix	malin
man	John	saw-suff	woman	Mary
	S	V	O	

it is John who saw Mary

The session will then continue with questions about how rigid the word order is and whether or not subjects of intransitives and objects of transitives can also be preposed for emphasis. One of the key sentences containing the answer to the first question will be the ungrammatical sentence elicited by the linguist:

*xil	ix	malin	naj	łuwan
saw	woman	Mary	man	John
V	O		S	

John saw Mary

which shows that the order of subject–object is rigid in nonemphatic sentences. The answer to the second question is that subjects of intran-

sitives or objects of transitives may be preposed for emphasis and that the
verb does not take any special marking then, as in:

naj   ɬuwan xul   ewi
man John   came yesterday
   it is John who came yesterday

ix   malin xil   naj ɬuwan
woman Mary   saw   man John
   O   V   S
   it is Mary that John saw

1.3.5 *Obtaining Reliable Data*   Even though direct elicitation is
considered an efficient way of obtaining the desired data, this method of
investigation must be handled with care. One of the prerequisites is that
the linguist have a good command of the working language—the
language common to linguist and informant—in order to minimize
misunderstandings. In this case, the linguist was fluent in Spanish,
although she had to become familiar with the Guatemalan Indian variety
of the language to be able to communicate efficiently with the informants. Problems may also arise when informants are asked to
respond to specific requests of linguists. As in all interview situations,
the questions should not be asked in such a way as to indicate what the
expected answer is, i.e., "Isn't it right that you cannot say ... ?" Informants may go along with whatever they think would please the
linguist. The notion of what is right and what is wrong, grammatical
or ungrammatical, is not reinforced in unwritten languages to the same
extent that it is through formal language education, grammar textbooks,
dictates of academies, and didactic grammars for standardized, official
languages. Although good informants are native speakers who have a
clear intuition about what is correct in a language and what does not feel
right, they may also have a benevolent attitude toward foreign linguists.
A linguist must learn to interpret the answers and judgments in the
context of a general scale of reference used by each informant.
    Using the following symbols: √ for an acceptable sentence, ? for
a somewhat awkward but still acceptable sentence, ?? for a more
questionable sentence, * for an ungrammatical sentence, and ** for
a very ungrammatical sentence that makes no sense, the two principal
informants for Jacaltec had the judgment patterns sketched below for
three critical sentences:

	Sentence 1	2	3
A.M.	**	*	√
T.M.	??	?	√

The scale of judgment for T.M. was:

√   "yes, it is good"

?   "I would not say it, but I guess others might" or "I have heard others say it"

??   "I have not heard it said that way, but if you wanted to say it that way, I guess you could" or "It does not make any sense to *me*, but if that is what *you* want to say, you can say it that way"

On the other hand, A.M. had a more conservative scale. He recognized sentences as either grammatical or ungrammatical, and did not identify marginal sentences, those sentences that could be said to be grammatical but, at best, were awkward.

Both informants, therefore, used parallel scales of evaluation although each expressed it in a different manner. T.M., who had no formal education, did not say that sentences were right or wrong; she based her scale on whether or not she herself used the form, always allowing for other speakers to do as they pleased. A.M., on the other hand, who had had many years of education and had spent years working on his own on a grammar of Jacaltec, was very prompt at determining whether or not a form was correct.

Linguists who rely on translation techniques in direct elicitation also have to be careful that the pattern of the sentence to be translated not merely be duplicated by informants as was shown to happen in the session of direct elicitation.

Field workers should always bear in mind that being an informant is very demanding; it can be tedious, tiring, boring, and frustrating, although hopefully it is also interesting and even exciting at times. Informants are human beings, they too have good days and bad days; in order to ensure that the data obtained are reliable, sessions of elicitation should not last too long and should be interspersed with breaks whenever the attention of the informants seems to be failing. It is a very discouraging experience to have an informant give different judgments of the same sentence on different days. Many times this happens because the informant is tired and does not understand the question or does not care one way or the other and says whatever the linguist seems to be asking for.

Finally, although informants should be encouraged to participate in the investigation, the ultimate responsibility of the analysis lies with the trained linguist. Some informants will show an excessive eagerness in finding an answer for everything, often offering explanations beyond the realm of linguistics. One must always remember that being a native speaker does not necessarily mean being a native linguist.

1.3.6   *Filing Data*   Thus, after hours of covering pages of a note-book with notes, scribbles, question marks, and arrows, the time comes to neatly file all the data gathered. This paper work is another necessary, tedious and time-consuming part of field work. All the information contained in the texts and the notes from elicitation sessions must be filed in order to be more readily accessible for further analysis. Every field worker develops somewhat idiosyncratic field methods, different types of interviews, and different filing systems. All the new data should be transcribed neatly on cards, with the appropriate set of references. It is important to note which informant provided which sentences and the date on which the data were collected. As familiarity with the language and the informants' personalities increases, transcription and judgment usually become more accurate. The references also allow for quick check-back with the original notes. A misfiled card, or a card with inadequate reference, is very much like a book misplaced on a library shelf.

1.4   Methodology

There exists no standardized guide book *How to Do Field Work*, nor will there ever be. Much of the style of field methods depends on the people involved, the personalities and training of the linguists, the personalities and training of the informants. Some linguists work with informants all day long, some for only a few hours a day. They hire one informant or several informants; they do everything themselves—taping, transcribing, interviewing—or they give an active role to the informants. Some field workers do a great deal of inspired, improvised, direct elicitation; others patiently organize and prepare their interviews. Some linguists take very neat notes and do little filing afterward; others need to file all the material away soon after it is gathered for fear they will not understand their hasty scribbles if they wait too long. Informants may be literate native speakers who are interested in learning linguistics them-selves, or they may be untrained, illiterate, but perceptive informants and unable, at least at the start, to take the initiative and participate actively in the work.

A working session can never be planned exactly. Some sessions will seem to get nowhere—they ramble on for hours without focus or solution to any of the questions raised—while others will be over-whelmingly rich in new and interesting material. The field workers must always be alert to pick up that mumbled comment from an informant that might lead to the answer and be able to judge on the spot the significance of an unexpected response. Some linguists lead sessions at a brisk pace and are quick at preliminary analysis; others work slowly and gather a lot of data that they analyze in between sessions.

Over an extended period of time in the field, one should expect to live through active, productive periods of work interspersed with depressing ones when everything sits at a standstill or boils into a frightening confusion.

In any case, when it is time to leave the field after weeks, months, or years of field work, the linguist carries back texts, notes, papers, and cards that usually contain much more information on the language than he/she has been able—or had the leisure—to analyze. Gathering linguistic data is an endless process that is difficult to stop while working in the field. One often needs literally to take some distance to concentrate on analyzing what has been gathered, thus avoiding the temptation of continually opening new areas of inquiry.

2   THE JACALTEC LANGUAGE

The major characteristic of Jacaltec sentences is their word order. Jacaltec is a VSO language, that is to say a language with a verb–subject–object word order. This word order is uncommon among the languages of the world and is one of the reasons for studying Jacaltec. Another characteristic of the language is the complex structure of its verbs. Jacaltec verbs contain information about aspect and mood, subject and object, and direction of the subject or of the object. Consider, for example, the verb form *xcin hatenic'toj* "you pushed me aside" and all its components:

xc-	completive aspect expressing a finished action
-in-	object marker "me"
ha-	subject marker "you"
-ten-	verb stem "move"
-ic'-	directional "to the side"
-toj	directional "away from the agent"

The system of subject and object marking is of special interest because it represents one of the comparatively infrequent instances among the languages of the world of an ergative case-marking system. This phenomenon of ergativity will be discussed in a separate section. The system of directionals, which is a phenomenon common to many American Indian languages, will also be the topic of a section.

Following the complex verb form in a sentence are the noun phrases. Jacaltec noun phrases have two characteristics. First, nouns are accompanied by a noun classifier; this interesting system of noun classification will be the last topic of this presentation of the Jacaltec language. Second, as is usual in verb initial languages, demonstrative articles, adjectives, and relative clauses follow the noun. Notice the presence of a noun classifier and the position of the adjective and of the demonstrative in the following example:

no'	*txitam*	*b'ak'ich*	*tu'*
Classifier	Noun	Adjective	Demonstrative
animal	pig	fat	that

that fat pig

2.1 Jacaltec as an Ergative Language

Languages typically have a way to signal the function of their noun phrases so that it is understood which one is the subject and which one is the object in a sentence. The most common ways are to assign subjects (S) and objects (O) to a particular position in the sentence, as in English:

John	*saw*	*Mary*
S	V	O

Mary	*saw*	*John*
S	V	O

and/or to mark the nominals themselves with a particular case, nominative for the subject and accusative for the object, as in German. (For the description of a language that has case marking on a similar pattern, which is to say with a distinct marker for subjects and a different one for objects, see the chapter in this volume on Japanese by Kyoko Inoue; for another, see the chapter on Russian by Bernard Comrie in the companion volume.)

der Mann sah	*den Jungen*
S-Nom	O-Acc

The man saw the boy

der Junge sah	*den Mann*
S-Nom	O-Acc

The boy saw the man

In English, only the personal pronouns are marked for case:

I	*see*	*him*	*I*	*laugh*
S-Nom		O-Acc	S-Nom	

he	*sees*	*me*	*he*	*laughs*
S-Nom		O-Acc	S-Nom	

In Jacaltec the functions of subject and object are marked both by word order and by case markers, although the case markers are inserted in the verb form instead of being on the nominals. Observe the subject and object case markers in the verb and the order of subject and object in the following examples ("Ø" in these examples stands for "zero" object markers, ones with no audible representation):

> *x-Ø-s-mak   naj   ix*
> Asp-O-S-hit   he   her
> > he hit her
>
> *x-Ø-s-mak   ix   naj*
> Asp-O-S-hit   she   him
> > she hit him

Since the personal pronouns in first and second person are not used in normal speech except for special emphasis, the case markers in the verb are often the only indication of who is the subject and who is the object:

> *ch-in   ha-colo*
> Asp-O   S-help
> > you help me
>
> *ch-ach   hin-maka*
> Asp-O   S-hit
> > I hit you

Not only does Jacaltec mark both subject and object on the verb, but it also marks them in a particular way illustrated in the examples below:

> (a) *ch-ach   wayi*
> Asp-you   sleep
> > you sleep
>
> (b) *ch-oñ   munlayi*
> Asp-we   work
> > we work
>
> (c) *ch-oñ   ha-maka*
> Asp-us   you-hit
> > you hit us
>
> (d) *ch-ach   cu-maka*
> Asp-you   we-hit
> > we hit you

In examples (a) and (b), the subjects of the intransitive verbs—those verbs that do not take objects—are:

> *(h)ach*   "you"   and   *(h)oñ*   "we"

The notation (*h*)*ach*/(*h*)*oñ* means that the full form of the case markers is *hach* and *hoñ* but that the initial *h* is lost when the case marker is suffixed to the aspect marker. In examples (c) and (d), the subjects of the transitive verbs—those verbs that take an object—are:

> *ha*   "you"   and   *cu*   "we"

Therefore, in Jacaltec not all subjects take the same case marker. One has to distinguish subjects of transitives from subjects of intransitives and assign them a different case. Furthermore, the case marker of the object of a transitive verb is the same as the one of the subject of an intransitive. Note how the object markers of examples (c) and (d) are the same as the subject markers of examples (a) and (b):

> (*h*)*ach* : "you"   and   (*h*)*oñ* : "us"

Jacaltec is said to have an *ergative* case-marking system, a system in which subjects of transitive verbs are assigned a case called *ergative*, while subjects of intransitives as well as objects of transitives are assigned a different case called *absolutive*.

As is usual in ergative languages, the absolutive is also used to mark subjects when there is a passive construction:

> *xc-oñ*   *mak'laxi*
> Asp-we   be hit
> > we were hit

> *xc-ach*   *collaxi*
> Asp-you   be helped
> > you were helped

and it is used to mark the subject of a stative predicate, in which case it appears behind the predicate:

> *sonlom*   **hach**
> marimba   you
> > you are a marimba player

> *meb'a*   **hoñ**
> poor   we
> > we are poor

The ergative case is also used as the possessive marker:

> **ha**   *mam*   **cu**   *mi'*
> your   father   our   mother

Ergative languages are not as common as nominative languages. Among the languages of the world that have been identified as ergative are Basque, Eskimo, Caucasian languages, the Mayan languages, and almost all the languages of Australia. (See the chapter in this volume by John Haviland on Guugu Yimidhirr; for another instance of ergative case marking, see the chapter on the Hua language of Papua New Guinea by John Haiman in the companion volume.) There is a certain amount of variation among these languages in the details of their case-marking systems (whether only nouns are marked ergatively and not the pronouns, whether the case markers are on the nouns or the verbs, etc.), but they all share the pattern of case assignment diagrammed below. In the following example, the nominals that have the same marker are in italics and the one that has a distinct marker is boxed:

Nominative System	*Ergative System*
The boy broke the pot	The boy broke *the pot*
The pot broke	*The pot* broke

EXERCISE 2

How would you say the following sentences in English if English happened to be an ergative language?

(a)   he hit me   _____ hit _____
       and I cried.   and _____ cried.

(b)   I pushed him   _____ pushed _____
       and he fell.   and _____ fell.

The foregoing sketch of the ergativity of Jacaltec is an example of descriptive linguistics that is meant to show how a system functions without losing the reader in the intricacies of the real speech situation. However, a field worker analyzing Jacaltec would have to deal with a whole array of additional facts. For example, there are two sets of ergative markers, one used with consonant initial stems and another with vowel initial stems, and the existence of these two sets alone could cause an unwarned field worker a moment of confusion. Furthermore, in this specific situation, one has to contend with the often inaudible nature of the case markers. For instance, as we have seen, the third-person absolutive marker is a "zero" marker (written $\emptyset$), which means that there is no audible morpheme for it, while the third-person ergative marker used with vowel initial stems is dropped when the object is a third person. All this means that a form like:

> x-Ø-y-il   ix   naj
> Asp-A3-E3-see she   him
>   she saw him

is said:

> xil   ix   naj

Finally, the first-person absolutive and the first-person ergative used with consonant initial stems are homophonous, both sounding (h)in. All these factors combined make it difficult at times for the field worker learning Jacaltec to identify the case markers and later to write about them, when it is best to use only selected forms that do not obscure the demonstration of the mechanism of the Mayan ergative case-marking system.

2.2 Directionals

Another characteristic of the Jacaltec language is its use of directional particles on verbs to express with precision movement of persons and objects. This characteristic is shared by many languages of the Mayan family. Similar directional particles are used in many languages of the world. In English they correspond to the verbal particles *out, in, off*, etc. as in *to go **out**, to come **in**, to walk **up**, to climb **down***, etc. (see Table 1.2).

The first two directionals express motion away from or toward the speaker or the agent. They are the most common directionals, found in the last position in the verb when other directionals and suffixes are present.

The next four directions (3–6) represent the four cardinal directions of the old Mayan civilization. -(*o*)*c* corresponds to the direction of the east. The verb *oci* "to enter" is the verb used to say that the sun comes up, -(*o*)*c* indicates therefore the direction of sunrise. -(*e/i*)*l* corresponds to the direction of the west, the verb *eli* "to exit" being used to say that the sun sets. -(*e/i*)*l* is therefore the direction of sunset. The four directionals are recognizable in the four adverbial expressions:

cehtu'	(*ah*)	upward
ceytu'	(*ay*)	downward
cectu'	(*oc*)	eastward
celtu'	(*el*)	westward

TABLE 1.2 *Inventory of Jacaltec Directionals*

The directional particles are the reduced forms of intransitive verbs.

(1)	*-toj*	x⟶	"away from" from *toyi* "to go"
(2)	*-tij*	x⟵	"toward" from *tita* "to come"
(3)	*-(a)h*		"up" from *ahoj* "to ascend"
(4)	*-(a)y*		"down" from *ayoj* "to descend"
(5)	*-(o)c*		"in" from *oci* "to enter"
(6)	*-(e/i)l*		"out" from *eli* "to exit"
(7)	*-(e/i)c'*		"passing, through" from *ec'i* "to pass, go"
(8)	*-pax*		"back, again" from *paxi* "to return"
(9)	*-can*		"remaining, still" from *cani* "to remain"
(10)	*-cañ*		"up, suddenly" (the expected verb *cañi* was not found in the language)

The directional *-(e/i)c'* (7) is the first directional that does not imply a point of origin or an end point, but rather a motion to the side, or through a particular point. Since it functions like the above directionals, directionals 3 through 7 inclusive will be referred to as the *cardinal directionals*.

The last three directionals (8–10) form a semantic group somewhat apart from the others. The first one, *-pax*, means to have gone somewhere and have returned "here." It corresponds semantically to the combination of *-toj* "away" and *-tij* "toward here." *-can* (9) expresses the absence of movement, meaning "remaining," "to go somewhere to stay," or "to be left behind." *-cañ* (10), the least used of the directionals, indicates an upward direction, the motion of something thrown up in the air that is expected to fall back down. It is semantically related to the word *satcañ* "sky," and does not specify point of origin or end point. These last three directionals are frequently used with secondary meanings: *-pax* "also, too," *-can* "once and for all," and *-cañ* "suddenly."

2.2.1 *Intransitive Verbs of Motion*   Intransitive verbs of motion are generally composed of two directionals. The first one refers to the direction taken by the agent, i.e., the person or the object being spoken about. It is one of the four cardinal directionals (3–6). The second directional specifies whether the movement is away or toward the speaker:

> *x-Ø-ah-toj*   *naj swi' te' ħah*
> Asp-he-up-away he   top   the   house
>> he climbed on top of the house (away from where I stand)

> *x-Ø-ah-tij*   *ix yul ha' ha'*
> Asp-she-up-here she   in   the   water
>> she came out of the water (here, where I stand)

2.2.2 *Getting Around Jacaltenango*   Jacaltenango is built on a narrow ledge down from the other Jacaltec town of Concepción. Across the gorge where the Río Azul (Blue River) runs is the Jacaltec village of San Marcos (see Figure 1.4). If John (naj ƚuwan) were going down to the river from Jacaltenango, Mary (ix malin) would say of him:

> *ch-Ø-ay-toj*   *naj ƚuwan*
> Asp-he-down-away   man John
>> John is going down there

while if he were going from Jacaltenango to San Marcos, Antonio (ya' antun) would say of him:

> *ch-Ø-ec'-tij*   *naj ƚuwan*
> Asp-he-aside-here   man John
>> John is coming across

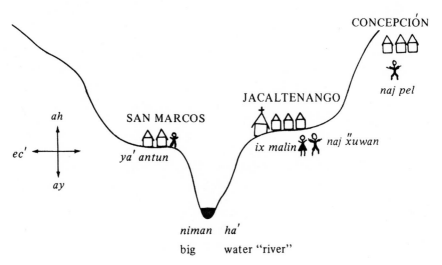

niman ha'
big   water "river"

FIGURE 1.4   *Jacaltenango and Its Environs*

It is not difficult to understand how Jacaltec directionals function; it is more difficult, however, to acquire a sense of the imperative precision of the language in this domain without trying to "think in Jacaltec." This is the purpose of the following exercise.

EXERCISE 3

(Refer to people and places in Figure 1.4)

(a) the speaker is in Jacaltenango, what is the most likely destination of the traveler/subject in each of these cases?

        chaytij   naj pel
        chahtoj   naj ƚuwan

(b) the speaker is in Jacaltenango, who could the traveler/subject be?

        chec'tij _____
        chahtoj _____

(c) <u>where</u> is the speaker?

        chaytij   naj ƚuwan
        chaytij   ya' antun

2.2.3 *Transitive Constructions*   While in intransitive verb forms the cardinal directionals $(a)h/(a)y/(o)c/(e/i)l/(e/i)c'$ "up/down/in/out/to the side" express the movement of the actor/subject, in transitive verb forms they refer to the movement of the object/patient:

xc-ach   *hin-ten-ic'-toj*
Asp-you   I-push-aside-away
    I pushed you aside (*you* moved *aside*)

While in intransitive forms the referential directionals *toj/tij* "toward/away from" express the direction of the movement with respect to the position of the speaker, in transitive forms they refer to the position of the actor/subject:

xc-ach   **hin-ten-ic'-toj**
Asp-you   I-push-aside-away
    I pushed you aside (*away* from *me*)

EXERCISE 4

Fill in the spaces with the appropriate directionals, remembering that:

Use the full form of the directionals (ah/ay) after a consonant, and the short form (h/y) after a vowel:

(a)   you threw the garbage down the cliff

    xabej-____ – _____   k'alem   sat   pajam
    you threw   garbage   on   cliff

(b)   I threw the ball on top of the house

    xwa-____ – _____   pelota   swi'   te'   ħah
    I sent   ball   top   the house

2.2.4 *Jacaltec Prepositions*   A discussion of the expression of movement and directionality in Jacaltec would not be complete without a remark about the nature of Jacaltec prepositions. Unlike English prepositions, Jacaltec prepositions express only the point of contact between two objects and do not express movement or directionality. To illustrate this point, compare the elements expressing directionality in the Jacaltec and English sentences below:

(a)   *xcin haten-ic-toj*   *yul*   *carro*
      you moved me-in-away   in   truck
          you *pushed* me *into* the truck

(b)   *xcin haten-il-tij*   *yul*   *carro*
      you moved me-out-toward   in   truck
          you *pulled* me *out of* the truck

(c)   *xcin haten-ay-tij*   *yul*   *carro*
      you moved me-down-toward· in   truck
          you *pulled* me *down from* the truck

The inventory of words expressing directionality in these three examples is shown below:

Jacaltec	English
Directionals	**Directional particles**
ic/il/ay	*in/out/down*
tij/toj	
	Verbs
	push/pull
	Prepositions
	to/of/from

The striking feature of this inventory is the diffuseness of the English system, which uses directional particles, verbs, and prepositions to express directionality, as compared with the concentration of all the directional meaning in the directionals in Jacaltec. The static nature of the Jacaltec prepositions, which indicate the point of contact before or after the action, is further shown in the pairs of examples below:

*xwacoj   k'ap camixè   **yul**   te'   cała*
I put   the   shirt   inside   the   chest
  I put the shirt *in* the chest

*xwilij   k'ap camiłe   **yul**   te'   cała*
I took out   the   shirt   inside   the   chest
  I took the shirt *out of* the chest

*xwahtoj   tx'otx'   xih   **yib'añ**   k'a*
I put up away   the   pot   on   fire
  I put the pot *on* the fire

*:waytij   tx'otx'   xih   **yib'añ**   k'a*
I put down toward   the   pot   on   fire
  I took the pot *off* the fire

The systematic use of directionals and the conciseness of the system are the two main features that characterize the expression of directionality in Jacaltec. From the point of view of a field worker, it means difficulty in picking out the short directionals in complex verb forms and difficulty in remembering to use them, which prompts the informants to reject sentences because they sound unnatural to native Jacaltec speakers.

2.3 Noun Classifiers

It is common for natural languages to organize their nouns in different classes. In European languages it takes the form of gender assignment. All nouns are assigned a gender; some languages have two genders, like French and Spanish, others three, like German. These genders are partly assigned on semantic grounds. For example, in Romance languages the gender of all animate nouns is determined by sex—masculine for males and feminine for females:

	French	**Spanish**	
M	*un enfant*	*un niño*	a male child
F	*une enfant*	*una niña*	a female child
M	*un chat*	*un gato*	a tomcat
F	*une chatte*	*una gata*	a she-cat

All inanimate nouns, however, have arbitrary genders which have to be learned and memorized by all speakers:

	French		**Spanish**	
M	*le sel*	**F**	*la sal*	salt
F	*une fourchette*	**M**	*un tenedor*	a fork
M	*un ongle*	**F**	*una uña*	a fingernail

The Jacaltec noun classifier system resembles a gender system in that it assigns nouns to different classes; however, it differs from a gender system in several ways. First, it assigns nouns to classes strictly on semantic grounds, which means that it is possible to predict from its meaning to which class a noun belongs. Second, while languages have two or three genders, the noun classifier system counts with twenty-five classes. A third difference is that not all nouns are classified. The system applies only to concrete nouns and provides an organization of the material world that ignores abstract nouns, with a few exceptions. Thus words with concrete meanings such as "man," "horse," "flower," and "rock" will be preceded by noun classifiers, but not words with abstract meanings such as "story," "night," "truth," or "strength." Finally, while genders typically trigger an agreement phenomenon with articles and adjectives, what we call noun classifiers ordinarily do not.

Noun classes are expressed by a noun classifier placed in front of the noun. Most of the noun classifiers are derived from nouns themselves. For examples, the classifier for woman is *ix*, and the word for woman is also *ix*. Thus the equivalent of "the woman" is *ix ix*. A classified noun is always accompanied by its noun classifier. The combination of noun classifier + noun corresponds to the combination definite article + noun of English, although the noun classifier cannot be said to be a definite article since it is still present with the indefinite article:

Classifier	Noun	
no'	*txitam*	
animal	pig	the pig

Indefinite Article	**Classifier**	**Noun**	
hune'	*no'*	*txitam*	
a	animal	pig	a pig

The noun classifiers fulfill a very active role in the grammar of Jacaltec, since they provide pronoun forms for the nouns they classify:

xul	*naj*	*pel*	*yaj*	*mach*	*xcan*	*naj*
came	man	Peter	but	not	stayed	man

   Peter came but *he* did not stay

swatx'e	*ix*	*malin*	*ixim*	*wah?*
made	woman	Mary	corn	tortillas?

ho'	*swatx'e*	*ix*	*ixim*
yes	made	woman	corn

   did Mary make the tortillas? yes, *she* made *them*

2.3.1 *Noun Classifiers for Persons* Noun classifiers for persons are assigned on the basis of three variables: sex, relative age, and kinship. Persons, including humans and deities, are classified in the following manner:

cumam	he (deity)
cumi'	she (deity)
ya'	he/she (older generation)
unin	he/she (infant)
ho'	he (equal age, kin)
xo'	she (equal age, kin)
naj	he (equal age, non-kin)
ix	she (equal age, non-kin)

Most of these classifiers are specific to one sex, with the exception of *ya'* for an older person and *unin* for an infant. *ya'* refers to a person who is older than the speaker and commands respect, such as parents, godparents, and authorities. *ho'* and *xo'* refer to male and female siblings and cousins. *naj* and *ix* refer to men and women no older than, and unrelated to, the speaker. The classifiers reflect the particular relationship of age and kinship that holds between the speaker and the person referred to. This will be illustrated by the example of the Camposeco and the Montejo families (see Table 1.3).

TABLE 1.3   The Camposeco and Montejo Families

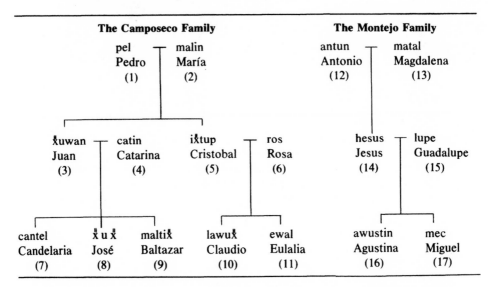

José (8) will refer to his sister as *xo' cantel* (7), to his female cousin as *xo' ewal* (11), and to their friend as *ix awustin* (16). He will talk about his brother as *ho' maltix̱* (9) and his male cousin as *ho' lawux̱* (10) but about Agustina's brother as *naj mec* (17). José (8) will also refer respectfully to his parents as *ya' hin mam* "my father" (3) and *ya' hin mi'* "my mother" (4), to his uncle as *ya' hin mam ix̱tup*—literally "my father Cristobal" (5)—and to his aunt as *ya' hin mi' ros*—literally "my mother Rosa" (6). He will also respectfully call Agustina's father *ya' hesus* (14).

Rosa (6) will be referred to by her parents (1–2) and her husband (5) as *xo' ros*, by her children (10–11) as *ya' hin mi'*, by her neighbor Guadalupe (15) as *ix ros*, and by her neighbor's children (16–17) as *ya' ros*.

EXERCISE 5

(a)   How does Cristobal (5) refer to

his brother (3)? _____	*x̱uwan*
his neighbor (14)? _____	*hesus*
his neighbor (12)? _____	*antun*

(b)   How is Guadalupe (15) referred to

by her father (12)? _____	*lupe*
by her neighbor Rosa (6)? _____	*lupe*
by her neighbor Eulalia (11)? _____	*lupe*

2.3.2 *Insults and Compliments* In special circumstances, to express strong feelings of dislike or anger, of close friendship or admiration, another set of rules of usage determines the choice of classifier. Classifiers normally used for kin also carry with them the expression of closeness, respect, and admiration, while classifiers for non-kin are sensed as more distant, potentially expressing negative feelings. The classifiers *xo'* and *ho'* are therefore used for non-kin (instead of *naj* and *ix*) to mark special affection or a feeling of admiration. Conversely, the distant classifiers *naj* and *ix* normally used with non-kin are used for kin with whom one feels particularly angry and unhappy. Similarly, when the classifier *naj* or *ix* is used for an older person, instead of the expected *ya'*, it carries with it the weight of an insult. One may not insult in that way one's own parents and grand-parents, however. The very strong code of respect for one's family does not allow such expression.

EXERCISE 6

Keeping in mind the dynamics of the classifier system illustrated below, fill in the appropriate noun classifiers in the monologue of the angry Candelaria (7):

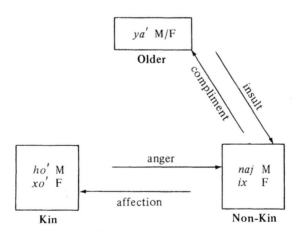

"Do you know what my unbearably stupid cousin _____ ewal (11) did? She is only ten and always starting nasty gossips! She told my friend _____ awustin (16) that I had met with her fiancé Lucas. It is not true. I really like _____ awustin (16) like a sister and I would not do that to her. I can tell that _____ ewal (11) is just going to become like the old witch of _____ Casimira who is so old and has such a poisonous tongue!"

This field worker learned to appreciate the nuances of treatment conveyed by the choice of classifiers. In general she was called *ix* Nicolasa; the children and the adults who wanted to express deference for her education—or her money—called her *ya'* Nicolasa; and a few people, on occasion, would call her *xo'* Nicolasa, always with a clear overtone of affection.

2.3.3 *The Supernatural and the Human Condition*   The pantheon of Jacaltec deities includes the following:

cumam	*dios*	God
cumam	*tz'ayic*	sun
cumam	*c'uh*	lightning
cumam	*sarampio*	measles
cumam	*hik'ob'*	whooping cough
cumi'	*virgen maría*	Virgin Mary
cumi'	*x'ahaw*	moon
cumi'	*ixim*	corn

Naj is used as the classifier of human contingency, and it is found with the following words:

naj cak'e	wind
naj witz	mountain
naj ya'b'il	disease
naj howal	fight, war
naj b'isc'ulal	sadness
naj tx'ixwilal	fear
naj meb'a'il	poverty

Deification applies to phenomena which either bring death (measles, whooping cough) or symbolize life (corn). The familiar gods of Mayan mythology are the sun, the moon, and lightning. The human classifier *naj* applies to all events and feelings of human condition (war, disease, sadness, happiness, poverty), and to semigods with which one is more familiar and feels closer, like the spirit of the mountain and that of the wind.

2.3.4 *Noun Classifiers for Objects of the Physical World* The physical world is divided into the following categories:

atz'am	(from *atz'am* "salt")
	atz'am atz'am "salt"
ch'en	(from *ch'en* "rock") stone, rock, glass, metal, and objects made of same material
	ch'en yojech "cooking stone," *ch'en melyu* "money"
ha'	(from *ha'* "water") water
	ha' ħab' "rain," *ha' pam* "lake"
ixim	(from *ixim* "corn") corn, wheat and all products made of corn and wheat
	ixim awal "cornfield," *ixim wah* "tortilla"
k'ap	(from *k'ape* "cloth, material") cloth
	k'ap chaħe "corte, skirt of the Jacaltec women"
	k'ap wełe "pants for men"
k'a'	(from *k'a* "fire")
	k'a k'a "fire"
metx	for dog only
	metx tx'i' "dog"
no'	(from *nok'* "animal") for all animals except dogs, and products made of animal material
	no' mis "cat," *no' txitam* "pig"
te'	(from *te'* "plant") for all plants except corn, and all products from plant material except rope, thread, and cloth
	te' hub'al "black beans," *te' tx'at* "bed"
tx'al	(from *tx'al* "thread") thread, woven material made of thread
	tx'al sintae "hair band," *tx'al faja* "sash"
tx'aħ	(from *tx'aħ* "rope") fiber rope, objects made of rope
	tx'aħ txim "cargo net," *tx'aħ lasu* "rope"
tx'otx'	(from *tx'otx'* "ground, land, earth") ground, dirt, made of dirt or clay
	tx'otx' xih "earth pot," *tx'otx' loc'* "adobe"

Each noun class contains a specific type of object as well as objects derived from them. For example, wooden objects fall into the plant class such as *te' tx'at* "bed," *te' ħah* "house" (from the time houses were made of cane and thatch roof); metallic objects fall into the stone/metal/glass class such as *ch'en melyu* "money," *ch'en limeta* "glass bottle," and *ch'en machit* "machete"; and animal products fall into the animal class such as *no' ceso* "cheese," *no' ƚapun* "soap" (made with animal fat and ashes and used to wash hair).

The classifiers therefore always point to the primary substance out of which a product is made, as illustrated by the list of the drinks available in Jacaltenango:

ha' ha'	"water," which is not recommended for drinking
no' lech	"milk," less and less available for the children of Jacaltenango as the population grows and more building grounds are needed—at the expense of cow pastures
te' uc'e	"aquavit," alcohol made from sugar cane on which people get drunk to celebrate happy events and forget their miseries
te' cape	"coffee," the main drink of Guatemala which is always served sweetened with raw sugar and flavored with cinnamon
ixim ulul	"atol," thick drink made of corn, also seasoned with sugar and cinnamon

Since the classification of nouns in Jacaltec is semantic and predictable, a learner can assign nouns to their class provided he/she knows what the primary substance of the object is.

EXERCISE 7

Think of what the objects are made and assign them to the appropriate class among the following: *no'* animal, *te'* plant, *ch'en* stone/glass/metal.

_____	*carro*	car
_____	*chib'e*	meat
_____	*oñ*	avocado
_____	*campana*	bell (church-)
_____	*hum*	book
_____	*chamarra*	woolen blanket
_____	*son*	marimba
_____	*ome*	earrings
_____	*xañab'*	sandals
_____	*meƚa*	table

One can even find in the language a few pairs of nouns distinguished by their different classifiers:

te' cuchara	wood spoon	**vs.**	*ch'en cuchara*	metallic spoon
te' ŝila	chair	**vs.**	*no' ŝila*	saddle
te' ak'b'al	flower	**vs.**	*no' ak'b'al*	candle

Therefore, Jacaltecs view a horse saddle as an animal-matter (i.e., leather) chair, and a candle as an animal-matter (i.e., pig fat) flower stem.

2.3.5 *The Classification of the Jacaltec World* Several comments may be made from the inspection of the noun classifiers on the state of religious beliefs and scientific knowledge of the old Mayan civilization at the time during which this system of noun classification arose. As already mentioned, the elements that take god-like and human-like classifiers point to the powers that governed the old Mayan world. They were the sun, the moon, lightning, the life-supporting corn, and the deadly diseases such as measles and whooping cough. They were also the more human spirits that inhabited the world such as the wind and the mountain and the milestones of human life.

The three noun classifiers that are used with only one noun may also isolate important cultural objects of the life of the old Mayas. The dog, for example, is isolated from all other animals and given its own classifier. Dogs are the best companions of the men in the fields; every Jacaltec goes to the cornfield carrying his machete and followed by his dog.

Salt is classified by itself, rather than being assigned to the rock category, maybe to indicate its religious significance. During the days before the harvest when food becomes very scarce, it is not uncommon for poor families to survive for weeks on a miserable diet of a few meager tortillas, if any at all, greens collected in the mountains, and salt. People of Jacaltenango say that in the poor village of San Marcos across the gorge, some people survive on salt alone when there is no more food to be had.

The third classifier that is used only for one noun is that of fire, but this may be simply due to the fact that products made from fire do not exist. Notice how the word for lightning is not classified with the classifier for fire. As was said above, lightning is treated like a deity, with the classifier assigned to gods.

Although the ancient Jacaltecs identified the two natural elements of water and fire, they did not identify the third one, the air. While water and fire were assigned a classifier, air, not recognized as a substance in itself, was not. The noun that is used to refer to static air is the same as the one used for the wind—*cak'e. cak'e* is used with the classifier of human contingency *naj* when it refers to the spirit of the wind. Such use reflects the belief that the wind is a spirit that causes many diseases; Jacaltec mothers always entirely cover their babies to protect them from the spirit of the wind, which gives headaches and earaches. But when the word *cak'e* is used to refer to the natural element air/wind, it remains unclassified.

The other substances left unclassified in Jacaltec include smoke, cloud, and dust, which were not assigned to the expected categories of fire, water, or earth/dirt. Similarly, the stars and the sky do not fall into any category. These unclassified nouns are:

cak'e	air/wind
satcañ	sky
tx'umel	star
ñub'	smoke
asun	cloud
pojoj	dust

The classification of natural elements of the world is therefore very incomplete in Jacaltec, particularly for the faraway phenomena. When some of those elements were classified, it was into the categories of gods or spirits as for the sun god (*cumam tz'ayic*), the lightning god (*cumam cuh*), the male spirit of the wind (*naj cak'e*), and the female spirit of the moon (*ix x'ahaw*)—which is sometimes treated as a goddess (*cumi' x'ahaw*). As the imprint of man on nature becomes more marked, the classifiers become more specific. Next to the unclassified or deified natural elements that escape human control are some natural phenomena that are classified simply by their appearance. For example, both ice and hail are classified as hard substances in the stone category: *ch'en chew* "ice" (literally, stone cold), *ch'en sajb'at* "hail" (literally, stone hail). This happens in spite of the fact that Jacaltec can observe that both melt into water.

As the people gain control over the world that surrounds them and start using its products, the classifiers come to identify objects not by their appearance but by their matter. For example, all products derived from animals are assigned to the animal category. These products include some that do not undergo any processing like *no' lech* "milk," *no' hos* "egg," or *no' chib'e* "meat" and some that are manufactured such as *no' xañab'* "sandals," *no' ǩila* "saddle" made from the skins, *no' chamarra* "woolen blankets" made from the wool, *no' ǩapun* "soap," and *no' ak'b'al* "candle" made from animal fat.

The domination of man over the vegetable world is apparent in the sudden proliferation of classifiers referring to materials derived from plants. There are five classifiers for the plant world. The corn *ixim* is set aside from other plants with its undeniable cultural and religious importance. The classifier *te'* designates all other plants and classifies all objects made of wood, such as pieces of furniture, doors, and windows. Three classifiers identify materials that require a more elaborate manufacturing process. They are *tx'añ* for rope and rope products, *tx'al* for thread and thread products, and *k'ap* for fabric and clothes.

Therefore, the language is explicit about the fact that to make a table, one needs a tree:

(1)   *te' te'*   tree ⟶ (1')   *te' mexa*   table

that to make a net bag, one needs first to have made rope, which is made from the agave plant:

(1)   *te' ch'ech*   agave ⟶ (2)   *tx'añ tx'añ*   rope ⟶
(2')   *txañ txim*   net bag

and that to make a shirt, one needs fabric, which is made from thread, which is made from the cotton plant, with the resulting chain of classifiers:

(1)   *te' tenok*   cotton ⟶ (2)   *tx'al tx'al*   thread ⟶
(3)   *k'ap k'ape*   cloth ⟶ (3')   *k'ap camiłe*   shirt

2.3.6 *A Frozen System of Classification*   The noun classifier system of Jacaltec is anthropologically interesting. It seems to reflect aspects of the culture of the old Mayas—their view and understanding of the world. The system used to be a productive part of the language, open to change and addition. It shows signs of its adaptability at the time of the conquest and early colonization. A study of how Spanish loanwords were incorporated in the noun classifier system of Jacaltec reveals that the system is now more and more limited and less productive, adapting less and less to the technology of the modern world.

At first, loanwords underwent extensive phonological adaptation. Spanish sounds and combinations of sounds that did not exist in Jacaltec were replaced:

Spanish	Jacaltec	
puerta	*pulta*	door
banco	*pancu*	bench
padre	*pale*	father (priest)

Later on, loanwords were borrowed with no adaptation, and new sounds were introduced in the speech of Jacaltecs:

vaso	*baso*	glass
carro	*carro*	car
avion	*abyon*	airplane

Whenever possible the loanwords were assigned to their natural classes:

te' pulta	wood door
ya' pale	respected father
tx'otx' ƚalu	earth jug (from Spanish *jarro* "jug")

Some classes were extended to accommodate loanwords. This was the case for the corn class, which was expanded to incorporate the imported wheat:

ixim trigo	corn wheat (from Spanish *trigo* "wheat")
ixim pan	corn (wheat) bread (from Spanish *pan* "bread")

Wheat is used mostly to make sweet rolls, which are served with coffee at fiestas and receptions and is also consumed by the Ladino population.

The rock class was also expanded to include metal and glass objects:

ch'en machit	metal machete
ch'en baso	glass/metal cup
ch'en carro	metal car

Notice how this part of the industry did not develop into a complex classificatory system comparable to the one observed for the weaving industry.

The most recent loanwords are not classified. The system of noun classifiers is becoming a frozen system that is not following the evolution of the lexical part of the language. There is no further extension of category and no invention of new classifiers to deal with the wave of new loanwords that reflect the advances of modern technology. Words like *cerveza* (beer), *Pepsi-Cola* and *Coca-Cola* are now commonly used, but without classifiers for lack of appropriate classifier and lack of identification of their ingredients. Most striking is the invasion on the market of plastic objects all of which remain unclassified. Although the words *plástico* and *naylo* have been borrowed, they are not being used as classifiers for the plastic goods of very common use and great popularity in Jacaltec households nowadays:

no' sapato	leather shoes	**vs.**	*sapato*	plastic shoes
ch'en baso	metallic cup	**vs.**	*baso*	plastic cup
tx'otx' ƚalu	earth jug	**vs.**	*ƚalu*	plastic jug

In order to specify that an object is made of plastic, the compound (noun + *plástico*) may be used, as in *baso plástico* "a cup made of plastic," although the use of the word without classifier is understood to mean that the cup is plastic and not metallic. These new loanwords increase the number of nouns that remain unclassified in Jacaltec, which include nonconcrete words (word, story, song), nouns indicating location rather than concrete building (church, marketplace, town hall, school), time expressions (hour, month, year), and body parts.

The three features of the Jacaltec language presented in this section offered some examples of the variation encountered across the languages of the world in three different domains of grammar. Among the languages that use case marking to signal the functions of subject and object, the majority function on a nominative/accusative system while Jacaltec represented an interesting example of the less common ergative system. Although all the languages have the means to express notions of directionality, in some languages—such as most of the American Indian languages—the expression of directionality constitutes an essential part of the verb complex, as was shown with the Jacaltec system.

Finally, while nouns are classified in many languages into either genders or noun classes, in Jacaltec they are organized into an elaborate system that provides interesting insights into the world as the Jacaltec speakers view it.

3 THE LINGUISTIC HORIZONS OF JACALTEC SPEAKERS

As people acquire a language and learn how to use it, they also acquire attitudes and beliefs toward that language and toward other people's languages. These attitudes and beliefs are generally shared by the members of the linguistic community and form an integral part of the culture. It sometimes takes months for the field worker to discover, through local incidents, comments from informants, confrontations, and puzzled looks, what these attitudes and beliefs are for a given community.

3.1 Spanish and Jacaltec

Jacaltec is spoken exclusively by Indians, although in the past this was not always the case. Until not long ago, the isolated Spanish-speaking Ladino families used to acquire some speaking knowledge of the local languages. They did it out of necessity; they were the school-teachers and officials of one sort or another, and they needed to communicate with a population that did not speak Spanish. Nowadays only in the most isolated villages would Ladino children still learn the local Mayan languages.

Spanish is the official language of the country and the language of prestige. In recent years it has been steadily spreading among the Indian population, to the extent that men go to serve in the army, and listen to the Spanish radio, and the children attend school. In their eagerness to help their children find a place in the dominant culture, some Indian parents of Jacaltenango may also decide to speak only Spanish to them, even if they themselves are not fluent in it.

Considered from a Ladino point of view, Jacaltec and the other Mayan languages are but "dialects"—a word associated with primitive ways, lack of education, superstitious beliefs, and poverty. Many believe these dialects to be breaking down, inadequate for education, and without grammar. Ladinos expressed such feelings by being half-amazed and half-scornful of a foreigner coming to study the grammar of Jacaltec. They thought that there was no grammar to be studied and were critical of the attention given to a language that they believe will and should be replaced in most situations by Spanish.

The attitude of Jacaltec speakers toward their native language is in part influenced by the pervasive attitude of the Ladinos. Most Jacaltec speakers agree with Ladinos in regarding Spanish as the language of prestige and social betterment, a notion heavily reinforced through schooling. So the Jacaltec speakers also were very curious and puzzled about the intrusion of a foreign linguist who presumed to tell them that their language indeed has a grammar, as do all languages, and that it was well worth studying. Some were apologetic, saying their language had broken down, accusing themselves of not learning it and respecting it as had their parents and ancestors. Although this is what they say to a foreigner and what they have come to say in the presence of Ladinos, it does not mean that Jacaltec speakers among themselves do not feel love and respect for their language as it is spoken today. Through centuries of white colonization and domination they have come to keep to themselves the pride they feel for their language and their culture. It was months before they shared their feelings about their language with the foreign field worker. By then, they expressed more and more openly their profound attachment to it and their strong identification with it.

In the town of Jacaltenango itself, the linguistic situation is steadily moving toward generalized bilingualism. A pattern that assigns a different role and function to each language is beginning to emerge. Spanish is the formal language of education and of dealings with public officials, while Jacaltec is the home language, that of private conversation. It is the language of mothers, the language of courtship, the language of idle talk and heated argument, and that of animated conversation of those sitting by the doorstep in the moonlight. Popular comedies are performed in Jacaltec at fiestas, and young Jacaltecs—inspired by Mexican movies—have begun to compose Jacaltec songs. Both the comedies and songs tell of the life of the Jacaltecs and are sources of obvious delight and pleasure for the people.

3.2 T.M.'s Feelings Toward Her Language

The bilingual informants were all very proud speakers of Jacaltec. They felt more at ease and more expressive in Jacaltec than in Spanish. They all experienced a deep satisfaction and enjoyment at being given the chance to work with, write in, and analyze their native language. T.M. was the most passionate about it. But as many other Jacaltecs, she had fallen prey to the widespread belief that Jacaltec was a second-class language. She gave as proof of this that it was not a written language and that it had no grammar.

T.M. had the notion that language was a very personal means of expression and that there were no right and wrong ways to use it—just personal differences. At first she resisted the idea of learning to write and read it, being convinced that it took special skills that could only be acquired by children through years of formal schooling. Once she began writing, she went through a period during which she would write and translate only her own texts and would refuse to transcribe and translate texts recorded by other people. She would argue that she could not do it because she would probably betray them, since she would not be able to guarantee that what she had heard and understood would be that which they had really meant to say.

This attitude corresponded to the way she judged sentences during sessions of direct elicitation. Her judgments reflected the same distinction between the secure instinctive knowledge she had of her own speech and her perception of other peoples' speech as their property—the expression of their free will for which she had an interpretation, but not necessarily the meaning that the speaker had intended. Her hesitations and scruples in dealing with more than her own speech and her attitude toward language in general stemmed from both the status of her language as an unwritten language and her lack of formal education. With a writing tradition, languages acquire standardization. Norms are set by recognized authorities; they are printed in books and taught in schools. The dialect of a certain group of speakers or a certain location is taken as the standard form, and this standard form is then shared, mostly through writing, by the speakers of all variants of the language. It is mostly through formal education that speakers acquire the feeling they all share the "same" language, in spite of noted differences of speech. But T.M.'s attitude toward language emphasized the reality of the variation found in unwritten languages, languages that exist only through the speech of individuals.

3.3   Jacaltec Dialects and the Surrounding Mayan Languages

There is no standard form of Jacaltec or of any Mayan language. This means that there are as many variations of the language as there are settlements of Jacaltec speakers, although the Jacaltec language exhibits little dialectal variation compared to other Mayan languages. Such variation is found in all speech communities of the world; however, it is not reflected in the written language, as noted earlier. And as in all the communities of the world, the variations—of accent, intonation, vocabulary, or grammar—are not all perceived as just linguistic variations. In Jacaltenango, as well as anywhere else, certain reactions, feelings, and prejudices are attached to them.

Jacaltec speakers from Jacaltenango consider that the dialect of Concepción is provincial, even though it is spoken by the second largest settlement of Jacaltec speakers. They also make fun of the dialect of San Marcos, the village across the gorge. The accent and speech of San Marcos are considered laughable, and they impersonate peasants in jokes—in the same way that Americans tell Polish or other ethnic jokes.

In addition to their fellow Jacaltec speakers, Jacaltecs have frequent dealings with speakers of two closely related languages—Acateco from the village of San Miguel Acatán, beyond San Marcos, and Kanjobal from the towns of Solomá and Santa Eulalia, a further distance away over the mountains. These three languages form a chain of dialects with unclear boundaries in which Acateco stands halfway between Jacaltec and Kanjobal. This means that Acateco shares as many features with Jacaltec as it does with Kanjobal. For example, it has the same negation word as Kanjobal but the same aspect markers as Jacaltec.

Although linguistically the Jacaltec language has more in common with Acateco than with Kanjobal, the Jacaltecs feel a much closer affinity with the Kanjobal speakers. They say that they understand Kanjobal, while they pretend to be unable to communicate with Acatecos, and it is not uncommon to hear scornful remarks from Jacaltecs as Migueleños go by on their way to or from the market.

The last language with which Jacaltecs are in close contact is Mam, a language from a different branch of the Mayan family of language. Mam speakers from the town of Todos Santos have come down from their inhospitable land to settle at the edge of town where they work for the Jacaltecs. They are socially discriminated against and constitute the poorest segment of the population. Jacaltecs make fun of their singing intonation and often behave very rudely toward them. It is, of course, the burden of these Todosanteros to learn Jacaltec and/or Spanish in order to communicate.

3.4 The Linguistic World of Jacaltecs

Positive (+), negative (−), and neutral (=) attitudes toward the languages and dialects that compose the linguistic world of the Jacaltecs are summarized in Table 1.4. The linguistic world of the Jacaltecs is, therefore, a patchwork of different dialects and languages toward which they have extremely varying attitudes. There is the prestigious Spanish, the despised Mam, the unintelligible Acateco, the preferred Kanjobal, and within the Jacaltec community itself, the provincial Concepcionero and the peasant Marqueño.

TABLE 1.4   Attitudes Toward Other Languages and Dialects

Spanish	+
Dialects of Jacaltec:	
Jacaltenango	+
Concepción	=
San Marcos	−
Other languages of the Kanjobalan branch:	
Acatec	−
Kanjobal	+
Chuj	=
Languages of other branch of the family:	
Mam	−

EXERCISE 8

Describe your own linguistic world and analyze your feelings and attitude toward the languages with which you are or have been in contact. Describe the attitude of the general public toward those languages.

3.5   T.M. and the Tzutujils

Although it might seem easy to think of all the Indians of Guatemala as Mayan, such a unifying concept does not correspond to the reality of a Jacaltec speaker who identifies himself or herself as "Jacaltec" and has little notion of the existence of a Mayan community. Even within their Jacaltec world, people perceive their differences more than their similarities. While linguists talk of the Mayan family of languages and label them as Jacaltec, Kanjobal, Mam, Quiché, or Cakchiquel, these languages are all referred to as *lengua* "tongue, or language" in Spanish and in each language with the common word for "tongue."

Jacaltecs say *w-ab'xub'al* "my language" or *j-ab'xub'al* "our language" to mean Jacaltec and *y-ab'xub'al naj/ix* "his/her language" for somebody else's language, but they have no specific names for Mayan languages.

This situation had never bothered T.M. until she went on a trip to Lake Atitlán where people speak Tzutujil, a language of still another branch of the Mayan family, as distinct from Jacaltec as Mam. There, in the market, the women were very intrigued by her, her native costume marking her clearly as a stranger. They tried to talk to her in Tzutujil, and she could not understand them. She tried Jacaltec, and they could not understand her. She came home one day looking very disturbed and asked what those women were speaking, what it was called, and what her language was called so that she could tell them. And she learned that outsiders call her language "Jacaltec" after the name of the linguistic center of the language, her town of Jacaltenango.

SOLUTIONS TO EXERCISES

2. (a)   he hit me and *me* cried
    (b)   I pushed him and *him* fell

3. (a)   Jacaltenango, Concepción
    (b)   ya' antun/ix malin *or* naj ɫuwan
    (c)   the speaker is down by the river

4. (a)   xabej-*ay-toj* (down away)
    (b)   xwa-*h-toj*   (up away)

5. (a)   3: *ho'* ɫuwan
            14: *naj* hesus
            12: *ya'* antun

    (b)   12: *xo'* lupe   by her father
            6: *ix* lupe   by her contemporary neighbor
           11: *ya'* lupe   by her younger neighbor

6. *ix* ewal (instead of *xo'*)
    xo' awustin (instead of *ix*)
    ix ewal
    ix Casimira (instead of *ya'*)

7. *ch'en* carro   *no'* chamarra
   no' chib'e   *te'* son
   te' oñ   *ch'en* ome
   ch'en campana   *no'* xañab'
   te' hum   *te'* meł̵a

SUGGESTIONS FOR FURTHER READING

On Linguistics Field Methods

Samarin, William. *Field Linguistics: A Guide to Linguistic Field Work*. New York: Holt, Rinehart & Winston, 1967.

On the Jacaltec People

LaFarge II, Oliver and Douglas Byer, *The Year Bearer's People*, Tulane University Middle American Research Series, no. 3. New Orleans: Tulane University Press, 1931.

On the Jacaltec Language

Craig, Colette G. *The Structure of Jacaltec*. Austin: University of Texas Press, 1977.

Day, Christopher. *The Jacaltec Language*, Indiana University Publications, vol. 12. Bloomington, Ind.: Indiana University Press, 1973.

_____. "The Semantics of Social Categories in a Transformational Grammar of Jacaltec." In *Meaning in Mayan Languages* [on noun classifiers], edited by Monro S. Edmonson. The Hague: Mouton, 1973.

II

Maninka

Charles Bird

Timothy Shopen

INTRODUCTION: MANINKA LANGUAGE AND SOCIETY

The Maninka language is spoken by people who spread over the savannah region of West Africa, from Upper Volta in the east to Gambia and Guinea on the Atlantic coast in the west, and from Mali and Senegal in the north down to the Ivory Coast in the south. The Maninka people are essentially the same in language and culture as those who have been called a variety of names including Bambara, Dyula, Malinke, Mandinka, Mandingo, and Wangara. (See Figure 2.1 for the set of names used most consistently by native speakers.) Maninka was the language of the great Mali empire of the thirteenth century, which, like the Ghana empire before it and the Gao empire after it, covered most of West Africa. It remains a language of first importance for social contact and trade.

Charles Bird is an American linguist teaching at Indiana University. His interests range from descriptive linguistics, with concentration on African languages, to sociolinguistics and stylistics, as well as the study of the role of language in education. He has been UNESCO visiting professor of applied linguistics in Mali since 1972.

Timothy Shopen is an American who teaches linguistics at the Australian National University. His work centers around describing languages and applying linguistics in education. He was a teacher in Mali from 1962 to 1964, and that is when he began his interest in Maninka and several other African languages.

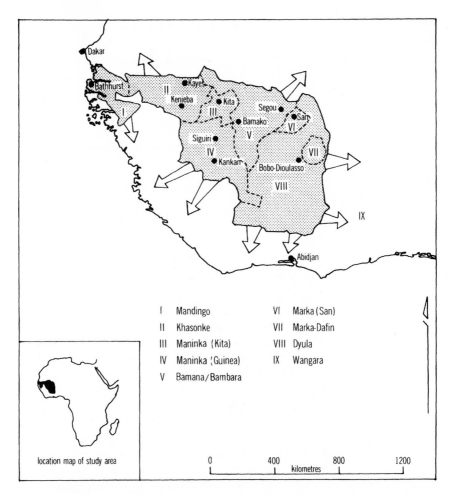

FIGURE 2.1   *The Maninka-Bambara Language Group and Its Various Names.*
The shaded area represents the greatest concentration of speakers, and the arrows show
the directions in which more widely spread communities are found.

The nucleus of Maninka society is the village. Villages range in size
from a few hundred to several thousand people. They are democratic,
governed by a chief who is responsible to a council of male elders that
represents each family in the village. The majority of a typical village
population are farmers who grow millet and rice as their staple crops,
some fruits and vegetables, and perhaps peanuts, cotton or tobacco as
cash crops. They may raise a few sheep, goats or cows, and there will
always be at least one blacksmith, a few weavers, perhaps a leather
worker, as well as some merchants, a few hunters and several bards
(more about the bards later). The women are the vegetable gardeners

and the ones who take the salable produce to the market, thereby getting more cash than the men. Most families are polygamous: many Maninka communities are Muslim, and they obey the Islamic law that limits each man to four wives. However, in areas where traditional beliefs predominate that were present before the arrival of Islam, some wealthy men have more than four wives. The children in Islamic areas usually attend a Koranic school where they learn to read and recite the verses of the Koran. In more traditional areas, the children are educated in initiation groups that teach them the fundamental principles upon which the culture is based. In the larger towns and cities, many children attend schools based primarily on the French system of education. Somewhat less than 30 percent of the children of school age attend these schools, and by the sixth grade, three-fourths of them are no longer students. There are no schools where Maninka children learn to read and write their own language.

This will be a discussion of what it means to be a speaker of the Maninka language. There will be two main parts: first, a discussion of some of the major characteristics of Maninka grammar, and second a discussion of the way language is used in Maninka culture.

1 MANINKA GRAMMAR

1.1 Learning Maninka

Consider the situation of a newcomer who has just taken up residence in a Maninka village and is starting to learn the language. Like speakers of all languages, Maninka people continually use sentences to communicate new messages to each other, and for the most part they do so not by knowing the sentences themselves but by sharing vocabulary and a systematic set of rules for combining words into sentences. They create sentences on the spot as the need arises. The vocabulary and the combinatory principles constitute the grammar of Maninka, and this is what the newcomer will have to learn. The newcomer would never succeed by learning just the sentences; there is no limit to the number he or she might hear or want to say. Language learners are like linguists interested in giving a scientific description of the language: they need to discover the knowledge speakers share that enables them to construct and understand original sentences.

The principles of Maninka grammar have their reality in the minds of the people who speak the language—a varied group of individuals living in communities located over a wide area of West Africa. As with all languages, the grammar of Maninka changes from generation to generation, and there are a number of dialects. Maninka itself is descendent from a dialect of the Niger-Congo language, the common ancestor to the languages spoken by most of the people of Subsaharan Africa. Like languages all over the world, Maninka has borrowed words and other grammatical features from languages with which it has come into contact.

In its finer details, Maninka is unlike any other language in the world; it is in this sense a unique cultural artifact. At the same time, in its broader outlines there is much about it that would be familiar to a speaker of any other language that wanted to learn it. Much of its particular shape at this point in its ongoing history is not accidental, and can be understood as representative of characteristics that all languages tend to have; these are characteristics that we can assume are due to the genetically determined nature of the human mind and vocal tract. This is why discovering the grammatical principles of each particular language contributes to an understanding of all languages. It is also why the more that is learned about the range of languages spoken by the people of the world (the more that is learned about what is possible as a human grammar and what is not), the more there will be a basis for defining an important aspect of human nature.

Like all languages, Maninka has a double level of structure: a small set of distinctive sounds combining to form meaningful units (phonology) and then ways in which these meaningful units are combined to express larger meanings (syntax). It has words that express events and states of being; one can assume that any language will have a way of saying things like "The child is sleeping," "The girl saw the boy," and "The man gave a bowl to the woman," and that any language will have a way of signaling who is sleeping, who saw whom, and who gave what to whom. Someone learning Maninka will find all this and more easy to recognize; what remains is to learn that which is different from the grammar of his or her native language.

1.2   How to Describe Events in Maninka

1.2.1   *Events with One Participant*   Let us assume a newcomer has heard:

Na!   Come!
Ta!   Go!

and from this has figured out that *na* means "come" and *ta* "go." His host's name is *Baba*, and his host's wife is named *Fanta*. Upon hearing the sentence:

Baba be ta.

and seeing Baba going somewhere, he assumes this means "Baba is going." He guesses how to say "Baba is coming":

Baba be na.

and he is right. He devises two more sentences:

Fanta be ta.
Fanta be na.

He has formed a generalization about how to describe ongoing events; he uses *be* along with the name for an event, and he identifies a participant. The participant comes first (*Baba* or *Fanta*), then *be*, then the name for the event (*ta* or *na*). (Note: the letter *e* represents a sound in Maninka close to the "ay" in English "say." Thus, Maninka *be* is pronounced like English "bay.")

When the newcomer learns *sigi* "sit down" and *da* "lie down," he can construct the following sentences and know what they mean (the reader should also be able to understand these sentences):

Baba be sigi.   Fanta be sigi.
Baba be da.   Fanta be da.

When he learns *sunogo* "sleep," *don* "come in," and *bo* "go out," he knows how to use them in simple sentences. (The reader is invited to make up some sentences with these words such as "Baba is sleeping," "Fanta is going out," etc. and proceed as a language learner through the rest of this discussion.)

The newcomer now knows seven *verbs*, words that describe events, and two *nouns*, words that can be used to name participants in those events. Combining these words with *be*, there are fourteen sentences he can produce, which are represented in Table 2.1.

TABLE 2.1 Possibilities for Fourteen Sentences

Sentence	=	Noun	*be*	Verb
				ta
				na
		Baba		sigi
		Fanta		da
				sunogo
				don
				bo

Central to what one has to know to speak any language is how to group nouns around verbs to describe events, and here the notions 'participant' and 'role' are useful. In the sense we intend, these terms apply to inanimate as well as animate beings. In "Baba is cutting wood" we would say there are two roles, one for the cause of the event and the other for the entity that is affected by it; *Baba* and *wood* are the participants playing these roles. Note the three participants assigned different roles in "Fanta is putting rice in a bowl" and the four roles and participants in "Baba bought a chicken from a woman for one hundred francs." Verbs define roles, and nouns name participants. The noun *Fanta* in itself has the same meaning in all the sentences *Fanta be bo*, *Fanta be don*, *Fanta be da*, and *Fanta be sunogo*; the participant is the same, but the roles are different. The sentences *Baba be sigi* and *Fanta be sigi* have the same role but different participants.

With another word that can refer to a participant, there are seven more sentences that are possible. Upon hearing:

i be ta

And understanding "You are going," the newcomer is able to construct these additional sentences:

i be na	i be sunogo
i be sigi	i be don
i be da	i be bo

He has correctly understood that *i* means "you" (note: the letter *i*, represents a sound in Maninka close to the "ee" in English "heel," "feet," etc.). When he learns that a speaker refers to himself as *ne* ("I, me"), he can produce the Maninka equivalents of the following seven sentences. (The reader is invited to do so.)

I am going
I am coming
I am going out
I am coming in
I am sitting down
I am lying down
I am sleeping

He learns that *a* refers to someone or something that speakers assume to be identifiable and not in need of naming ("he, him, she, her, it") and that *u* has the same function in the plural ("they, them"). He learns that *an* means "we, us," while *au* means "you" plural ("you all").

He has learned all the *personal pronouns* of Maninka, and with these there are six sentences the learner can compose with any of the verbs he knows, here shown with the verb meaning "sit down":

ne be sigi   an be sigi
i be sigi   au be sigi
a be sigi   u be sigi

All languages have the means of referring to participants this way, by pointing to them as it were, rather than naming them, and personal pronouns are by far the most commonly used for this purpose. Personal pronouns are employed as much for designating the participants of events in Maninka as all nouns put together. Pronouns often refer to the protagonists of a story once their identity has been clearly established, as in the following narrative about Baba:

Baba be na. A be don. A be sigi. A be da. A be sunogo.

Furthermore, people talk a good deal to each other about themselves, and ordinarily the only way for speakers to designate themselves or their addressees is with personal pronouns. If Baba wants to announce that he is going out, he doesn't say *Baba be bo*, but rather *ne be bo*. If Fanta were speaking to him about it, she wouldn't say *Baba be bo* either. She would say *i be bo*, or perhaps *Baba, i be bo*. This makes the personal pronouns some of the most useful words in the language. We will henceforth refer to all the expressions used to designate participants in events, nouns and pronouns included, as *noun phrases*.

1.2.2   *The Productivity of the Grammar*   The language learner has discovered not only what individual words and some particular sentences mean, but also a principle of sentence formation. He has learned that the parts of sentences belong to different categories and that the categories come in a particular order. Put first the expression identifying a participant in an event and the word naming the event at the end, with a third kind of word, *be*, in the middle:

Sentence = Noun Phrase   *be*   **Verb**

Knowing this principle, he does not have to have heard a sentence before in order to understand it or produce it himself. If he wants to say "They are going" and he knows this principle plus the words "they" and "go" (*u* and *ta*), he can form the sentence: *ta* names the event so it comes at the end; *u* names the participant in that event so it comes first,

TABLE 2.2   Fifty-Six Sentences

Sentence	=	Noun Phrase	*be*	Verb
		Baba		ta
		Fanta		na
		ne		sigi
		i		da
		a		sunogo
		an		don
		au		bo
		u		

and *be* comes in the middle, *U be ta*. With his present vocabulary and this principle, there are fifty-six sentences that the newcomer can create if the need arises. This is shown in Table 2.2.

1.2.3   *Recursion*   Now when the newcomer learns that:

U be ta nga Fanta be sunogo.

means "They are going but Fanta is sleeping," where *nga* means "but," his understanding of how conjunctions like *but* work in his own language leads him to formulate the following principle:

Sentence = Sentence   *nga*   Sentence

In other words, he has devised the principle that two sentences like "They are going" and "Fanta is sleeping" can be conjoined with *nga* to form a larger sentence as can be seen in Figure 2.2.

This is in fact a fully productive principle in Maninka. The descriptions of events linked together by *nga* do not have to be just *U be ta* and *Fanta be sunogo*, they can be any of the sentences he has learned to form, providing of course that they make sense. There is now a myriad of new sentences he can construct, for example, the Maninka equivalents of:

You are sitting down but I am lying down.
Baba is going out but Fanta is coming in.
They are coming but we are going out.

With his present vocabulary and the contrasting principles he has discovered, the newcomer can now construct something over 2,500 sentences! When he learns just one more conjunction, *sabu* "because,"

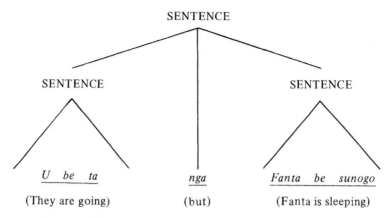

FIGURE 2.2 Sentence Conjunction

he can not only say things like *Fanta be bo sabu Baba be don* (Fanta is going out because Baba is coming in), but he can construct even longer sentences with multiple conjunctions such as *Ne be sigi sabu u be da nga Baba be bo sabu Fanta be don* (I am sitting down because they are lying down but Baba is going out because Fanta is coming in), and the number of sentences he can now create is *minimally* on the order of 50^4 or 6,250,000. He is now in a position to produce Maninka sentences that not only has he not heard before but that most Maninka speakers as well will not have heard!

The feat of being able to create so many sentences with the addition of only two more words is due to the 'recursive' use of sentences—the principle whereby sentences can occur within sentences, which in turn can be inside still larger sentences. The language learner has adopted a rule something like the following:

Sentence = Sentence   Conjunction   Sentence

where the conjunction can be either *nga* "but" or *sabu* "because." The principle can apply over and over again so that it allows the construction of "multitiered" sentences. The structure of our example sentence is as in Figure 2.3.

All languages have recursive devices such as this. Our language learner has acquired the ability to produce an astronomical number of sentences with a very small vocabulary—eighteen words. One can imagine how many more sentences the native speakers of Maninka and other languages have the capacity for. Instead of just eighteen words, they have vocabularies with many thousands of words, and they use many more sentence constructions besides the ones examined here.

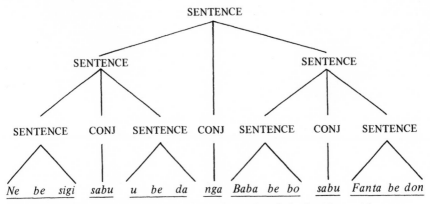

(I am sitting down because they are lying down, but Baba is going out because Fanta is coming in.)

FIGURE 2.3 *Multilevel Sentence Conjunction*

1.2.4 *Auxiliaries* When it is learned that:

Fanta ka ta.

means "Fanta should go," then a principle can be formulated defining *be* and *ka* as auxiliaries, similar in some way to English auxiliary verbs (see Table 2.3).

Now one can begin to imagine how meanings such as "will go" and "have gone" are expressed in Maninka: with the expressions meaning "will" and "have" coming between the noun phrase and the verb. This is in fact the case:

Baba bena ta.	Baba will go.
Baba bara ta.	Baba has gone.

What the person learning Maninka has come up with so far is a

TABLE 2.3 *Maninka and English Auxiliary Verbs*

Noun Phrase	Auxiliary	Verb
Fanta	*be*	*ta*
Fanta	is	going
Noun Phrase	**Auxiliary**	**Verb**
Fanta	*ka*	*ta*
Fanta	should	go

principle of word order that makes Maninka look very much like English. For both languages, the following principle obtains:

Sentence = Noun Phrase   Auxiliary   Verb

1.2.5 Events with Two Participants   Suppose now that the newcomer has learned the meaning of the following sentences:

Fanta be daga sigi.	Fanta is setting down the pot.
Fanta be ji sigi.	Fanta is setting down the water.
Fanta be kini sigi.	Fanta is setting down the rice.
Fanta be daba sigi.	Fanta is setting down the hoe.

It is clear that *daga* means "pot," *ji* means "water," *kini* means "rice" and *daba* means "hoe." It is reasonable for the language learner to identify *sigi* "sit down" and *sigi* "set down" as the same word. The most important discovery is that of word order when there are two participants in an event:

Sentence = Noun Phrase   Auxiliary   Noun Phrase   Verb

There is a noun phrase at the beginning of the sentence, just as before, but a second one comes before the verb (V). The noun phrase at the beginning of the sentence is the subject (S), and the second one, if it occurs, is the object (O). English has the order SVO, while Maninka is SOV: in this respect Maninka is like many other languages, including Hindi and most of the other languages of India, Japanese and Korean, and very many of the native languages of North America. SOV languages are the most common in the world. Among these, the most frequent type is like Japanese (see Chapter 5) where not only direct objects precede the verb but all other constituents as well. Maninka belongs to a comparatively smaller group that has subjects and direct objects before the verb but other constituents after it. To say "The girl put the book on the table" in Japanese, one places the verb "put" at the end of the clause; in Maninka "the girl" and "the book" precede the verb, but the expression "on the table" follows it.

In all languages, an object noun phrase, when it occurs, tends to be the participant with the role most closely affected in the event described by a verb. So it is with the verb for "break" in Maninka, *ti*. One can say either "The pot has broken" or "Fanta has broken the pot": *the pot* is the participant most closely affected in the event in either case (it is changed from something whole to something in pieces). *The pot* shows up in subject position when it is the only participant mentioned, but it moves over to object position when two participants are identified:

Daga bara ti.	*The pot* has broken.
Fanta bara *daga* ti.	Fanta has broken *the pot.*

The tendency for objects to be the participants most closely affected in the events described by verbs is an extremely general characteristic of the languages of the world. A speaker of English would have to learn a different word order to say "Fanta has broken the pot" in Maninka, but he would have nothing new to learn about which of the participants, *Fanta* or *the pot*, is to go in the object position.

Just as Maninka objects are similar to those of other languages, so are the subjects. It is typical that when a cause is expressed for an event, it appears as subject. So it is that in the sentences that say that Fanta has caused the pot to "sit down" or to break (*Fanta bara daga sigi, Fanta bara daga ti*), *Fanta* shows up in subject position. There is a pervasive tendency among the languages of the world for subjects to come before objects: besides SVO and SOV, the only other word order that is common is VSO. Given the tendency for causes to be expressed in subject position, this means (reasonably enough) that causes tend to be expressed before effects. For example, in *Fanta bara daga ti, Fanta* is the cause of the event and comes before *daga ti* (pot-break), which is the effect.

Subjects tend to be understood as the 'topic,' and the rest of the sentence as a 'comment' on that topic. Thus in either "Fanta is sitting down" or "Fanta is setting the pot down," there is a tendency in either Maninka or English to understand that something is being said "about" Fanta. Both languages prefer to have their topics as subjects. If we were talking in English "about" the pot, we would usually make it the subject and say "The pot is being set down by Fanta"; Maninka would do something similar saying in effect "The pot is setting down" (a construction we will examine in a moment). A language that has a remarkable system for keeping topics in subject position is the Austronesian language Malagasy (see Chapter 3). Maninka is a Niger-Congo language, and English is Indo-European; these two families generally have a strong notion of subject with a tendency to put topics in subject position. Maninka word order is more fixed than English so that subjects invariably come first in the sentence, which makes their topic function all the more prominent.

Not all languages have so strong a link between the notions of subject and topic. Japanese has a fully systematic means of marking any participant as topic, the subject or any other. Chinese has a fully productive means of moving objects to first position in the sentence and thus topic status, and Russian can do this easily with any noun phrase (see Chapters 3 and 6 in the companion volume *Languages and Their Status*). New York City English is somewhat like Chinese in that it freely allows sentences such as "That movie I saw yesterday," and

"Apples I like," while Old English was more like contemporary Russian in allowing any noun phrase (subject or not) to come first in the sentence when it was the topic. Depending on what his native language is like, the learner will find more or less that is familiar in the placement and function of Maninka subjects and objects.

Now we have two sentence types, *intransitive* sentences with only one participant expressed, the one in subject position; and *transitive* ones with two participants expressed, one in object position as well as in subject position:

Sentence = Noun Phrase   Auxiliary   Verb
Sentence = Noun Phrase   Auxiliary   Noun Phrase   Verb

We can express these two principles as a single generalization by using parentheses to designate the possibility of an object noun phrase:

Sentence = Noun Phrase   Auxiliary   (Noun Phrase)   Verb

Now as the newcomer learns more vocabulary, he is able to construct a number of transitive sentences. When he learns *tobi* "cook," *dumu* "eat" and *min* "drink," he can say things such as the following. (The reader is invited to make up these sentences. Recall that "rice" is *kini* and "water" is *ji*.)

Fanta is cooking the rice.
They are drinking the water.
You all should drink the water.
We have eaten the rice.
I will cook it.
You have broken them.
Baba will eat it.
Baba should set me down.

Here are the corresponding Maninka sentences, but in a different order: *Baba bena a dumu, U be ji min, Ne bena a tobi, Baba ka ne sigi, Au ka ji min, Fanta be kini tobi, An bara kini dumu, I bara u ti.*

When he learns *dila* "repair," *ye* "see" and *fo* "greet," he can say (recall that "hoe" is *daba* and "pot" is *daga*):

They are repairing the pot.
We have seen Baba.
You should greet Fanta.
I have seen the hoe.
You should repair the hoe.

Baba will see them.
Fanta is greeting us.
I will repair the hoe.

Here are these same sentences in a different order: *I ka Fanta fo, Ne bara daba ye, Ne bena daba dila, I ka daba dila, An bara Baba ye, Fanta be an fo, Baba bena u ye, U be daga dila.*

A summary of the Maninka grammar learned so far is presented in Table 2.4.

The language learner now commands sentences such as the following:

(1) They will go out.
(2) Baba is greeting them.
(3) I have broken the hoe.
(4) Fanta will see you all.
(5) You should lie down.
(6) They are eating the rice.
(7) You should drink the water.
(8) Fanta will cook the rice because Baba is coming.

TABLE 2.4 Summary Grammar

Vocabulary					
Verbs				**Nouns**	
bo	go out	*na*	come	*Baba*	(man's name)
da	lie down	*sigi*	sit/set down	*Fanta*	(woman's name)
dila	repair	*sunogo*	sleep	*daba*	hoe
don	come in	*ta*	go	*daga*	pot
dumu	eat	*ti*	break	*ji*	water
fo	greet	*tobi*	cook	*kini*	rice
min	drink	*ye*	see		
Auxiliaries				**Pronouns**	
bara	perfect	*bena*	will	*ne*	I
be	continuous	*ka*	should	*i*	you
				a	he, she, it
Conjunctions				*an*	we
				au	you all
nga	but	*sabu*	because	*u*	they

Combinatory Principles

Sentence = Noun Phrase Auxiliary (Noun Phrase) Verb
Sentence = Sentence Conjunction Sentence

(9) They are coming in but we will sleep.
(10) You should sit down because Baba is sitting down.
(11) Baba has gone but he has repaired the hoe.
(12) I will repair the pot because you have broken it but Fanta should cook the rice.

Here is the Maninka for sentences 1–7, in a different order: *I ka da, U bena bo, Ne bara daba ti, U be kini dumu, Baba be u fo, I ka ji min, Fanta bena au ye.*

And here are sentences 8–12, in a different order: *I ka sigi sabu Baba be sigi, Fanta bena kini tobi sabu Baba be na, Baba bara ta nga a bara daba dila, Ne bena daga dila sabu i bara a ti nga Fanta ka kini tobi, U be don nga an bena sunogo.*

The number of sentences the newcomer can now form and understand with this very small part of Maninka grammar is truly astronomical. We stopped counting at a point where the number was *minimally* 6,250,000, and by now the number is many times higher. Most of the sentences he uses will be ones he has never heard before, and many will be ones that are new as well for the Maninka speakers with whom he communicates. The grammatical principles they share make this possible.

1.2.6 *How Maninka Speakers Say "Baba Is Eating"* The language learner's ability to describe events in Maninka will depend in part on his discovering a principle governing the formation of intransitive and transitive sentences. Rules often have exceptions, and this is as much the case in Maninka as in English; however, this one is completely regular, as the reader will see once he has discovered it for himself. The rule may not be immediately apparent to someone who is familiar only with a language like English; but once discovered, it is easy to remember because of its elegant simplicity.

Like all languages, Maninka has verbs that can be used only intransitively, and this seems to be because they describe events that people can only conceive of as involving one participant—verbs such as *na* "come," *sunogo* "sleep," and *sa* "die." Notice the parallel to English. Asterisks indicate sentences that are ungrammatical—not possible in Maninka, or English.

Maninka	**English**
Fanta be na.	Fanta is coming.
*Fanta be Baba na.	*Fanta is coming Baba.
Fanta be sa.	Fanta is dying.
*Fanta be Baba sa.	*Fanta is dying Baba.

In the Maninka verbs that can be used transitively, we appear to have another instance where there are similarities between languages because of the way people think. These verbs describe events people can conceive of as involving two participants (or more). Maninka, like English, has verbs that can be used both intransitively and transitively. For example:

Maninka	English
Daba bara ti.	The hoe has broken.
U bara daba ti.	They have broken the hoe.
Kini bena tobi.	The rice will cook.
Fanta bena kini tobi.	Fanta will cook the rice.

In English and many other languages, some verbs can be used freely only in transitive sentences, for example, *greet*. English speakers do not ordinarily accept sentences such as "Bill greeted." In Maninka, on the other hand, all verbs can be used intransitively. Recall that *min* means "drink" and *ji* means "water." One can say:

Ji be min.

Word-for-word this translates as "The water is drinking," but one can reasonably suppose that some other meaning is entailed. Indeed, a couple of hundred years ago people used to say things in English like "The bridge is building," but that kind of construction was opposed by the purists of the time and is not in use anymore. (*Time* magazine, however, used to play on the old construction for stylistic effect.) The best way to approximate the Maninka meaning in today's English would be with the passive tense, such as "The water is being drunk." Recall that the English passive is a way of getting the object of a transitive sentence into subject position. We see here that Maninka can do the same thing, but without changing the form of the verb.

English	Maninka
They are drinking *the water*.	U be *ji* min.
The water is being drunk.	*Ji* be min.

Given the following sentences:

U bena daba dila.	They will repair the hoe.
U bara daga sigi.	They have set down the pot.
U be kini dumu.	They are eating the rice.
U ka daba ye.	They should see the hoe.
U bena Baba fo.	They will greet Baba.

one can see how the following sentences would be formed. (The reader is invited to form these sentences himself):

The hoe will be repaired.
The pot has been set down.
The rice is being eaten.
The hoe should be seen.
Baba will be greeted.

Here are the sentences in a different order: *Daba ka ye, Daga bara sigi, Baba bena fo, Kini be dumu, Daba bena dila.*

An English speaker would think that one could say things in Maninka like "Fanta is eating," "We will drink," and "I will cook." But the sentences an English speaker might think would have these meanings in fact have different meanings. One can say *Kini be dumu* (The rice is being eaten), and *Fanta be kini dumu* (Fanta is eating the rice), but if one said *Fanta be dumu*, it wouldn't mean "Fanta is eating" but rather "Fanta is being eaten." Given the sentence:

An bena ji min.   We will drink the water.

and following our intuitions in English, we would think that one could also say *An bena min* and mean "We will drink." But this would only be understood by a Maninka speaker as meaning "We will be drunk," not in the sense of "inebriated," but rather in the odd sense of our being ingested as some kind of liquid. On the other hand one can say *Ji bena min*; while the English speaker might think that this has the nonsensical meaning of "The water will drink," it in fact means something close to "The water will be drunk."

The word for "meat" is *sogo*. One can say *Ne bena sogo tobi* (I will cook the meat). Following intuitions in English, one would guess correctly that *Sogo bena tobi* is a possible sentence and that it means "The meat will cook." However, one might be misled into thinking that *Ne bena tobi* was also possible as a way of saying "I will cook" (perform the cooking), but it can only mean "I will cook" in the sense of "I will be cooked."

Someone learning Maninka will have to discover what principle is involved here, or he will make a lot of mistakes. The reader is invited to carry out a piece of scientific inquiry to see if with the data that is presented it is possible to find a hypothesis that will explain which intransitive sentences can occur in Maninka and what they mean. Following are some examples of the kinds of intransitive sentences that are allowed in Maninka. Some are formed with verbs that can be used only intransitively and some with verbs that can be used transitively as well:

(1) Ne ka ta.   (5) Daba be ti.
(2) Fanta bara na.   (6) Ji bena min.
(3) Baba bara sa.   (7) Kini ka dumu.
(4) A bena bo.   (8) Sogo bara tobi.

Translations: 1) I should go. 2) Fanta has come. 3) Baba has died. 4) He/she/it will go out. 5) The hoe is breaking. 6) The water will be drunk. 7) The rice should be eaten. 8) The meat has cooked.

Here is the kind of intransitive sentence that is *not* possible:

To express the concept:	One can*not* say:
(1) Baba is eating.	*Baba be dumu.
(2) We have eaten.	*An bara dumu.
(3) Fanta should eat.	*Fanta ka dumu.
(4) They are drinking.	*U be min.
(5) Baba should cook. (perform the act)	*Baba ka tobi.
(6) Baba is breaking. (something)	*Baba be ti.
(7) He will repair. (something)	*A bena dila.
(8) Fanta has greeted. (someone)	*Fanta bara fo.

Sentences of this form are possible in Maninka but with different meanings. It will perhaps clarify the issue if we observe that English has a rather complicated state of affairs in regard to intransitive sentences; it may be that Maninka appears complicated here because it is being seen through English translation. To begin with, one has to remember which English verbs can be used intransitively and which ones cannot. One can say "John gave," but "John donated" is not easily accepted; one can say "Mary taught," but it doesn't sound good to say "Mary advised"; one can say "Bill shoved," but not "Bill put." In addition to this state of affairs, there are three different patterns in English among verbs that can be used either transitively or intransitively. These three patterns can be illustrated by *break*, *eat*, and *cook* respectively. They are patterns for 'active' sentences and not 'passive' ones, that is, sentences like "Baba is breaking the pot" or "The pot is breaking" but not ones such as "The pot is being broken by Baba" or "The pot is being broken."

With the English *break*, the situation is as follows: only the same participant that would show up as object in a transitive sentence can serve as subject in an intransitive sentence. We will be concerned here in each set of examples with intransitive sentences that refer to the same event as the transitive one:

Baba is breaking *the pot.*
The pot is breaking.
*Baba is breaking.

With *eat,* only the same participant that would show up in subject position in a transitive sentence can serve as subject of an intransitive one:

We are eating *the meat.*
**The meat* is eating.
We are eating.

Finally, with *cook,* either the subject or object participant of a transitive sentence can serve as subject of an intransitive one that refers to the same event:

Fanta is cooking *the rice.*
The rice is cooking.
Fanta is cooking.

A reader interested in this aspect of English grammar could here undertake a research project. One might wonder how this part of the structure of English is learned by successive generations of English speakers. Does someone learning English have to remember on an individual basis what intransitive pattern (if any) is possible for each of the many thousands of transitive verbs in the language? Is there some more general principle? To investigate this question one could find more verbs that operate like *break,* more like *eat,* and more like *cook* (as a start one could consider the verbs *study, fly,* and *boil*); in addition, one could list more verbs like *put* that do not easily allow any kind of intransitive usage. Then one could consider whether there is a likely explanation for why these verbs pattern the way they do. If it is entirely random, then this part of English grammar must be exceedingly hard to learn; if on the other hand there is a reasonable generalization that can predict new data not yet considered, then it may be in terms of such a generalization that people have learned to speak English.

Now we will compare the same examples *break, eat,* and *cook* to the corresponding examples in Maninka (see Table 2.5).

Recall that the meaning of the intransitive sentence *Sogo be dumu* is such that it can refer to the same event as the transitive *An be sogo dumu* (We are eating the meat); *Sogo be dumu* does not have the

TABLE 2.5   Paradigms for **Break, Eat** *and* **Cook**

English	Maninka
Baba is breaking *the pot.*	Baba be daga ti.
The pot is breaking.	*Daga* be ti.
*Baba is breaking.	*Baba be ti.
We are eating *the meat.*	An be *sogo* dumu.
The meat is eating.	*Sogo* be dumu.
We are eating.	*An be dumu.
Fanta is cooking *the rice.*	Fanta be *kini* tobi.
The rice is cooking.	*Kini* be tobi.
Fanta is cooking.	*Fanta be tobi.

improbable meaning that the meat is eating something, but rather that the meat is being eaten. These examples with *ti, dumu,* and *tobi* accurately reflect the general situation in Maninka, a single completely regular pattern.

The verb meaning "hear" in Maninka is *men.* The noun *bara* means "work" (not to be confused with the auxiliary verb *bara*). Consider:

I bena bara men.   You will hear the work.

One can predict the intransitive sentence with *men* that could refer to the same event:

English	Maninka
You will hear *the work.*	I bena *bara* men.
The work will hear.	*Bara* bena men.
You will hear.	*I bena men.

The verb *gwen* means "chase" and *mina* means "grasp" or "take." *Saga* means "sheep." Given the sentences *Baba be saga gwen* (Baba is chasing the sheep) and *Baba bara saga mina* (Baba has taken the sheep), the reader should be able to tell which intransitive sentences with *gwen* and *mina* can refer to the same events. Neither "chase" or "take" can be used intransitively to describe these same events in English, but it should be recalled that all verbs can be used intransitively in Maninka. (The reader is invited to complete the paradigm):

English	Maninka
Baba is chasing *the sheep*.	Baba be *saga* gwen.
The sheep is chasing.	_____
*Baba is chasing.	_____
Baba has taken *the sheep*.	Baba bara *saga* mina.
The sheep has taken.	_____
*Baba has taken.	_____

Now notice the verb *ke* "do":

A be bara ke.   He is doing the work.

Here again is the set of eight concepts given as examples of the kind that could not be expressed with intransitive sentences. One expresses them in Maninka with this same verb *ke*. This is how Maninka speakers say things like "Baba is eating":

To Express the Concept:	One Says in Maninka:
(1) Baba is eating.	*Baba be dumuli ke.*
(2) We have eaten.	*An bara dumuli ke.*
(3) Fanta should eat.	*Fanta ka dumuli ke.*
(4) They are drinking.	*U be minli ke.*
(5) Baba should cook. (perform the act)	*Baba ka tobili ke.*
(6) Baba is breaking. (something)	*Baba be tili ke.*
(7) He will repair. (something)	*A bena dilali ke.*
(8) Fanta has greeted. (someone)	*Fanta bara foli ke.*

Notice that the forms *tili* (related to *ti* "break") and *tobili* (related to *tobi* "cook"), etc., can occur as subjects and objects in other kinds of sentences:

Tobili bara ye.	The cooking has been seen.
Ne bena tobili ye.	I will see the cooking.
Foli bara men.	The greeting has been heard.
U bena foli men.	They will hear the greeting.
Tili bara men.	The breaking was heard.
Au ka dilali ye.	You all should see the repairing.

TABLE 2.6   Deverbal Nouns in English

Verb	+	Affix	=	Noun	Example Sentence
cook		-ing		cooking	The cooking was fun.
create		-ion		creation	John's creation is beautiful.
revive		-al		revival	We are glad about the recent revival of handicrafts.
argue		-ment		argument	I don't want an argument.

These forms with *-li* are in fact nouns. The affix *-li* is used to derive nouns from verbs. We have many nouns in English derived from verbs, for example as in Table 2.6.

In similar manner, the Maninka verb *ti* "break" combines with the affix *-li* to form the noun *tili* "the breaking," *tobi* "cook" combines with *-li* to form the noun *tobili* "the cooking," and so on. These nouns can serve as objects of the verb *ke* "do" in transitive sentences. The expressions "the eating," "the drinking," "the cooking," etc., are here a kind of participant in an event of "doing." Such transitive sentences are the means one has available in Maninka to say things like "Baba is eating." The most direct translation into English for the previous Maninka sentences 1–8 is as follows:

(1)	*Baba be dumuli ke.*	Baba is doing the eating.
(2)	*An bara dumuli ke.*	We have done the eating.
(3)	*Fanta ka dumuli ke.*	Fanta should do the eating.
(4)	*U be minli ke.*	They are doing the drinking.
(5)	*Baba ka tobili ke.*	Baba should do the cooking.
(6)	*Baba be tili ke.*	Baba is doing the breaking.
(7)	*A bena dilali ke.*	He will do the repairing.
(8)	*Fanta bara foli ke.*	Fanta has done the greeting.

We can now return to our examples with *break, eat,* and *cook* and see how similar concepts are expressed in English and Maninka. We want to see how each of the languages would form a transitive sentence where two participants are identified, and then see the normal way to refer to the same event identifying each of these same participants one at a time. The full paradigms are in Table 2.7.

There is then a principle having two parts that is discovered by every child becoming a native speaker of Maninka. It defines which intransitive sentences are possible and which are not; it defines when a description of an event must take the form of a transitive sentence with the verb *ke* and a noun like *tobili* "the cooking" or *dumuli* "the eating"

TABLE 2.7 *Revised Paradigms for* **Break, Eat** *and* **Cook**

English	Maninka
Baba is breaking *the pot.*	Baba be *daga* ti.
The pot is breaking.	*Daga* be ti.
Baba is doing the breaking.	Baba be tili ke.
We are eating *the meat.*	An be *sogo* dumu.
The meat is being eaten.	*Sogo* be dumu.
We are eating.	An be dumuli ke.
Fanta is cooking *the rice.*	Fanta be *kini* tobi.
The rice is cooking.	*Kini* be tobi.
Fanta is cooking.	Fanta be tobili ke.

as the object. It is a completely regular principle; children can and do apply it creatively with verbs that are new for them: they do not have to have heard a verb used in all of the kinds of sentences that are possible for it, and they do not have to be told what kinds of sentences are not possible for each verb. They soon know this aspect of the way individual verbs can be used to describe events because they have learned the general principle.

The reader is invited to try his hand at describing this principle. He might illustrate his generalization with a verb that is new for him, the verb *bugo* "hit," referring, for example, to the situation where Baba is hitting the sheep (*saga*). There should be three sentences: one identifiying both Baba and the sheep, one identifying only the sheep, and one identifying only Baba.

1.3 Maninka Pronunciation

Any newcomer to a language is immediately struck by what is aptly called "the stream of speech," and a stream it is. He has to learn how to parse that stream into meaningful units despite the fact that words in the speech flow of all languages run into one another with no obvious divisions between them. He has to learn what sounds are distinctive in the representation of meaning-bearing elements, and he has to learn how those distinctive sounds pattern. Two instances of sound patterning will be explored here, the first dealing with the way Maninka speakers pronounce the self-same deverbal nouns used to say things like "Baba is eating," or "Baba is hitting" (*Baba be bugoli ke*).

1.3.1 *The Pronunciation of Deverbal Nouns Ending in -li* Like the *-ed* ending on English verbs as in "helped," "rubbed," and "needed," the Maninka suffix -*li* has more than one pronunciation. Here are some examples:

	Spelling	Pronunciation
bugoli	the hitting	*bugoli*
dilali	the repairing	*dilali*
donli	the coming in	*donni*
dumuli	the eating	*dumuni*
foli	the greeting	*foli*
gwenli	the chasing	*gwenni*
minali	the taking	*minani*
sunogoli	the sleeping	*sunogoli*
tili	the breaking	*tili*

The reader is invited to state a hypothesis as to what principle is involved here. As a way of illustrating the generalization, the reader could state what the pronunciation would be for the following words (*famu* means "understand"):

	Spelling	Pronunciation
dali	the lying down	
famuli	the understanding	
menli	the hearing	
nali	the coming	
sali	the dying	
tobili	the cooking	

1.3.2 *Maninka Tone* One of the more befuddling aspects of Maninka grammar for English speakers has to do with tone and intonation. No natural language can be spoken without some sort of melodic contour on its sentences. We call this contour *intonation*. The differences depend on how the grammar plays a role in selecting the many possible melodic contours. In English, the melody of a sentence is defined by a highly complex relation between the organization of a sentence (its syntax) and the message the speaker wants to get across. For a given sequence of words, the intonation will vary according to 'functional sentence perspective' (see Chapter 3 in the companion volume for an introduction to this notion), where the same report or comment on an event can be made from different perspectives. One would say, for example, "John gave a book to Bill" with the main accent and highest pitch on "Bill" to answer the question "To whom did John give a book?", but with the main accent on "gave" if someone had just said "John sold a book to Bill" and one wanted to insist that it had been a gift, and so on. The reader can easily conceive of contexts where the melody of the sentence would foreground "book" or "John."

Like many languages of West Africa and other parts of the world, Maninka is a tone language. One way of understanding the difference between an intonation language like English and a tone language like Maninka is through the substitution of words into sentences. For example, in the English sentence:

Baba didn't buy a house.

we can assign the highest accent to the last word "house," in which case the sentence could be paraphrased "It's not a house that Baba bought." This would give us a sentence melody that can be represented by the following display, where each line represents the pitch of each syllable:

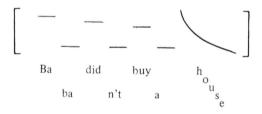

The melodic pattern or intonation is, in English, largely independent of the actual words that are in the sentence. This enables us to replace one word by another without affecting the melodic pattern. Thus, we can pronounce the following sentences with the same intonation pattern illustrated above.

Baba didn't buy a house.
Baba didn't buy a horse.
Fanta didn't buy a house.
Fanta didn't buy a horse.
Baba didn't see a house.
Baba didn't see a horse.
Fanta didn't see a house.
Fanta didn't see a horse.

All eight of these sentences can have the same melodic pattern:

For our stranger in Maninka country, the situation is quite different. The above sentences would be pronounced in Maninka as follows:

Baba ma so san.	[__ ‾‾ _]
Baba ma so san.	[__ ‾⁄_]
Fanta ma so san.	[‾_ ‾‾ _]
Fanta ma so san.	[‾_ ‾⁄_]
Baba ma so ye.	[__ ‾‾‾]
Baba ma so ye.	[__ ‾_‾]
Fanta ma so ye.	[‾_ ‾‾‾]
Fanta ma so ye.	[‾_ ‾_‾]

Each of the eight sentences results in a new melodic configuration, and what is more, this configuration cannot be changed as it can in English to accent different words. If the melody is changed in Maninka, the meaning of the words will change. The stranger soon learns that words have relatively fixed tone patterns in Maninka. That is, he will learn that a name like *Baba* is pronounced with a low pitch on both syllables [__] whereas with Fanta the first syllable will always be a higher pitch than the second [‾_]. Similarly, the word "house" *so* is pronounced with a high pitch [‾], whereas in most contexts, the word "horse" *so* is pronounced with a lower pitch [_]. Where *so* "horse" is not pronounced with low, level pitch, it is pronounced with a rising pitch [⁄]. The stranger would have to figure out what conditions this variation. That is, he would have to discover the grammar of tone in Maninka. In some ways, this is relatively simple. We can work out a set of instructions sort of like a road map that will account for all eight intonation patterns of the Maninka sentences.

1. A low-tone syllable following a low-tone syllable in the same word will have the same level of pitch:
   Baba [__]   *fila* two [__]

2. A low-tone syllable or word following a high-tone syllable or word will have a level of pitch lower than the high tone:
   Fanta [‾_]   *ma so* didn't horse [‾_]

3. A high-tone syllable or word will remain on the same level of pitch as a preceding high-tone syllable or word:
   ... *ma so ye* [‾‾‾]
   ... didn't house see

4. A high-tone syllable or word following a low-tone syllable or word will be at a level of pitch higher than the low tone:

Baba ma... $\left[\,_{\_\_}{}^{-}\,\right]$
Baba didn't ...

"Lower" and "higher" are relative terms, and the same absolute pitch is not usually maintained for all high and low tones throughout an utterance. In fact, when high tones are separated by low tones, there tends to be an overall "downstep" shape to the speech with successive highs separated from each other by lows and descending in their absolute pitch. This sometimes happens to the intermittent lows as well. Here is a likely realization of "Fanta didn't see a horse":

Fanta ma so ye $\left[\,^{-}{}_{\_}{}^{-}{}_{\_}\,\right]$

A correlated detail is that a high after a low tends not to be as high as a high at the beginning of a sentence. Thus the high of *ma* after low tone *Baba* $\left[\,_{\_\_}{}^{-}\,\right]$ won't be as high in absolute terms as a high at the beginning of a sentence that starts with *Fanta* $\left[\,^{-}{}_{\_}\,\right]$.

The above rules are comparatively straightforward, and they account for six of the eight intonation patterns. The only sequences for which we have not yet uncovered a principle concern the relation between a word that has low tone in some contexts and rising tone in others. Our newcomer would probably eventually note that *ye* "see" is a high-tone word and that *san* "buy" is a low-tone word and that the word "horse" has a low pitch before *ye* and a rising pitch before *san*. He can now make a hypothesis concerning when *so* "horse" will be low and when it will be rising:

5. A one-syllable low-tone word will rise in tone when preceding another low-tone word.

If this hypothesis is correct, it will account for the two remaining intonation patterns. This hypothesis must be tested. It turns out that the numerals have different tones, for example:

one	*kelen*	$\left[\,^{--}\,\right]$
two	*fila*	$\left[\,_{\_\_}\,\right]$
three	*saba*	$\left[\,_{\_\_}\,\right]$
four	*naani*	$\left[\,^{--}\,\right]$
five	*duuru*	$\left[\,^{--}\,\right]$

If the rules are correct, we should be able to predict the melodic contours of the Maninka equivalent of the following English examples:

one house
two houses
one horse
two horses

It turns out that they have the following contours:

so kelen   [¯¯¯]

so fila   [¯__]

so kelen   [_---]

so fila   [∕__]

The last example demonstrates that our rule is correct, as far as it goes. It turns out that with a few modifications, these rules will account for the overwhelming majority of Maninka sentences.

Try to mark the melodic contours of the following sentences. An underlined vowel will be considered a low tone. Unmarked syllables will be high tones.

Ali	*bara*	*namasa*	*kelen*	*san*	*bi*.
Ali	has	banana	one	buy	today

     Ali has bought one banana today.

Fanta	*bara*	*na*.
Fanta	has	come

     Fanta has come.

u	*be*	*ji*	*min*.
they	do	water	drink

     They drink water.

ne	*bara*	*ji*	*min*	*bi*.
I	have	water	drink	today

     I drank water today.

1.4 Other Features of Maninka Grammar

In the same manner, the newcomer will continue to discover the principles of syntax and pronunciation in Maninka. He will learn how to express other kinds of concepts besides events, such as states of being (Fanta is tall); existence (There is a man in the field); location (The man is in the field); possession (Fanta has a pot, The pot is Fanta's); equation

(Baba is a farmer); and so on. He will learn that Maninka has *postpositions*. To say "She has gone into the house," words have the order She–has–gone–house–into. (*Kono* is the postposition meaning "into," and *so* is "house".)

A bara ta so kono.

To say "I have set the hoe on the table" (table is *tabili* and *kan* is the postposition meaning 'on'), we have:

Ne   bara   daba   sigi   tabili   kan.
I   have   hoe   set   table   on.

The great majority of languages that are like Maninka in having objects before verbs also have postpositions rather than prepositions; conversely, the great majority of languages that are like English in having objects after verbs also have prepositions rather than postpositions. Thus, one tends to get Hoe–set–table–on (or Table–on–hoe–set) and Set–hoe–on–table but not the other conceivable orders. English is prolific in the use of prepositions, but it has a few expressions that are postpositional. There are several words, such as *ago*, one could call postpositions: compare "*in* two years," "*for* two years," and "two years *ago*." In addition one sees postposed prepositions in compounds such as "here*after*," "where*fore*," "there*to*," and "home*less*."

A notable characteristic of Maninka is that word order is highly fixed. Whereas English changes word order to ask a question about an object, for example, "What have you seen?" or "What have you set the hoe on?" (changing word order, notice, not only in respect to the object, but the subject and the auxiliary verb as well, giving "have you" instead of "you have"), Maninka uses the same word order in such questions as in a statement. (See Table 2.8 [the Maninka word for "what" is *mun*].)

TABLE 2.8   *Interrogated Objects in English and Maninka*

	English
Statement:	You have seen *the hoe.*
Question:	*What* have you seen?
Statement:	You have set the hoe on *the table.*
Question:	*What* have you set the hoe on?
	Maninka
Statement:	I bara *daba* ye.
Question:	I bara *mun* ye?
Statement:	I bara daba sigi *tabili* kan.
Question:	I bara daba sigi *mun* kan?

Maninka relative clauses are formed in several ways. Here is an important one. To say "I have greeted the woman that has come," one says:

Muso	*min*	*bara*	*na*	*ne*	*bara*	*o*	*fo.*
woman	who	has	come	I	have	that one	greeted.

To say "I have greeted the woman that you saw" one says:

I	*bara*	*muso*	*min*	*ye*	*ne*	*bara*	*o*	*fo.*
you	have	woman	who	seen	I	have	that one	greeted.

There are three main ways that relative clauses are formed among the languages of the world. English exemplifies one type, where the 'head,' the noun being modified by the relative clause, comes to the left of it (the woman *that you saw*); Japanese exemplifies a second type where the head noun comes to the right of the relative clause that is modifying it (*that you saw* the woman); and finally the above construction exemplifies the third main type, where the head noun being modified by the relative clause occurs within the relative clause itself. If the newcomer's native language happens to be one with the same type of relative clause formation, it will be comparatively easy to learn this aspect of Maninka grammar; otherwise, additional effort will be required.

2   THE USE OF LANGUAGE IN MANINKA CULTURE

Se-ci ni kalan-ci te kelen ye.
Ability-work and study-work are not one.

—A Maninka Hunters' Proverb

(What one is able to do and what one has studied to do are not the same.)

2.1   Ability-work and Study-work Are Not One

The newcomer will in a reasonable period of time learn Maninka words and the rules of their combination well enough to form a large number of grammatically correct sentences. This knowledge alone, however, no matter how perfect, will never make him a good enough speaker of the language to become a full-fledged member of the community. He is also going to have to learn a good deal about the society and the appropriate use of language in particular situations. There are many things that one *could* say in Maninka in a given context, but not all of them would constitute acceptable cultural behavior. As in every culture, there are *social* principles that make certain kinds of linguistic acts desirable and others undesirable.

2.1.1   *Greetings and Leave-takings*   Consider a context in which a greeting takes place: someone is fifteen minutes late for work and in hurrying to his job comes upon a friend he has not seen for three days. What might transpire in our society is shown in Table 2.9.

This dialogue could be translated into Maninka, but if it ever took place in a Maninka community it would be viewed as unthinkably bad social behavior.

Let us analyze what has happened. Two friends have met, greeted each other, and then taken leave to go on their respective ways. Greetings and leave-takings are a common event in all societies. A verbal encounter typically begins with an opening remark that signals someone's intent to start a conversation, followed by a response that shows a willingness to proceed ("Hello.—Hi there . . . ," "Hey you!— What? . . ."); it ends when someone indicates a desire to bring the conversation to a close and the other speakers agree (". . . Well . . . I'll see you later.—O.K. Bye-bye."). A great deal of what is communicated is inferred rather than explicitly stated; for example, people on good terms with each other will not end a dialogue saying "I do not want to talk with you any more now," but someone says enough to imply just that; it may be enough to say something like ". . . Well . . ." or if that doesn't work, one can usually give a reason for having to leave; if the conversation is face-to-face there may be a change in body posture that indicates a shift of attention away from the conversation. What is said will be interpreted differently depending on the occasion and who is

TABLE 2.9   *Verbal Encounter When Fifteen Minutes Late for Work*

Hello Ed!

    —Hi! How are you?

Sorry, I'm in a hurry.

    —Yeh, me too.

See you on Saturday.

(Time elapsed: 5 seconds. The two people cross paths without breaking stride.)

talking to whom: one can consider under what circumstances there is a pleasurable reaction when someone starts a dialogue with "Hi there!" or "Hey man!" or when someone calls a person "Dick" or "Richie" instead of "Richard" or "Mr. Jones."

Greetings and leave-takings can perform other functions besides simply starting and stopping the conversation. Strangers identify themselves; people indicate their reasons for speaking; they reveal emotional attitudes; they express personal recognition, friendship, intentions that are friendly or otherwise, family or group affiliations, professional or social status, and so on. People will be greeted differently depending on how others perceive their status, age, and cultural identity, and they will feel complimented or not depending on how the greeting matches their expectations. There may be reference to conditions surrounding the encounter: one says "Good morning" or "Good afternoon" depending on the time of day, "Merry Christmas" or "Happy birthday" depending on the time of year; a conversation can be initiated with a reference to the weather ("Is it hot enough for you?" "Cold day, isn't it?"); depending on varying degrees of familiarity, conversations may end with salutations such as "Good-bye darling," "Good luck on the exam!", "Have a good time at the beach!" "Say hello to Bill for me!" and so on. Greetings and leave-takings always orient the speakers in respect to the conversation itself, and they frequently communicate a good deal that has to do with the time, place, and social setting for the encounter.

We can define a common kind of verbal encounter as follows:

Verbal Encounter = Greeting
                   (Conversation)
                   Leave-taking

TABLE 2.10 Greeting and Leave-taking

Greeting	Hello Ed! —Hi! How are you?
Leave-taking	Sorry, I'm in a hurry. —Yeh, me too. See you on Saturday.

This is to say that there will always be a greeting and a leave-taking and that there may or may not be a conversation in between. The five-second encounter given as an example has simply a greeting and a leave-taking (see Table 2.10).

Let us take a comparable exchange in a Maninka town or city where one person is fifteen minutes late for work. What people do in their greetings and leave-takings may reveal important principles governing the use of language in their culture. This is very much the case in Maninka society where greetings and leave-takings are highly developed. The reader is invited to consider what kinds of cultural values might be motivating the speakers here. Mamodou Diarra is fifteen minutes late for work and in hurrying to his job meets his friend Sedou Kanté:

Ah Sedou, you and the morning.

—Excellent. You and the morning.

Did you sleep in peace?

—Only peace.

Are the people of the household well?

—There is no trouble.

Are you well?

—Peace, praise Allah. Did you sleep well?

Praise Allah. You Kanté.

—Excellent. You Diarra.

Excellent.

—And the family?

I thank Allah. Is there peace?

—We are here.

How is your mother?

—No trouble.

And your cousin Fanta?

—Only peace. And your father?

Praise Allah. He greets you.

—Tell him I have heard it.

And your younger brother Amadou?

—He is well. And your uncle Sidi?

No trouble, Praise Allah . . .

Where are you going?

—I'm going to the market. And you?

My boss is waiting for me.

—O.K. then, I'll see you later.

Yes, I'll see you later. Greet the people of the household.

—They will hear it. Greet your father.

He will hear it.

—May your day pass well.

Amen. May the market go well.

—Amen. May we meet *soon.*

May that "soon" arrive in good stead.

(Time elapsed: 46 seconds. The two come together to shake hands before going on.)

Maninka people are very concerned about the overt manifestation of respect for social ties. This is a concern that influences all forms of social behavior: the greatest importance is attached, for example, to presence by members of a community at events giving public expression to social ties—events such as marriages, baptisms and funerals; in verbal encounters the most overt manifestation of respect for social ties takes place in greetings and leave-takings.

People make an elaborate display of respect for social ties in Maninka society, and much of that reflects the deep and extensive development of those relationships. For example, a marriage is not simply a union between a man and a woman, it is the union of the man's family with the woman's family; rights and obligations are defined for both the man and the woman in regard to both families. Failure on the part of one to show respect for any member of the other's family would most likely lead to conflict in the marriage. Just as there must be an outward display of respect in relationships defined by marriage, so also in friendship. Friendship for Maninka people is not a once-in-a-while thing. The bonds of friendship must be continually reinforced, and they are given the highest priority in all social interactions. It is more important to show respect for a friend or a kinsman than to be on time for work, and thus we have the example of Mamadou Diarra above, already fifteen minutes late for work and not hesitating to be even later in order to greet a friend in the proper manner. First things first, and there is no question for the Maninka people about what is most important.

In our society friendships are formed rather easily because they tend to be relationships with very few obligations. For someone from our society, having a Maninka friend presents a formidable set of obligations since the friendship is not a casual thing and involves his or her entire family. Not only is it necessary to be able to identify the members of the friend's family, which may easily involve forty to fifty people, one must also remember all their names; failure to remember someone's name is understood as a failure to recognize their significance and is therefore a serious social insult. Notice that in the greeting the friends cite each other's names and make specific reference to members of each other's family by name. This is an important part of a greeting between friends.

2.1.2　*Badenya and Fadenya*　One part of the above dialogue is indicative of a major principle for behavior in Maninka culture: it is the way in which Mamadou Diarra takes leave of his friend Sedou Kanté after greeting him. Although he is in a hurry, he will not express this directly lest Sedou infer that their friendship does not have the highest priority. However, in order to convey the idea to Sedou that he is in a hurry, he asks him where he is going in hope that Sedou will ask him the same question. Sedou does, and in response Mamadou is able to say that his boss is waiting for him. This illustrates the principle of the avoidance of conflict, one of the major precepts incorporated in the notion of social cohesion. Maninka people have a word for this notion: it is called *badenya*, which translates as "mother-child-ness." *Badenya* includes such notions as politeness, modesty, and unselfishness; conflict is to be avoided at all costs, but if there has to be conflict, every attempt should be made to avoid direct confrontation. The English word *comity* has some of the meaning of *badenya*, but only some of it, and it is not a commonly used or widely known word. There is no one word in English forming part of everyday vocabulary that conveys what *badenya* does, and that fact shows the relative importance of the concept in the two cultures.

There are a number of consequences to the fact that people want to avoid direct confrontation: one of them involves the situation where someone is in a position to tell someone else what he may or may not do. The exercise of authority cannot be carried out in such a way as to imply either criticism or a manifestation of power. The Maninka of course recognize power relationships, but within the framework of *badenya*, people attempt to give as little overt expression to them as possible. Consider a dialogue between an American father and a teenage son where a power relationship is openly expressed:

Teenager: But why can't I have the car tonight, Dad?

Father: Because I said so!

This situation in a Maninka context might be transformed as follows:

Teenager: But why can't I have the car tonight, Dad?

Father: Ah my son, the words of the elders are like the droppings of the hyena. Grey when fresh, they become clear with time.

The Maninka father has used a proverb to respond to his son. The same task has been accomplished, the son has been firmly rebuffed in his request for the family car, but the father has avoided a direct assertion of his power over his child. He has instead called on the wisdom of the ancestors. The proverb is traditional wisdom. The person who utters it is not considered responsible for its meaning, only for the context in which it is used. The son no longer has only his father's opinion to contend with, but also the wisdom of many past generations.

There is a counterforce to *badenya* called *fadenya*, "father-child-ness." It is occasionally manifested in the way people speak Maninka, and when it is, it draws a lot of attention. This force is characterized by competitive individuality as opposed to cooperation and collectivity. *Fadenya* is above all the search for a name, a name that people will remember. In Maninka culture, people are remembered primarily through notable deeds, the most notable of which are new, different from the ordinary, and sometimes dangerous. However, the performance of notable deeds frequently does not lead to social stability; quite to the contrary, it often leads to disequilibrium.

Contemplate what acts are likely to be reported to others in our society. They can be acts of hard work, imagination, perseverance, and service to the community, but these are not indispensable ingredients; the essential ingredient is for the act to be unexpected. If behavior has nothing unexpected about it, it is usually considered not much worth talking about. People like to avoid getting the response "So what?" This expression indicates that someone has reported something uninteresting and of no consequence. Consider:

David was nice to his brother.

—So what?

Now compare:

> Harry punched his baby sister in the face and broke her nose.
>
>   —He did?!!

More people will probably hear about Harry than David. Daredevil stuntsmen on motorcycles are remembered by name far more often than are truck drivers who go long hours without sleep to transport food and other needed goods. More renown has gone to the violent men of the old West, the lawmen like Wyatt Earp and the outlaws like Billy the Kid, than to steady, hard-working ranchers and homesteaders. Outstanding leaders and innovators become famous, but so do outstanding gangsters and deviants. The names of ordinary people and those who make quiet innovations, no matter how successfully, are usually not remembered. To gain a hero's status one has to not only do something valuable, but also have it reported and remembered in the community.

The performer of notable deeds in Maninka society is often ruthless, lacking in respect for his traditions and his kin, thus violating the principles of *badenya*. This is frequently the kind of person who would say disagreeable things bluntly to people. He would typically have a great sense of self-importance and might not take the time to go to a baptism or to greet a friend properly. He might think he had more important things to do, and indeed sometimes he does; and when these deeds are noticed, his name is remembered in praise songs. This kind of person is called *ngana* (ŋana), which translates as either "hero" or "rebel." There is a proverb that characterizes the importance of the *ngana* (hero-rebel):

> The *ngana* is welcome only on troubled days.

In *badenya* there is harmony, but it only occurs within traditionally defined activity. When the society is threatened, there is the need for innovation that *badenya* cannot provide. At this point, the society seeks the *ngana*.

2.2 The Bard

In every Maninka community there are bards who are responsible for a significant number of verbal acts. They are the historians of the society, preserving the histories of the families and the genealogies of kings and emperors. They are the singers of praise and they act as intermediaries between families.

As singers of praise, the bards often function to encourage the performance of notable deeds and to reinforce the quest for a name.

FIGURE 2.4 The Famous Bard Batourou Sekou Kouyate from Mali. He is shown here building Koras, the instrument he plays as a background to many of the Malian epics. The Kora is a twenty-one string harp lute.

There are few, if any, Maninka people who would not like to become the subject of a praise song. The content of the songs is clearly oriented towards *fadenya*. Some of these songs of praise have developed into heroic epics comparable to the Homeric epics of ancient Greece, *The Iliad* and *The Odyssey*; *The Song of Roland* of medieval France; the *Kalevala* of Finland; the sagas of Iceland, or the contemporary epics of the Serbo-Croatian bards in Yugoslavia.

Examples of this sort of praise can be found in *The Songs of Seydou Camara*, Volume I, *Kambili*. (Full reference is given in the "Suggestions for Further Reading" section at the end of the chapter. A photograph of Seydou Camara appears at the beginning of this chapter.) *Kambili* is a heroic epic of the Maninka hunters. The hero is a *fadenya*-oriented figure who represents a model of behavior for the hunters. The hunters are unusual in that they are committed above all to the performance of memorable deeds, rather than to the stability of the village. In this passage (line 95 ff.), the first line says "A name is to be paid for . . ." meaning that the exchange for renown is deeds:

A name is to be paid for; a name is not to be forced . . .
I've seen a hunter; I've seen my friend.
I've seen a hunter; I've seen my brother.
Look to the Fresh Heart-Cutter for the Fresh Liver-Cutter.
Killer of the Ruthless and Killer of the Hardy!
Green Head Smasher and the Green Eye Gouger! . . .
The jealous one doesn't become a hunter . . .
A woman-chaser doesn't become a hunter either.
The great lover does not become a hunter,
Nor does he become a man of renown.
A name is a thing to be paid for; a name is not to be forced.

There are also political and historical epics sung in Maninka society in which the hero is a model for the governance of the society and where there must be an interplay between the forces of *fadenya* and *badenya*. Perhaps the most famous is the epic of *Sunjata*, the founder of the great Mali empire of the thirteenth century.

This epic contains much information about the beliefs and customs of the Maninka people. The part of the epic telling the story of Tira Magan, one of Sunjata's generals, is particularly interesting in describing the role of the bard as an intermediary in cases where conflict might otherwise break out. One can see *fadenya* in this episode in the terrible temper of Sunjata, so much to be feared, and also *badenya* in the way in which the bard prevents a confrontation.

Sunjata had sent some of his men to the country of the Serers to get some of their fine horses for his cavalry. On their return, his men were waylaid by Jolofin Mansa, the king of the Wolof people. Jolofin Mansa told the men that Sunjata was only a poor bush hunter who had no need of horses. He took the troop of horses and gave the men a pack of dogs to give to Sunjata with the message that Sunjata should continue to run his dogs in his part of the country.

A messenger returned to report the news of what had happened, but he could not bring himself to tell Sunjata directly since the latter's temper was well known. More than one simple messenger had fallen victim to that temper and perished by bringing bad news. The messenger went to Sunjata's bard and asked him for help. The next morning, the bard went to Sunjata's hut singing:

Who has ever seen it?
Who has ever seen a goat bite a dog?
Who has ever seen it?
Ah! But we have seen it!
A goat has bitten a dog!
Yes, a goat has bitten a dog!

Sunjata, amused and curious, asked the bard to explain the meaning of his song, and thus the news was made known to him in a way that softened the feared reaction of his terrible temper. The expression "A goat has bitten a dog" has become a proverb, used to describe actions where people have behaved out of character and have done something beyond their ability to control ("They've gotten in over their heads," "They've bitten off more than they can chew").

As intermediaries between families in contemporary society, bards serve to resolve conflicts. If a member of a particular family has a grievance against a member of another family, rather than expressing his grievance directly, the person can tell a bard about it; the bard will convey the message to the other party in a most elegant and inoffensive manner; the grievance will thus be negotiated without bringing the offended parties together.

2.3 Proverbs

Since proverbs are used widely in Maninka culture, a large inventory of them will have to be learned by any stranger wanting to become a good speaker of the language. In addition, it will be necessary for the newcomer to learn how to recognize the situations in which each proverb can be used appropriately.

Imagine our language learner as a man talking to an old Maninka gentleman, speaking with a control of the language that is obviously that of a newcomer; that is to say, he is making lots of mistakes. The old man indulges in a bit of ironic humor, saying something with a meaning that is the opposite of what would seem appropriate for the situation:

The old man: Ah, you are becoming a Maninka.
You speak the language just like one of us.

If the newcomer is gullible, here is how the dialogue might go:

The old man: Ah, you are becoming a Maninka.
You speak the language just like one of us.

The newcomer: Gee, do you really think so? Thank you very much.

The newcomer will have fallen into the old man's trap and come out looking close to a total fool. In a society where insults are taboo, one becomes very sensitive to levels of praise. Given the context, what the old man has said would best be interpreted as the opposite of its literal meaning and, by implication, a criticism. If the newcomer accepts what has been said to him at face value, then he in effect accepts the criticism.

With more sophistication on the part of the newcomer, the dialogue might go something like this:

The old man:	Ah, you are becoming a Maninka. You speak the language like one of us.
The newcomer:	No matter how long a log lies in the water, it never becomes a crocodile.

This is really the kind of response the old man is looking for. As an ingratiating way of expressing his admiration for the newcomer's knowledge of Maninka culture, the old man might respond with another proverb:

The old man:	Ah my son, a log lying in the water is still the cause of fear.

Most of the concepts that people communicate to each other in any language are new ones, and the sentences that result are original combinations of words, creations that are produced on the spot. Proverbs, on the other hand, are a stock of traditional sayings that are used over and over again. There is variation in the form of Maninka proverbs. If "A stitch in time saves nine" were a Maninka proverb, one might also hear "You would save nine stitches if you did one at the right time," or "Nine stitches are saved by one at the right time." Instead of "There is no use crying over spilt milk," one might hear "No use weeping about the milk that is on the floor." There is this kind of variation, viewed as a kind of stylistic elegance, but the fact remains that essentially the same literal meaning is being expressed in each case. In this sense, the saying of a proverb is different from saying something new, and this is especially so when there is as strong a sense as there is in Maninka culture that by so doing one expresses traditional wisdom. A typical proverb is something old, and one wants to say in essence what was said the time before, and the time before that, and back into past generations, as if the proverb had always existed and was never spoken for the first time. Maninka speakers know many proverbs, many more than do most present-day English speakers, and they use them often. So familiar are a number of proverbs that Maninka speakers frequently communicate them in abbreviated form. Instead of saying the full "A log lying in the water is still the cause of fear," one might say just "A log lying in the water," or even just "A log."

It is the *use* of proverbs rather than their form that requires the most on-the-spot creativity. They are often employed in a wide variety of contexts to convey not just concepts associated with their literal meanings, but often concepts that can be understood only by quite original metaphorical extensions. There are pithy sayings called 'aphorisms' or 'maxims' the use of which is directly related to their literal meanings. For example, the comment "Children should be seen and not heard" will typically be used in reference just to children; on the other hand, if one uses the English proverbs "Barking dogs don't bite" or "A bird in the hand is worth two in the bush," it would not usually be for a situation involving dogs or birds. Just so, when the old man says "A log lying in the water is still the cause of fear," the message has nothing to do with logs, water, or fear. It is rather something to the effect that even though the newcomer is not a native-born Maninka, he is behaving enough like one to be respected as a member of the group.

At least two factors contribute to the expressive power of proverbs in Maninka culture: the first is their indirection; there is little value in arguing with the literal meaning of most proverbs because the point being made in any particular instance will be only indirectly related to the literal meaning. The second and complementary factor is that since proverbs represent traditional wisdom, they call forth respect for the point being made by the speaker, or at least for the manner in which it is presented. These two factors together make it impossible to condemn what has been said directly: no one in Maninka society replies to a proverb saying "That's a lot of nonsense." The only viable counter-attack is to address oneself to the reasoning underlying the use of a proverb; polemics are channeled towards the ideas being advocated rather than towards the manner of their expression or the proponents of the ideas. Proverbs thus play an important role in the outwardly peaceful tone of most conversation and debate (*badenya*)—people may be inwardly just as personally involved, just as competitive, and ambitious, and just as resentful of those who disagree with them as in other societies, but this culture makes it harder for them to manifest such feelings openly.

An obvious situation where what is said might cause offense or anger is when someone decides to give someone else a piece of advice. This can be done by either suggesting a course of action, or by criticizing behavior already being carried out. In either case, the person receiving the advice might conclude that his sense of judgement and his character are being called into question. If a course of action is suggested, he can infer that the speaker thinks he isn't smart enough to know what is good for him; if the advice amounts to criticism of decisions already made, there is the possible inference that the speaker thinks he should have known better in the first place. Thus, there is in either case the risk that the advice could be interpreted as an insult and that a personal confrontation could follow. This is a situation made to order for proverbs. Even if the person receiving advice feels resentment, it is difficult for him to show negative feelings when the advice is given in the form of a proverb. Here are some Maninka proverbs that can be used to give advice. Some are relatively easy for outsiders to understand; others depend on culturally defined references. The reader is invited to imagine how the following proverbs might be used:

The donkey always wants the salt that is on its back.

The hoof of the bull broke the pot of honey.

One takes the body, one takes the shroud; nobody takes them both.

The hyena chasing two antelopes will go to bed hungry.

The last two in this set have meanings that are appropriate for a similar set of situations. Coincidentally, they both have something to do with hyenas. The one about the hyena chasing two antelopes is no doubt the easier one for most uninitiated people to understand. The one beginning "One takes the body" makes reference to a cadaver; the hyena will steal away a dead body, the thief will steal the cloth used to wrap the corpse for burial, but nobody takes them both. The sense is something like "You can't have your cake and eat it too." The main difference in the situations to which these two proverbs apply would appear to be one of timing. "One takes the shroud" applies to situations where someone already has a prize in hand and is tempted to add on still more. By contrast, in "The hyena chasing two antelopes," no one has yet accomplished anything, but there is someone who is tempted to go after more than one prize or objective at the same time. A proverb is typically a comment on a situation; either of these two could be used to comment on a situation in which neither the speaker nor the hearer is involved; the comments they communicate can become advice when they are applied to situations for which the hearer bears responsibility.

The proverb "The donkey always wants the salt that is on its back" concerns the matter of trust and one's reputation in the community. One entrusts a load of salt to the donkey and the donkey wants to eat it himself. If someone has been entrusted with something and takes advantage of the situation for personal gain, that person will be viewed by others in the community as no more than a donkey. The proverb "The hoof of the bull broke the pot of honey" is a comment appropriate for a context in which someone is attempting either to ingratiate himself with or bribe another person. A note of caution: more than one can play that game; one person may give a pot of honey, but someone else may give a bull quite capable of breaking the pot of honey.

It is a common experience for all people to be touched by events that are so serious that it is difficult to talk about them openly. There are various kinds of verbal art that allow people to approach these problems indirectly. The value of many folk tales is that they present ideas on an abstract level that make it possible to get at important truths without frightening or alarming an audience. The Maninka are like people around the world in having a rich inventory of stories that describe events in a world where the main characters are animals such as rabbits, turtles, foxes, lions, monkeys, and hyenas that talk to each other and act out anthropomorphic dramas. With these stories it is possible to convey a great deal about human experience and cultural values and probably much more so than would be possible if stories were told only about "real life" people in the community. This is especially true where young children are concerned. Drama in the theater has a similar quality. It provides a kind of aesthetic distance for the presentation of ideas that can then be applied to personal experience. The Maninka are like other West African people in having a well-developed tradition of improvised theater: plots are acted out without the actors having memorized their lines verbatum, and part of the delight for the audience comes in the unexpected ways that a particular actor will portray a role. The poetry of the bards is still another instance: it states a world view that people can take as a point of reference for their lives, but without mention of details that might be painful or embarrassing. Proverbs are bite-sized pieces of verbal art that do the same thing. Since they are short, they do not require a special performance or telling, and they are woven into everyday conversation. They comment on situations abstractly, and it is up to the people communicating to make their own inferences as to which "real-life" people and events are being pointed at. Just so, a delicate way to advise someone to take a trust in a responsible manner might be with the proverb "The donkey always wants the salt that is on its back"; the most effective way to warn someone about trying to bribe someone might be with the proverb "The hoof of the bull broke the pot of honey."

The great legitimacy of proverbs is illustrated in another part of the Sunjata epic. Dankaran Tuman was Sunjata's half-brother and king of Mali before Sunjata. There has always been great tension between half-brothers, and the relation between Dankaran Taman and Sunjata was no exception. When Sunjata was still a young man, Dankaran Tuman forced him into exile.

Without Sunjata's prowess as a warrior and leader, Dankaran Tuman's kingdom became vulnerable to attack. From the north came the following proverb message, sent by Sumanguru, the great blacksmith king of the Soso:

Should you kill your vicious dog, someone else's will bite you.

This was his declaration of war. He descended with his armies to conquer Mali and drive Dankaran Tuman from the throne, opening the way for Sunjata's eventual return.

By using a traditional proverb as a declaration of war, Sumanguru was in this way legitimizing his attack on Dankaran Tuman. Dankaran Tuman had violated traditional wisdom, the heritage of the ancestors, and had therefore made himself vulnerable to attack.

It should be noted that proverbs have connections to the other forms of verbal art commented on here. Just as the proverbs "A goat has bitten a dog" or "Should you kill your vicious dog" recall passages in the *Sunjata* epic, so there are proverbs that bring to mind various folk tales. Some folk tales appear to have come into being as elaborations on proverbs; in other cases there are proverbs that come from folk tales. A commonly used Maninka proverb goes "That's just a case of the scorpion and the fish." This is a reference to the following story:

> The scorpion asked the fish to take him across the river. The fish said "No, I'm afraid of you. You might sting me."
>
> The scorpion said "I'd be a fool to sting you. If I did then we'd both die."
>
> The fish thought for a while and then said "All right. I'll take you across."
>
> They got to the middle of the river and the scorpion stung the fish. The fish said "What did you do that for?"
>
> The scorpion replied "Just to teach you that you are a fool to trust anyone."

This is an extreme case of someone "cutting off his nose to spite his face."

Here are some more proverbs:

> The axe blade cannot cut a tree without a handle.
>
> You can't crush the head of a fish without touching its eyes.
>
> He who has gotten a bad name does not pick up a dead sheep in the bush.
>
> The goldfish told the carp that not all water was to be struck with its tail.
>
> The sides of an old well fall down into it.
>
> If you fall on a log it will hurt you; if the log falls on you it will hurt you.
>
> If you are afraid of the wind you will hide under a thorn tree.
>
> A ripped garment can be sewn, but an old garment can't be sewn.
>
> The pot may be tipped but it hasn't spilled yet.

The last two, "A ripped garment" and "The pot" have to do with the notion of process but with opposite viewpoints. "The pot" says in effect "Things may be bad but they are not hopeless." "A ripped garment can be sewn but an old garment cannot be sewn" emphasizes the importance of doing things at the right time and not when it is too late. In English one might have said "You should have struck while the iron was hot": the time when something could have been done is passed; the garment is too old to be mended, and the situation is irreparable. One would use "The pot" to urge action but "The ripped garment" to counsel someone to resign himself to the way things have come to pass.

"The axe blade cannot cut the tree without a handle" is a comment on the need that a leader has for his followers. Another proverb says

"It's only the axe blade that knows the strength of the tree," implying that only the leader is in a position to fully understand the problems facing a community. However, "without a handle" implies that without support from the rest of the group, the leader will not be able to do anything.

"You can't crush the head of a fish without touching its eyes" has a variant that goes "You can't break someone's head in his absence." Either of these will be used in a situation where a conversation has been initiated on matters concerning one not present. Someone listening will use one of the proverbs to say in effect "This concerns so and so. We shouldn't talk about it in his absence. Let's wait until he can give his side of the story."

"He who has gotten a bad name does not pick up a dead sheep in the bush" is a warning to people who already have bad reputations not to perform acts that could be interpreted as evil. If someone with a bad reputation were to pick up a dead sheep in the bush, people would say that he had killed it, whether or not he in fact had.

The proverb "The goldfish" is about discretion and secrecy. The slapping tail of the carp is to the surface of the water as someone's wagging tongue is to the public. The message is "Be careful to whom you tell this."

"The sides of an old well fall down into it" is about treachery: a traitor usually destroys himself with his own evil deeds.

The proverb "If you fall on a log" is a warning: "Don't mess with so and so. No matter what you do, he will hurt you."

"If you are afraid of the wind you will hide under a thorn tree" is as much as to say "Be careful that you don't jump out of the frying pan and into the fire."

More proverbs are presented in the appendix.

2.4 A Research Topic

The reader is invited to consider what are the differences between Maninka culture and English-speaking culture in respect to the proverbs that are available in the two languages and the way they are used. What in the nature of the two cultures might account for these differences? As part of this investigation, one ought to list all the proverbs in English he can think of and specify for what kinds of situations each one is appropriate. Another consideration would be what kinds of English-speaking people are most likely to use proverbs.

A word of caution: While one's first reaction can easily be to think proverbs are far less important in contemporary English than in Maninka (that is absolutely correct), one should not pass over proverbs that are in fact part of the living language. People perhaps underrate the number of proverbs in their own language because they tend not to recognize many of them as proverbs. The stranger's proverbs may actually seem "more proverbial" because they are unfamiliar.

2.5 Conclusion

The social principles discussed here are an essential part of what someone has to know to be a speaker of Maninka in its natural setting. They are cultural attitudes that manifest themselves in the speaking of Maninka but in other ways as well. When Maninka people speak other languages in the West African context, they behave in similar ways, or as nearly so as they are able given the limitations they find in speaking other languages. A Maninka person expressing himself in French will typically display many of the same cultural values that he does when he speaks Maninka: there will be extensive greetings and leave-takings, respect for the bonds of friendship and marriage, and a similar concern for the principles of *badenya*. But these cultural values cannot be fully expressed without the Maninka language.

As in all societies, the language has names for concepts that have traditionally had importance for its speakers. Proverbs and the expressions used in greetings and leave-takings express ideas that come to the foreground again and again in Maninka life and thought. These ideas would have to take deep roots in new languages before they could approach anything like the same force in translation. Similarly, there is no easy way to translate words such as *badenya*, *fadenya* and *ngana* into a language like French or English because they are part of a world view that is systematically different from that of most French and English speakers. The best one can do is to explain those words, which is what we have attempted to do here. Languages neighboring on Maninka in West Africa reflect much closer cultural values and so in that sense are easier to translate into and easier for Maninka people to learn.

Maninka has a term *koro*, which means "older person with common grandparents": someone's *koro* is an older brother, older sister, or older cousin. Another term *dogo* means "younger person with common grandparents." Someone's *dogo* is a younger brother, younger sister, or younger cousin. Just as there are no single words in English to translate *koro* or *dogo*, so Maninka has no single words to translate English *brother*, *sister*, or *cousin*. This does not mean that a Maninka cannot distinguish between his siblings and his cousins or think of his older and younger brothers together as a single category, any more than it means that an English speaker is incapable of grouping in two categories all the older and younger relatives with whom he has common grandparents. It does, however, illustrate how a language tends to focus attention on categories that have through time been of greatest importance to a people. Age groups and the extended family are of central importance to a Maninka child, and relationships between older and younger children in an extended family (cousins included) are more important than those between just siblings. Learning a language is intimately connected with learning about the way people think and the way they organize their culture.

There are a number of reasons why Maninka society would benefit from having some of its members learn French in schools (or English in the case of Maninka people living in Gambia). One could also argue, however, that the best program of classroom instruction would be a bilingual one, with both Maninka and the European language being used for government administration. The best language for international contact may be the European one, but the best one for daily life and work within the society is the language that the people speak. Therefore, the best hope for using classroom instruction to help meet new economic and environmental challenges—instruction that can be relevant to improvements in agriculture, animal husbandry, and health care—is through a program that makes major use of Maninka.

Most of the area in which Maninka is spoken was colonized by the French in the last century and received its independence in the early 1960s. Until now the independent governments have tended to rely almost exclusively on French as the language for classroom instruction of the young. However, in the seventies, literacy in Maninka has been spreading as a part of adult education programs in rural areas, and more than one government made preparations for the use of Maninka and several other West African languages, along with French, in the primary schools.

SUGGESTIONS FOR FURTHER READING

The best book available today giving a general picture of life in urban and rural Maninka settings is Claude Meillassoux's study entitled *Urbanization of an African Community: Voluntary Associations in Bamako.* Nicolas Hopkins also has an outstanding study of current life in a small town in Mali, *Popular Government in an African Town: Kita, Mali.*

Nhemia Leotzion gives us a historian's view of the great empires of the Maninka past in his study entitled *Ancient Chara and Mali.*

Samples of the rich Maninka literature can be found in *African Folklore,* edited by Richard M. Dorson, where Charles Bird has some translations as well as an article entitled "Heroic Songs of the Wasulu Hunters."

Charles Bird, Bourama Soumaoro, and Mamadou Koita have done a translation of a hunter's epic from the Wasulu region on the Mali-Guinea border, *The Songs of Seydou Camara: Vol. 1, Kambili.* The introduction to this volume contains further discussion of several themes touched on in this chapter, including hunters' societies, bards, the *ngana*, and the forces of *badenya* and *fadenya*. The life and art of the great bard Seydou Camara is commented on.

For those students who would like to learn more of the intricacies of the Maninka language, we can suggest the volumes on the mutually intelligible dialect called Bambara by Charles Bird, John Hutchison, and Mamadou Kanté, *An Ka Bamanankan Kalan: Introductory Bambara* and by Bird and Kanté, *An Ka Bamanankan Kalan: Intermediate Bambara.*

See the excellent account by Bernard Dumont of the functional literacy program he directed in Bambara in the Republic of Mali, educational work closely linked to a program of agricultural development: *Functional Literacy in Mali: Training for Development.*

Bird, Charles. "Heroic Songs of the Wasulu Hunters." In *African Folklore.* Edited by Richard M. Dorson. New York: Doubleday, 1972.

Bird, Charles, and Kanté, Mamadou. *An Ka Bamanankan Kalan: Intermediate Bambara.* Bloomington: Indiana University Linguistics Club, 1977.

Bird, Charles; Hutchison, John; and Kanté, Mamadou. *An Ka Bamanankan Kalan: Introductory Bambara.* Bloomington: Indiana University Linguistics Club, 1977.

Bird, Charles; Soumaoro, Bourama; and Koita, Mamadou. *The Songs of Seydou Camara: Vol. 1, Kambili.* Bloomington: Indiana University African Studies Center, 1974.

Dumont, Bernard. *Functional Literacy in Mali: Training for Development.* New York: UNESCO Educational Studies and Documents No. 10. UNESCO Publications Center, P.O. Box 433, Murray Hill Station, New York, 10016, 1971.

Hopkins, Nicolas. *Popular Government in an African Town: Kita, Mali.* Chicago: University of Chicago Press, 1972.

Leotzion, Nhemia. *Ancient Chara and Mali.* London: Methuen, 1973.

Meillassoux, Claude. *Urbanization of an African Community: Voluntary Associations in Bamako.* Seattle: University of Washington Press, 1968.

APPENDIX

More proverbs (explanations follow):

1. You can pretend to yawn but you can't pretend to sweat.
2. The old man seated knows everything about dancing; once standing he forgets it all.
3. Even if the rabbit has become your enemy, you will still say he is fast afoot.
4. If night has fallen and something bad gets in your eye, it is your fault.

5. The tortoise might want to dance, but it has no muscles in its neck.
6. You can't see a bird in the air and tell whether it has got an egg.
7. Teeth are white, but there is blood underneath them.
8. The eye cannot see whether the sauce is salty; it can only see its grease.
9. Although the deaf man doesn't hear the thunder, he'll see the rain.
10. When you hear the canoe go crunch, it has arrived on the sand.
11. There is no canoe so big that it will not sink.
12. Once you have planted a tree and it grows up, you no longer can pull it out.
13. Only the little tree can be straightened.
14. Sickness comes on a stallion and leaves on a tortoise.
15. It's better knowing the time to run than to say "I'm fast afoot."
16. You don't ask to borrow the sandals of someone you are travelling with.
17. If you are putting monkeys in a basket, you should expect to hear the noise.
18. You can't put cows in all the barns that your mind has built.
19. It's better to destroy the home you're living in than one you're going to move to.
20. Don't light a lamp for a blind man.
21. Don't ask a hungry man to wash his hands.
22. Rinsing your mouth with water doesn't cut your thirst.
23. A pail left in the house won't catch water.
24. The bullet doesn't turn, it goes straight to the mark.
25. When you come to a stream, before trying to walk around it, put your foot in it.
26. Even if you don't like your buttocks, you still won't sit on your knees.
27. Should you give birth to a snake, you'll still tie it around your waist.
28. One stream crossed, another is ahead.
29. The scrubby bush can give birth to a giant tree.
30. Fresh excrement is a joy for flies.
31. A lion will starve to death rather than eat flies.
32. When you invite a blind man, you invite two people.
33. If the red monkey can't reach the fruit, he says it is rotten.
34. If you hear someone say "I was tricked," you know there has been a person who said something he liked.
35. The colt has found the mare.
36. Smoke comes out of any roof (chimney).

37. One donkey got into the flour, and all the donkeys have white muzzles.
38. If you see an old man fill his mouth with flour, you know there is water nearby.
39. The lizard and the bat do not eat the same dish.
40. If you see a fire has jumped the river, it's trouble for the person trying to put it out.
41. The chicken's beak is too small to blow a horn.
42. The rolling stone is the pebble crusher.
43. Two big calabashes won't fit together.
44. No matter how good your horse, it still needs a bridle.
45. One finger can't pick up a pebble.
46. The man with fresh meat will look for someone with fire.
47. When you find fruit on the ground, raise your eyes to the tree.
48. If the people of the village are blind, the one-eyed man is the leader.
49. When the birds are gone, the fly becomes general.
50. Good sauce doesn't remain in the bowl.
51. If the drum is good, the dancers will be many.
52. You see millet fallen on the ground and you pick it up; if you see a man fallen on the ground, you pass.
53. There is no place the wise man can go to get away from fools.
54. One deed doesn't build a name.
55. When you have beaten the older brother, you look for the younger one.
56. Grass doesn't grow on the road.
57. If you hear a blind man say "Let's throw stones today," you know he is sitting on a pile of stones.
58. Sometimes you own the day; sometimes the day owns you.
59. Truth doesn't gouge your eyes, but it reddens them.
60. Eating a traditional dish is not an evil deed.

Explanations:

1. Someone can pretend to know how to do something but can't pretend to do it.
2. It is one thing to talk about something, another to do it.
3. It is better to be honest about the strengths of your adversary.
4. People are supposed to be asleep at night. If their eyes are open after dark, that means they are doing something they are not supposed to do.
5. Everyone has his limitations.

6. Everyone is limited in what he can see and know.

7. Appearances can be deceiving.

8. To find out if the sauce is salty, you have to commit yourself and taste it.

9. Even if you do not know the cause of something, you can still deal with it sensibly when it occurs (e.g., get in out of the rain).

10. It should be evident that you have gone as far as you can go.

11. Everyone is fallible, every problem has a solution, etc.

12. After a while there are commitments that cannot be revoked.

13. Act soon if you want to have an effect.

14. You have to be patient.

15. Stop bragging and be alert.

16. If you want someone to do something with you, don't expect him to get along with less than you are willing to get along with.

17. You reap what you sow.

18. Imagination is always bigger than reality.

19. It is better to have hardship now and a secure future than the reverse.

20. Don't make useless gifts.

21. First things first.

22. Don't do things half way.

23. The importance of initiative.

24. Consistency, perseverance.

25. Be bold enough to try.

26. Self-acceptance.

27. No matter what you create, you will be fond of it.

28. Keep a stiff upper lip.

29. Insignificant people can have great offspring and perform great deeds (Sunjata's mother was said to have been a small hunchback, the ugliest woman in the country).

30. That shows what kind of people they are. If they like it, they can have it.

31. Nobility.

32. For instance, when someone is complaining about a mother-in-law one could say, "You have no right to complain. When you married me you took on obligations to my whole family."

33. Sour grapes.

34. Deceiving flattery.

35. Now things are as they should be.

36. Everyone has troubles.

37. When one does wrong, the whole group gets blamed.

38. An old man is wise and knows that flour is dry; he wouldn't make a mistake about the situation. He knows what he is doing.

39. One man's meat is another man's poison.

40. Rumors are difficult to squelch.

41. The horn is a symbol of kingship and power; the king's words are considered more important than what comes from the mouth of a peasant. When the rich man speaks, people will listen. Do not try to take on a member of the Rockefeller family.

42. He who takes initiative gains power: *fadenya*.

43. Two powerful, ambitious people will not get along peacefully.

44. Strength must be tempered with wisdom.

45. No one is an island unto himself (if he wants to accomplish anything).

46. The opportunity for gain can lead to cooperation.

47. Thanks.

48. In the valley of the blind the one-eyed man is king.

49. Big fish in a little pond.

50. True merit will be recognized.

51. People join in if you are doing something worthwhile.

52. A criticism for someone's lack of charity.

53. The need for patience in working with others.

54. Patience and perseverance.

55. If you give them an inch, they will take a mile.

56. A criticism of sexual promiscuity.

57. A criticism of people who brag about situations for which they are not responsible.

58. You win some and you lose some.

59. Truth won't kill you, but it can make you angry. (Getting "red eyes" means to get angry.)

60. People should do what they know is fitting and proper, no matter what others may say.

Special thanks to Dwight Bolinger, Karen Courtney, Bob Dixon, Jim Fidelholtz, Peggy Good, Peg Griffin, Mary Haas, Mamadou Kanté, Ed Keenan, Mamadou Lamine Keita, Michael Noonan, Michael Ryan and Agnes Shopen for helpful comments and suggestions on this essay in an earlier form.

III

Becoming a Competent
Speaker of Malagasy

Edward Louis Keenan

Elinor Ochs

INTRODUCTION

In this chapter we will describe some of the major adaptations that a native speaker of a Western European language, like English, must experience in order to become a competent speaker of Malagasy, the language of Madagascar. Our understanding of these adaptations comes from our own experience, as we spent a year living in a peasant village in Madagascar precisely for the purpose of learning the language.

To be a competent speaker of a language in any culture, one must be able to perform successfully those social acts that require the use of language. This entails that a speaker be able to produce simple sentences and that he be able to apply those processes that form more complex

Edward Keenan, American, has taught extensively in Europe as well as in Israel and is currently professor of linguistics at the University of California at Los Angeles. His major work concerns logically based semantics for natural language and comparative syntax of world languages. His interest in world languages began with a year's stay, 1969–1970, in Madagascar.

Elinor Ochs received her Ph.D. in cultural anthropology from the University of Pennsylvania in 1974. Her dissertation focused on language use in Vakinankaratra, Madagascar. Currently she teaches in the department of linguistics at the University of Southern California. Her primary research interests lie in the organization of discourse across cultures and its acquisition by children.

FIGURE 3.1 The authors with the Razotovo family, who helped them find a residence in a small village and often served as language consultants. On the occasion of a visit to town (Antsirabe) June, 1970.

sentences from simpler ones. And the production of simple sentences requires that we know both the basic vocabulary of the language and which combinations of the vocabulary items yield understandable phrases and sentences. And finally, of course, we must know the basic sounds of the language and which combinations of sounds yield admissible words and phrases.

Competence in a language, however, requires much more than merely being able to form understandable sentences. A machine, however cleverly disguised as a human, which could only produce well-formed sentences on a random basis, would not be able, in general, to joke, tease, bargain, ask a favor, perform ritual oratory, or even, as we shall see, exchange ordinary information in a socially normal way.

To be a competent speaker of Malagasy (or of any language) then, one must be able to adhere to the complex norms of the society concerning language use in particular and personal interaction in general.

In the first part of the discussion to follow we shall concentrate on those aspects of word and sentence formation that are most novel to native speakers of English and hence require the greatest adaptation on their part. Later we shall discuss several social norms that make language behavior quite different from that prevalent in middle-class

American society. (We will have little to say about the sound system of Malagasy, as it presents few major difficulties for an English speaker. Malagasy sentences will be presented in the standard writing system, which corresponds overall quite closely to the pronunciation system. Occasional notes on spelling conventions will point out the few discrepancies.) First, however, we make some general remarks about the situation of the Malagasy people and language.

1 BACKGROUND

Malagasy, spoken in eighteen major dialects throughout the island of Madagascar (the large island off the east coast of Africa), constitutes a subgroup of the Austronesian family of languages (also called Malayo-Polynesian), and thus has a common ancestry with the languages of Indonesia, the Philippines, and Polynesia (see Figure 3.2). Our best evidence indicates that Madagascar was peopled early in the first millenium A.D. by settlers coming from somewhere in the Indonesian part of the world, probably travelling along the coast of the Indian Ocean, down the east coast of Africa, and across the Mozambique channel to what is now called Madagascar (or internationally, the Malagasy Republic—the name Madagascar itself is probably of Portugese origin). Trade along these routes was largely controlled by the Arabs, and the first references we have to the Malagasy people come from Arab sources of this period. The Malagasy language itself attests to many obvious Arabic borrowings such as the days of the week: *Atalata* "Tuesday," *Alarobia* "Wednesday," etc. In fact the first writing in Malagasy was done in an Arabic script, although it never gained widespread use.

The first substantial European contact came through the English missionaries in the mid-nineteenth century. They established the current writing system, and several Malagasy words pertaining to writing or Protestant Christianity derive from this influence, for example, *boky* from "book," *pastaora* from "Pastor," etc. In fact the spelling convention whereby the long *ee* sound is written as *y* at the end of a word, as in *boky* above, derives from English influence. In the interior of a word, this sound is written *i*.

At the end of the nineteenth century, however, the French took over colonial control of Madagascar, and some of the current technical and administrative vocabulary of Malagasy as well as that of Catholic Christianity, derives from French sources, for example *savony* from French *savon* "soap," *mompera* "priest" from French *mon père* "my father." It is interesting to note, however, that despite the onslaught of European culture in the twentieth century, Malagasy has overall borrowed relatively few words from European languages. As we shall see,

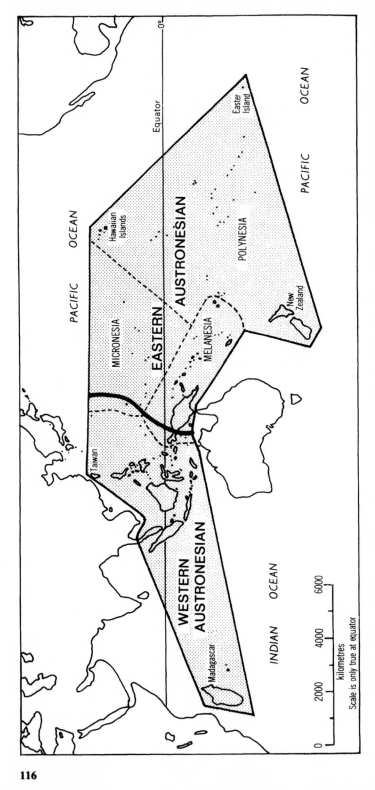

FIGURE 3.2 *The Area Within Which Austronesian Languages Are Spoken. There are also several Austronesian languages spoken by minority groups in the southern part of Vietnam.*

Source: Adapted with permission from "Austronesian Languages" in *Encyclopaedia Britannica*, 15th edition, 2:485, © 1974 by Encyclopaedia Britannica, Inc.

the structure of the Malagasy language enabled it to coin many of its words in a natural way for objects and activities of European origin. Currently, for example, schoolbooks in subjects such as geometry are written in Malagasy using largely words native to Malagasy.

2 FORMING SENTENCES IN MALAGASY

2.1 Simple Sentences

Let us consider a simple declarative sentence like (1) below, which might be used to express a statement of fact.

(1) *manasa   ny   lamba   amin'ity   savony   ity   Rasoa*
    wash   the   clothes   with this   soap   this   Rasoa
    Rasoa is washing the clothes with this soap.

Under the Malagasy sentence we have put a word-for-word translation and then given the most natural translation in everyday English. Sentence (1) presents several striking differences from its English translation. In the first place, the verb occurs in initial position and is followed by the major noun phrases. This is already unusual; probably not more than 10 percent of the world's languages place the verb in initial position in simple (unemphatic) sentences. (The most common position for the verb is in the final position, as in Japanese, Hindi, and Basque. A close second in terms of frequency is for the verb to occur in second position, preceded by the subject of the sentence, as in English, modern Hebrew, and Swahili. Together these two word order types account for about 90 percent of the world's languages.)

Even more unusual, however, is the fact that in Malagasy the subject phrase, for example *Rasoa*, a woman's name in (1), occurs in sentence final position. At most, about a dozen of the world's five-thousand-odd languages are known to regularly place the subject in final position. Yet it would be a mistake to assume that the subject phrase in Malagasy is in any way less important in Malagasy sentence construction than, for example, the subject phrase in English. As in English, Malagasy subjects refer to the doer of the action, or as we shall say, the *agent*, in cases where the verb expresses an action (like *wash*, as opposed to, say, *need*). And as in English, the subject normally refers to the main thing the speaker is talking about, or as we shall say, the *topic* of the sentence. Thus in (2) and (3) below, although the main predicate does not express an action, the subject phrase still expresses the topic of discussion and occurs in the final position of the sentence.

(2) *mpandrafitra   any   Antsirabe   Rabe*
    carpenter   there   Antsirabe   Rabe
    Rabe is a carpenter in Antsirabe.

> (3) *tany   Antsirabe   ny   mpampianatra*
>   there   Antsirabe   the   teacher
>   The teacher was in Antsirabe.

Further, as we shall see, much of the syntax of complex sentences in Malagasy depends on the behavior of subject phrases. Before considering this dependency, however, let us consider how to form verbs and noun phrases in order to combine them as illustrated in (1)–(3) to form simple sentences.

2.1.1 *Verbs* In several respects, the structure of Malagasy verbs seems quite simple compared to that of English. For example, in English and many European languages, the form of the verb varies with the person (first, second, or third) and number (singular or plural) of the subject. Thus we say "I sing" but "John sings," and "I am singing," but "we are singing." But in Malagasy the verb does not change form depending on the person and number of the subject. Thus "I sing" (or "I am singing") is *mihira aho* (lit.: "sing I"), and "John sings" or "John is singing" is *mihira Rajaona* (lit.: "sing John"), and "we sing" or "we are singing" is *mihira izahay* (lit.: "sing we").

As a second example, consider that English verbs may occur in a bewildering variety of forms together with auxiliary (or 'helping') verbs like "be," "have," and "do." Thus from a simple verb like "sing" we have "John sings, is singing, sang, did sing, has sung, was singing, will sing, will be singing, will have sung," etc. But in Malagasy there are no auxiliary verbs like "be," "have," and "do." In fact there is no simple verb "to be" at all. Tense, then, is indicated very simply by the initial consonant on the verb. Almost all present-tense verbs begin with *m-* (as *manasa* "wash" and *mihira* "sing" above). To form the past tense, simply replace the initial *m-* by *n-* (e.g. *nihira aho*, "I sang"). And to form the future, replace the initial *m-* by *h-*. Thus *hihira aho* is "I will sing." Further, Malagasy verbs do not distinguish progressive from nonprogressive forms (e.g. "I am singing" from "I sing"). Both receive the same translation in Malagasy, although if it is important to stress that an action is continuing, one can use independent adverbs like *mbola* "still." Thus to indicate that someone is in the process of singing now and hasn't yet stopped, you might say (4) below.

> (4) *mbola   mihira   izy*
>   still   sing   he
>   He is (still) singing.

Given a simple sentence like (5) below, the reader should now be able to form the Malagasy equivalents of "I drink milk," "I am still drinking milk," "John drank milk," "John was drinking milk," "He will drink milk," and "He will be drinking milk."

(5) *misotro   ronono   izahay*
     drink   milk   we
   We are drinking milk.

However, while some aspects of Malagasy verb structure appear simpler than English, others are clearly much more complex. The learner of Malagasy will be frustrated to find that almost none of the simple present-tense forms of verbs occurs as such in the Malagasy dictionaries (and there are some excellent ones). The reason is that verbs are in general formed by prefixing elements to what we shall call *roots*. For example, *mihira* "sing" is formed by adding the prefix *mi-* to the root *hira* meaning "song." There are about a dozen such prefixes, and most of them can combine with most roots to form verbs. So dictionaries simply list the roots and indicate which prefixes may apply and what the meaning of the derived verb is. Thus to look up a verb in the dictionary, it is necessary to be able to determine its root. In the case of *mihira* above, the problem is simple. Once we know that *mi-* is one of the verb-forming prefixes, we may assume that the rest of the verb is the root. And further, *hira*, the rest of the verb in this case, occurs as a noun with the meaning "song," so it is a form we know independently in the language.

But a more usual case is illustrated by *manasa* "wash." Here the prefix is *man-* and the root is *sasa*. *Sasa* does not occur independently in the language as a word, and further, when the prefix *man-* is added, the initial consonant *s-* of the root is lost. So we cannot simply read off the root form by eliminating the prefix from *manasa* for that would yield only *asa*, which is not the root. Thus, to find *manasa* in the dictionary, it might appear as though we would have to look up all roots of the form *Xasa* where X is any consonant (we would also have to check for a root *asa*, since a root beginning with a vowel does not change in any way when the prefix *man-* is added).

Fortunately our dictionary checking does not have to be quite this tedious, for not just any consonant at the beginning of a root is dropped. The ones most commonly dropped are *f, h, k, p, t,* and *s*. For example, *man-* + the root *tolotra* = *manolotra* "to offer," *man-* + *hadino* = *manadino* "to forget," etc. On the other hand, consonants like *g, b, d,* and *z* as well as *l* and *r* at the beginning of roots are not dropped when *man-* is added, although certain other changes in pronunciation may take place. For example, while *man* + *dinika* = *mandinika* "to study," we have *mandroso* "to progress" from *man* + *roso* and *mandeha* "to go" from *man* + *leha*, etc.

What principle can you give to describe, on the basis of the data at hand, those consonants that drop and those that don't?[1] Given the following roots, form the corresponding verbs:

man- + sorata = _____"to write"
man- + araka   = _____"to follow"
man- + haja   = _____"to respect"
man- + kaikitra = _____"to bite"
man- + lefa   = _____"to send"

Of the many verbal prefixes in Malagasy, *mi-* and *man-* are the most commonly occurring ones that apply directly to roots (although there are several others). And many roots accept both prefixes, in which case the verb formed from *mi-* usually has an intransitive meaning, and the one formed from *man-* has a transitive meaning. Thus from *sasa* we form the transitive *manasa* "to wash (something)" and also *misasa* "to wash (oneself)." And from *araka* we form the transitive *manaraka* "to follow (someone)" and the intransitive *miaraka* "to be or go together with."

However, even when we have formed verbs from *mi-* or *man-*, it is still possible to add further prefixes to the derived verb. In this case the initial *m-* of *mi-* or *man-* is dropped and the new prefix added. Thus from *manasa* "to wash (something)" we could add the reciprocal prefix *mif-* yielding *mifanasa* "to wash each other." Or we could add the causative prefix *mamp-* yielding *mampanasa* "to cause (someone) to wash (something)" and so on.

It should be clear then that verbal structure in Malagasy is quite complex, though in a different way from English. Furthermore, the complexity we have discussed so far only concerns active verbs, that is, ones in which the subject/topic is the agent of the action. But as we shall see, Malagasy, like the languages of the Philippines, has elaborate ways of making nonagents into subject/topics, much as the passive voice in English ("John was hit by Mary" is the passive form of "Mary hit John") makes a nonagent into the subject/topic of the derived sentence since "John" is not the agent of the action. Rather it is he who undergoes the action, or as we shall say, is the *patient* of the action.

2.1.2 *Nouns* As with the formation of verbs in Malagasy, we find that the formation of nouns lacks certain of the complexities associated with nouns in European languages. For example, Malagasy nouns do not in general change form according to whether they refer to one or many

---

[1]In general, roots that begin with unvoiced consonants, that is those that are not produced by making a noise with the vocal cords, like *t* as opposed to *d* or *k* as opposed to *g* etc., are dropped when the prefix *man-* is added. Roots beginning with voiced consonants generally either leave the consonant intact when *man-* is added or else change it in fairly systematic ways, e.g., *l* becomes *d* as in *mandeha* "to go" from *man-* + *leha*.

things. Thus *ny akoho* would translate, word for word, as either "the chicken" or "the chickens." Further, Malagasy lacks the gender system of languages like German and French. We don't have to know in Malagasy whether nouns are masculine, feminine, or neuter. Malagasy also lacks the case system of European languages. Thus, in general, we do not have one form of a noun (the nominative case form) if it functions as a subject and another form if it functions as an object. Compare for example (6) and (7) in which the two noun phrases in each sentence have the same form, differing only in position.

(6) *nahita   ny   voalavo   ny   akoho*
     saw   the   rat   the   chicken
     The chicken saw the rat.

(7) *nahita   ny   akoho   ny   voalavo*
     saw   the   chicken the   rat
     The rat saw the chicken.

On the other hand, Malagasy nouns do evidence a complexity of a different sort. While many common nouns are themselves roots in the language, a great many others that name common objects of everyday use are derived from more basic structures. We consider here a few types.

Notice that proper names of people we have mentioned so far, *Rabe, Rasoa, Rajaona* all begin with *Ra-*. *Ra-* in fact is a prefix that indicates that the construction in which it occurs is a proper name. (This use of *Ra-* is largely limited to the major dialect of Malagasy, *Merina*. It is used for men's or women's names, but not for children's. For a child's name, one uses the prefix *I-*). What follows *Ra-* is either an adjective or a verb phrase. Thus *be* is an adjective meaning "big," so *Rabe* might be translated as "Mr. Big." Similarly *soa* is an adjective meaning "beautiful," so *Rasoa* might be translated as "Ms. Beautiful." (Note that *jaona* in *Rajaona* has no Malagasy meaning. It is simply the name "John" borrowed from English, but the particle *Ra-* is still added because it functions as a proper name.) For reasons of space the adjectives we have used in proper names have been short ones, but typical Malagasy names are quite long and may contain whole verb phrases. Thus *Ramanandraibe* is about an average-length name and 'means' "Mr.-have-father-big" (*Ra-manana-rai-be*). Further, the systematic way of forming proper names from *Ra-* + predicates allows one to refer to someone with a name he has just made up using a predicate that is appropriate to the immediate situation. This is occasionally done in English, as when we say things like "Mr. Blabbermouth," although such use is unusual, perhaps childish. But in a Malagasy village, we might easily refer to an old white-haired woman whom we see in the fields but don't know as *Rafotsy* (Ms. White).

In addition to names of people, names of places are also all derived from other words in the language. The most common formula here is *an-* (a particle indicating location), followed by a common noun, followed by one or more adjectives. For example, in sentences (2) and (3) the name of the town *Antsirabe* was used. But this word really has three parts: The locative particle *an-*, the noun *sira* "salt," and the adjective *be* "big." Antsirabe is so named because of the many mineral springs located there. Similarly the capital of Madagascar, Tananarive, is in Malagasy *Antananarivo*, which decomposes into *an-* (locative particle) + *tanana* "village or country" + *arivo* "thousand." It is so named as it was a stopping point for a thousand soldiers during an early battle in the history of Madagascar.

Nouns that refer to locations exhibit another interesting property in Malagasy. Recall again sentence (2), *mpandrafitra any Antsirabe Rabe*, which is, word for word, "carpenter there Antsirabe Rabe." Locative nouns, whether common or proper, are obligatorily accompanied by an independent locative word like *any* "there." It is rather as though in English we could not say "John is a carpenter in Boston" but rather had to say "John is a carpenter there in Boston." The use of locative words like *any* "there" might seem redundant since, after all, it is already clear that nouns like *Antsirabe* name places. But in fact such locative words contain much information.

In the first place, *any* is but one of seven such locative words that could have been used in (2). And each such word indicates that the locative noun that follows it is at a greater or lesser distance from the speaker. Thus *any Antsirabe* means that Antsirabe is rather far from the speaker, but *aroa Antsirabe* would mean it was still farther, and *ary Antsirabe* would mean very far indeed. On the other hand, *atsy Antsirabe* would mean that Antsirabe was somewhat closer to the speaker, *ato* would mean closer yet, and *aty* would clearly mean that the speaker was in Antsirabe at the moment of speaking. Compare this to English with its twofold distinction in locative words—"here" vs. "there."[2] And since the use of these locative words is obligatory with place names, the European speaker who learns Malagasy must quickly learn to make many more judgments of relative distance than he is used to. Yet we have just begun to note the complexity in the use of locative particles!

In addition to marking seven degrees of relative distance, locative particles in Malagasy also mark whether the location referred to is visible to the speaker or not. All the locative words used so far indicate

---

[2]There is a seventh form, *ao*, which has a slightly specialized meaning. It not only means fairly close, occurring between *atsy* and *ato* in the series, but also usually implies "inside of something." Its use would not then be appropriate when referring to a city, which does not, by its nature, occur inside anything else.

that the location, Antsirabe, is not visible to the speaker. To indicate visibility, we simply change the initial *a-* of the locative word to *e-*. Thus had we said *eny Antsirabe* instead of *any Antsirabe*, that would mean that Antsirabe was pretty far away, but that the speaker could see it. Thus instead of merely seven locative particles we actually have fourteen! And our complications are still not over.

Note sentence (3) *Tany Antsirabe ny mpampianatra*, which we glossed word-for-word as "there Antsirabe the teacher." But the locative word *tany* is not one of those we have already considered. It looks like *any* except that it begins with a *t-*. Also, its meaning is close to that of *any* in that it indicates a fairly great distance and lack of visibility to the speaker. But in addition, the prefix *t-* indicates past tense so that the sentence means "The teacher was in Antsirabe." Had we said *Any Antsirabe ny mpampianatra*, we would have meant that the teacher is now in Antsirabe. And had we said *Ho any Antsirabe . . .* we would have meant that the teacher will be in Antsirabe. Note that in the English translations of these sentences, the tense marking is carried by the form of the verb "to be" ("is" for present, "was" for past, "will be" for future). But as we have seen, Malagasy has no such verb. And in sentences like those above, we feel no need for such a verb since the principal meaning that "to be" has there is to mark the time of the state referred to, and in Malagasy this is done by marking the locative particle. As all fourteen of the locative particles may occur with *ho-* or *t-* prefixed, we have in fact forty-two such forms from which a learner of Malagasy has to choose at a moment's notice when speaking!

We might also mention that words like "where," which question location may also be marked for tense. Thus *Aiza Rabe?* would mean "Where is Rabe?" whereas *Taiza Rabe?* would mean "Where *was* Rabe?" and *Ho aiza Rabe?* would mean "Where will Rabe be?" Even certain prepositions in Malagasy may be marked for past tense in this way. Thus if we put sentence (1) in the past tense, changing *manasa* to *nanasa*, we must change the present tense form of the preposition *amin-* "with" to *tamin-* "with (in the past)."

Finally we should note that the complex distance discriminations that are made in the system of locative particles extends as well to the system of demonstrative adjectives and pronouns. Here again English makes only a two-way distinction, "this" vs. "that." But Malagasy makes, in this case, a six-way distinction. Thus in sentence (1) the use of *ity* in *ity savony ity* "this soap" indicates that the soap is in the immediate presence of the speaker. The reader will note that the demonstrative adjective occurs on both sides of the noun phrase it modifies. For example, if the noun phrase contains an adjective, the demonstratives frame the noun + adjective construction, as in *ity trano fotsy ity* (literally, "this house white this") for *this white house*. On the other hand *io savony io* would mean the soap is somewhat farther away, *itsy savony itsy* still farther away, *iny savony iny* rather far indeed, *iroa savony iroa* still farther yet, and *iry savony iry* would mean that the soap is so far away from the speaker that he probably could not see it, so the use of this demonstrative would be bizarre, since the meaning of the demonstrative includes the idea that it is present to the speaker. Thus the visible/nonvisible marking is not so clearly differentiated in the demonstrative adjective series. It is possible nonetheless to infix *-za-* into most of the demonstrative adjectives, in which case the item need not be visible to the speaker. Thus from *io* we have *izao*, from *iny* we have *izany*, etc., but this infixing process is only of limited productivity.

Let us return now to some of the other ways of forming noun phrases. One common way is to replace the initial *m-* of a present-tense active verb (one in which the subject is the agent) by *mp-*. The resulting noun denotes "one who performs the action expressed by the verb." Thus from *manasa* we form *mpanasa* "one who washes," and from *mihira* we form *mpihira* "one who sings." Note that in sentence (2) the word for carpenter is such an agent noun. Thus from the root *rafitra* "something constructed" we add the *man-* prefix to form *mandrafitra* "to build, put together" and thence the agent noun *mpandrafitra* "carpenter, mason," etc. Such nouns are easy to form, but once again they are difficult to find in a dictionary, for in order to look them up, we must know the verb from which they are formed; and to find the meaning of the verb, we must know the root from which it is formed.

A second common way of forming nouns is by replacing the initial *m-* of active present-tense verbs with *f-*. Here the meaning of the derived noun is less systematically related to the meaning of the verb from which it is derived. But usually such nouns refer to some object closely associated with the action expressed by the verb. Thus from the root *vaki* "broken" we form the transitive verb *mamaky* "to cut, chop" (note that an initial *v-* in a root changes the *n-* of the prefix *man-* to *m*) whence we form *famaky* "hatchet." From the root *zaitra* we form *manjaitra* "to sew," whence we have *fanjaitra* "needle." (The *j* in Malagasy is pronounced like "dz" together.) Once again, then, to determine the meanings of such nouns, commonly used for names of everyday objects, it is necessary to be able to determine the meaning of verbs.

A final and even more productive way of forming nouns is based on what we shall call the circumstantial form of verbs. 'Circumstantial' here contrasts with active and passive. In an active verb, the agent is the subject. In a passive verb an object, usually the patient, is the subject. And in a circumstantial verb the subject is some circumstance of the action, such as the place or time at which the action was performed, the manner or purpose of the action, the instrument with which the action was performed, or the person for whose benefit the action was performed. Consider for example sentence (1), for convenience repeated as (8) below.

(8) | *manasa* | *ny* | *lamba* | *amin'ity* | *savony* | *ity* | *Rasoa* |
     |----------|------|---------|------------|----------|-------|---------|
     | wash | the | clothes | with this | soap | this | Rasoa |

Rasoa is washing clothes with this soap.

The verb in (8) is active, so the subject Rasoa denotes the agent of the action. In (9) below, however, the verb is passive and the subject, *ny lamba* "the clothes" is the patient of the action.

(9) | *sasan-dRasoa* | *amin'ity* | *savony* | *ity* | *ny* | *lamba* |
     |----------------|------------|----------|-------|------|---------|
     | washed-by-Rasoa | with this | soap | this | the | clothes |

The clothes are washed by Rasoa with this soap.

Note that in (9) the derived subject *ny lamba* "the clothes" occurs in sentence final position where subjects in Malagasy go. The agent phrase in this sentence tacks onto the end of the verb in a characteristic and rather complicated way. (The passive form of the verb without an agent tacked on would be *sasana*, formed by adding *-na* to the root *sasa*. But when we put in the agent phrase, the final *a* of *sasana* drops. This should yield a form like *sasan-Rasoa*. But in Malagasy *n* never occurs directly before *r*. In such cases a *d* is then inserted, yielding in this case *sasan-dRasoa*.)

Now, in the same way that passive verbs take patients as subjects, so circumstantial verbs take as subjects nouns that refer to some circumstance of the action. Thus in (10) below *ity savony ity* "this soap" is the subject.

(10) | *anasan-dRasoa* | *ny* | *lamba* | *ity* | *savony* | *ity* |
     |-----------------|------|---------|-------|----------|-------|
     | wash-with-by-Rasoa | the | clothes | this | soap | this |

This soap is washed clothes with by Rasoa. (Or in more natural English, "This soap is used by Rasoa to wash clothes".)

Again the derived subject "this soap" occurs in sentence final position and loses its preposition *amina* since subject phrases never occur with prepositions.

The circumstantial form of the verb is derived from the active form (not directly from the root as is the case with passive forms) by deleting the initial *m-* and adding the suffix *-ana*, moving the stress to the right. So from *mánasa*, which has the stress on *man-*, we form *anasa + ana* (two *a* sounds together collapse into a single *a* sound), which yields *anasána* with the stress on the *sa*. As with passive forms, when circumstantial forms combine with an agent phrase beginning with *r-*, the final *a* drops and a *d* is inserted yielding the form we see in (10). How deceiving was the original apparent simplicity of the Malagasy verb!

Now we may, and very commonly do, form nouns from circumstantial verbs simply by adding *f-*. The resulting noun refers to some circumstance of the action indicated by the verb, such as the purpose, place, time, manner, etc. Thus from *anasana*, the circumstantial form of *manasa*, we can form *fanasana*, which might be used to refer to the manner of washing. In such cases we may still retain the agent and the patient phrases, as illustrated in (11).

(11) *tena   ratsy   ny   fanasan-dRasoa   lamba*
      very   bad   the   washing-by Rasoa   clothes
        The way in which clothes are washed by Rasoa is very bad.

2.2 Adapting to European Vocabulary

Given the productive devices in Malagasy for forming verbs and nouns, we can now see how Malagasy survived the onslaught of European contact without having to borrow huge numbers of words designating concepts of European origin. For example, consider the general area of formal education. A few words like *boky* "book" and *sekoly* "school" were in fact borrowed. But most words pertaining to formal instruction are of Malagasy origin. Thus from a root *anatra* meaning "counsel, advice," we form the intransitive verb *mianatra* "to study, learn." And "student," of course, is just the agent noun *mpianatra*. The circumstantial form of the verb is *ianarana* (the final *-tra* part of roots usually drops or is modified in circumstantial forms, as are *-na* and *-ka*). And the circumstantial noun *fianarana* means "studying, learning, or studies." Further, if we form the causative verb from *mianatra*, we obtain *mampianatra* "to cause to study or learn," which is to say "to teach." The agent noun, *mpampianatra* then means, "teacher," and the circumstantial noun from this verb, *fampianarana*, as you might predict, means "instruction." Further, circumstantial nouns are often used to modify other nouns. Thus alongside *sekoly* "school" we can also use *trano fianarana* or *trano fampianarana* meaning "house for learning" and "house for teaching" respectively. This usage of circumstantial nouns is very common in naming the stores and shops introduced by European culture. From the root *varotra* we form *mivarotra* "to sell" and the circumstantial noun *fivarotana* "purpose, place, manner, etc. of selling." Combined with a noun like *trano* "house" we obtain *trano fivarotana*, which naturally means "house for selling" that is, "store." If we desire to specify what type of store, we merely retain the patient phrase of the verb from which the circumstantial noun is formed. Thus "bookstore" would be *trano fivarotam-boky*, "house for selling books."

3 MALAGASY SUBJECTS AND COMPLEX STRUCTURES

3.1 Subjects as Topics

In English, indeed in most languages, the subjects of simple sentences normally identify the main individuals (or objects) which the speaker is talking about—that is, the subject expresses the *topic* of the sentence. And perhaps more importantly, by identifying the topic, the subject phrase allows the hearer to guess how the *relevance* or *importance* of what is going to be said relates to what he already knows. Thus if I begin a sentence in English with "*John* . . . ." I assume the hearer knows who I am talking about and has some idea of the relevance of what I will say; this in turn depends on what the hearer knows about John, including what may have been said about him in previous discourse.

Given that subjects occur sentence-finally in Malagasy, we might expect that the relevance function of subjects would not be prominent. Indeed it is often the case that the hearer must wade through a complex predicate phrase before he has an idea of how what is said relates to what he already knows or cares about. For example, in (12) below, several individuals are mentioned before the topic "John":

(12)   *nahita   ny   vehivavy   izay   nanasa   ny   zaza   Rajaona*
       saw   the   woman   that   washed the   child   John
       John saw the woman who washed the child.

Nonetheless, subjects in Malagasy have perhaps a more prominent topic-relevance function than in English. Consider that to determine the relevance of what will be said, the topic phrase must succeed in identifying an individual (or individuals). Thus topic phrases are usually definite, as in proper names such as *John* and *Chicago*; or demonstrative noun phrases, such as *this man*; or noun phrases with a definite article, such as *the man* (which most usually serves to identify a man as the one already talked about in the discourse). On the other hand, indefinite noun phrases like *a man*, *some men*, *two men*, etc. do not identify individuals to the hearer and thus do not permit him to assess the relevance, or importance to him, of what will be said.

In English, however, it is quite possible for subjects to be indefinite, as in (13):

(13)   A woman was washing some clothes in the river.

Such a sentence is not primarily *about* some particular woman, since no such woman is identified. And upon hearing the phrase *a woman*, the hearer of (13) is not (usually) in a position to assess the relevance of what will be said. Thus *a woman* in (13) does not identify the topic of discussion nor does it serve as a relevance indicator. Yet the phrase *a woman* is clearly, syntactically speaking, the subject of the sentence (e.g. it takes nominative pronouns, controls verb agreement, occurs in initial position, etc.). So subjects in English are not consistently topics or relevance indicators. But in Malagasy they are. Subjects in Malagasy must be definite. Thus (14) is categorically ungrammatical.

(14) *manasa zaza   vehivavy
      wash   child   woman
      A woman is washing children.

How would we express the idea in (14) in Malagasy? The principal way would be to use an existential construction, as in (15).

(15) *misy*   *vehivavy* *manasa* *zaza*
      exist   woman   wash   child
      A woman is washing children. (Literally "[there] is a woman washing children.")

We note that *misy* is a normal verb taking present, past, and future tenses, having imperative forms ("let there be..."), circumstantial forms, etc. It usually translates the "hard core" notions of existence seen in (16) and (17).

(16) *misy* *liona* *any*   *Afrika*
      exist lion   there   Africa
      There are lions in Africa.

(17) *misy* *Andriamanitra*
      exist God
      God exists.

Sentences like (15) in English and Malagasy then lack topics and relevance indicators. And in Malagasy they also lack subjects. We note, for example, that *vehivavy* "woman" in (15) does not have the syntactic properties of subjects in Malagasy. For example, we cannot relativize it. That would yield the ungrammatical (18).

(18) *(ny) *vehivavy* *izay*   *misy*   *manasa* *zaza*
      the   woman   that   exist   wash   child
      The woman who there is washing children.

We should further note that if the agent phrase in sentences like (15) is fully indefinite, as *someone* in English, there would most usually be no noun phrase at all following the existence verb!

(19) *misy   manasa   zaza*
     exist   wash   child
          Someone is washing children.

This indeed is one of the ways of avoiding direct reference to in-dividuals, and as we shall see, avoiding direct reference to individuals is often very important in Malagasy society.

The role of subjects as topics gives us reason to believe that despite its final position, the category of subject is very important in Malagasy syntax. In fact, we have already seen another piece of evidence in support of this. For we can think of 'passive' and 'circumstantial' as ways of converting various types of nonsubjects into subjects. These operations, or as we shall say, transformations, move the appropriate nonsubject to subject position, sentence final; eliminate whatever pre-positions the noun phrase may have carried; and put the verb into a characteristic form. But there are no transformations in Malagasy that systematically convert, for example, nonobjects into objects, or nonin-strumentals into instrumentals. The only noun phrase into which others can be converted is the subject noun phrase. Further, many other ways of transforming certain sentences into others also apply, in one way or another, to subjects. We now consider examples of several such pro-cesses.

3.2   The Reflexive Construction

In English when we want to indicate in a simple sentence that the agent and the patient are the same, we normally put the sentence in an active form and present the patient phrase as a reflexive pronoun, as in "John likes himself" or "Mary killed herself." This process is usually described by saying that when two noun phrases refer to the same thing, the second can be replaced by a pronoun (in the above cases by a reflexive pronoun). But for English we could equally well describe this process by saying, as we did above, that in an active sentence the direct object (or the patient phrase) becomes a reflexive pronoun and the subject phrase remains as is. Since the direct object occurs after the subject, the two descriptions are equivalent for English. But in Malagasy the direct object occurs before the subject, so the two descriptions give different predictions in this case. If the second noun phrase were to become the reflexive pronoun, we would expect to say "likes John himself" for "John likes himself," whereas if the object noun phrase becomes the reflexive pronoun, we would expect to say "likes himself John." And it turns out that the subject-object distinction is more important in Malagasy than the left-right order distinction. That is, it is the object phrase that becomes a reflexive pronoun, not the second noun phrase that occurs. Thus we must say literally, "Likes himself Rabe" or "Killed herself Rasoa" as illustrated below.

(20)   *tia   tena   Rabe*   (21)   *namono   tena   Rasoa*
       like   self   Rabe   killed   self   Rasoa
       Rabe likes himself.   Rasoa killed herself.

(As with other pronouns in Malagasy the reflexive pronoun does not vary with the gender of the noun phrase to which it refers.) So it is that contrary to English and most European languages, Malagasy allows pronouns to precede their 'antecedents' in simple sentences.

3.3 Coordination

Similarly, when in certain closely connected contexts a noun phrase is understood to refer to the same entity more than once, we do not have to repeat it. This is the case, for example, if the topic of our discussion plays the role of subject in two coordinated clauses. In English instead of saying "John came early and John left late," we would usually say "John came early and left late," omitting the second occurrence of the subject "John." But in such a case in Malagasy it is the first occurrence of the subject that is normally omitted. Thus the most natural way to say (22a) below would be as in (22b)—waiting for the identification of the subject and topic "Rabe" until the very end. (Note that when two phrases, as opposed to sentences, are conjoined with "and" the conjunction used is *sy* rather than *ary*. *Ary* can only conjoin full sentences.)

(22) a.   *misotro   taoka   Rabe   ary   mihinam-bary   Rabe*
          drink   booze   Rabe   and   eat rice   Rabe
          Rabe is drinking booze and Rabe is eating rice.

     b.   *misotro   taoka   sy   mihinam-bary   Rabe*
          drink   booze   and   eat rice   Rabe
          Rabe is drinking booze and eating rice.

Again, it seems funny to the European ear to omit a noun from a fairly simple sentence before we know to what it would refer. However, in this respect, the Malagasy ear listens to a different tune.

3.4 Relative Clauses

Another common way in many languages of the world to form complex structures from simpler ones is by moving parts of a simpler one to other positions and perhaps inserting a few other 'grammatical' words. Consider, for example, a simple sentence such as "The woman washed the clothes." Suppose we want to talk about that woman, identifying her precisely as the one who washed the clothes. We might refer to her as "The woman *who* washed the clothes." We will refer to such structures as *relative clauses* and the noun that occupies the position of "woman" as the *head* of the relative clause. Notice that in the above example the head functions as the subject of the verb *washed* since it is the woman who is doing the washing. Had we relativized on the object of the verb, the resulting relative clause would have been "The clothes that the woman washed." So in this case the head of the relative clause would be functioning as the object of the verb.

Now, in English we may think of relative clauses as being formed from sentences by taking the noun phrase to be relativized and moving it to the front and perhaps inserting some grammatical words like "who" or "that." If we relativize on a subject, of course the noun phrase to be relativized is already at the front of the clause, so no movement is apparent. But when we relativize on an object, or any nonsubject, the movement to the front is apparent.

When we relativize on a subject phrase in Malagasy we also move that phrase to the front and optionally insert a particle *izay* "that." Compare the simple sentence in (23a) below with the relative clause formed on the subject in (23b).

(23) a. *nanasa   ny   lamba   ny   vehivavy*
         washed   the   clothes   the   woman
         The woman washed the clothes.

     b. *ny   vehivavy   izay   nanasa   ny   lamba*
         the   woman   that   washed   the   clothes
         The woman who washed the clothes.

However, if we attempt to relativize on the object, we find that the resulting relative clause is ungrammatical or nonsensical. Moving the object to the front and inserting *izay* would yield (24).

(24) **ny   lamba   izay   nanasa   ny   vehivavy*
       The   clothes   that   washed   the   woman.

(24) could only mean "the clothes that washed the woman," which would of course be comical since clothes can't wash people. In other words, in Malagasy the head noun of a relative clause *must* be understood to function as the subject of the verb.

But how then do we talk about "the clothes that the woman washed" in Malagasy? It might seem that we have a real gap in expressive power here. But such is not the case. We simply make the sentence from which we form the relative clause into the passive form, so that "the clothes" is the subject, and then we can relativize on "the clothes" yielding "the clothes that were washed by the woman." (25a) below illustrates the passive form of (23a) above, and (25b) the relative clause formed on "clothes."

(25) a. *nosasan'ny   vehivavy   ny   lamba*
       washed-by-the woman   the   clothes
       The clothes were washed by the woman.

     b. *ny   lamba   izay   nosasan'ny   vehivavy*
       the   clothes that   washed-by-the   woman
       The clothes that were washed by the woman.

Similarly in Malagasy it is not possible to relativize on any nonsubject noun phrase. If, for example, we want to relativize on an instrumental, as in "the soap that Rasoa washed clothes with," we must first put the verb in the circumstantial form so that the instrumental noun phrase is the derived subject, and only then may we relativize on it. In this way the thing we are talking about within the relative clause, the topic, is always the subject. Thus from (26a) below, we cannot directly relativize on "the soap," which would yield (26b), a meaningless expression in Malagasy. Rather we must first convert (26a) to the circumstantial form in (26c), where "soap" is the subject, and then relativize it, as in (26d).

(26) a. *manasa   lamba   amin'ny   savony   Rasoa*
       wash   clothes   with the soap   Rasoa
       Rasoa washes clothes with the soap.

     b. **ny   savony   izay   manasa   lamba   Rasoa*
       The   soap   that   washes   clothes   Rasoa

     c. *anasan-dRasoa   lamba   ny   savony*
       washes-with-by-Rasoa clothes the   soap
       The soap is used by Rasoa to wash clothes.

     d. *ny   savony   izay   anasan-dRasoa   lamba*
       the   soap   that   washes-with-by-Rasoa   clothes
       The soap used by Rasoa to wash clothes.

It turns out then that the system of verb voices—active, passive, and circumstantial—plays a much greater role in the syntax of Malagasy than does the more limited system of active vs. passive forms in English; and further, the role of 'subject' is much greater in Malagasy since only subjects can be relativized.

3.5 Information Questions

Furthermore, what holds of relative clause formation in Malagasy also holds, to a greater or lesser extent, for all processes that form complex structures from simpler ones by moving elements. Consider, for example, questions of the "who? what? when? where?" sort. In both English and Malagasy the principal way of forming such questions puts the question word in the front of the clause, as illustrated in (27) and its English translation.

(27) *Iza   no   nanasa   ny   lamba?*
      Who part washed the clothes
      Who washed the clothes?

Note that following the question word in Malagasy there is a grammatical particle *no*, which serves to isolate the question word and to emphasize it. Again however, (27) illustrates the case where the subject of the verb has been questioned. If we try to question the object by moving the appropriate question word forward we get the nonsensical (28). The only correct way to ask "What did the woman wash?" is as in (29) in which the question word "what?" functions as the subject of the verb, and the question is literally "What was washed by the woman?"

(28) ***Inona   no   nanasa   ny   vehivavy?*
      What part washed the woman
      What did the woman wash?

(29) *Inona   no   nosasan'ny   vehivavy*
      What part washed-by-the woman
      What was washed by the woman?

Once again then, in the simple cases cited, only subjects can be moved, in this case questioned, and once again the voicing system comes into play to make these noun phrases we want to question into subjects. Clearly then if we lost the voicing system in Malagasy, the rest of the syntax would have to change in radical ways. In particular the basic methods of forming questions and relative clauses would have to change. In English on the other hand, the loss of the passive voice would not entail many serious consequences for the grammar, for basically no major syntactic operations in English require the sentence on which they operate to be passive.

3.6 Raising

We conclude this section with consideration of a more complex example of Malagasy syntax that indicates the overwhelming role played by the notion of 'subject' in Malagasy.

Suppose someone claims "John thinks that Mary washed these clothes" and that sometime later we want to refer to those clothes. In English we may easily form the appropriate relative clause *the clothes that John thinks Mary washed*. But in Malagasy such relative clauses would seem impossible to form, since *clothes* is clearly not the subject of the main verb *think*. Further, we cannot use the passive or circumstantial voices to make it into the subject of *think*, since these voices would only apply to noun phrases that occur in the main clause, and *clothes* occurs in an embedded or subordinate clause. Thus *Mary washed the clothes* is itself a sentence that occurs embedded within the larger sentence *John thinks that Mary washed the clothes*. It might appear once more that Malagasy has an expressive gap. But such is not the case, for Malagasy has a very productive means of *raising* embedded noun phrases into main clauses, whence they can be made into subjects by the voicing system and then relativized (or questioned, or otherwise moved).

We shall illustrate the 'raising' first in English. In sentence (30a) the noun phrase *the woman* occurs within a sentence itself embedded within the entire sentence.

(30) a.   John thinks that the woman washed the clothes

b.   John thinks the woman to have washed the clothes

In (30b) however, the phrase *the woman* is presented as a direct object of the main verb *think*. Thus it occurs immediately after that verb, it takes accusative forms of the pronoun (to give *her* instead of *she* as in *John thinks her to have washed the clothes* as opposed to *John thinks that she washed the clothes*), and it can passivize the subject, as in *the woman was thought to have washed the clothes*. It appears clear then that the embedded noun phrase *the woman* in (30a) has been raised to main clause position in (30b).

This raising process in English, however, is of only limited productivity. Some native speakers of English find sentences like (30b) awkward or pretentious. Their acceptability varies with the choice of main verb.

Thus most speakers would probably not allow *the woman* to be raised from *John said that the woman washed the clothes*, which would yield *John said the woman to have washed the clothes*. Similarly, it would be unacceptable for most speakers to say *John hoped the woman to have washed the clothes* and *John doubted the woman to have washed the clothes*.

But in Malagasy the raising process is fully productive. Basically all verbs of thinking and saying allow an embedded noun phrase to be raised as an object of the main verb. We illustrate this in (31)[3], where (31a) indicates the underlying sentence and (31b) the derived one. The embedded sentence is indicated by brackets.

(31) a. *mihevitra*   *[fa*   *nanasa*   *ny*   *lamba*   *ny*   *vehivavy]*
      thinks   that   washed   the   clothes   the   woman

       Rajaona
       Rajaona

       Rajaona thinks that the woman washed the clothes.

    b. *mihevitra*   *ny*   *vehivavy*   *ho*   *nanasa*   *ny*   *lamba*
        thinks   the   woman   that   washed   the   clothes

       Rajaona
       Rajaona

       Rajaona thinks the woman to have washed the clothes.

Clearly *ny vehivavy* "the woman" looks and behaves like a direct object of the main verb *mihevitra* "think." Thus it immediately follows that verb, and it takes accusative forms of the pronoun, *azy* as opposed to *izy* (see example (4) for the use of the nominative form *izy* in a simple sentence). And finally of course, since *ny vehivavy* "the woman" is the object of the main verb, it can now passivize to the subject, as in (32).

(32)   *heverin-dRajaona*   *ho*   *nanasa*   *ny*   *lamba*   *ny*
       thought-by-Rajaona   that   washed   the   clothes   the

       vehevavy
       woman

       The woman was thought by John to have washed the clothes.

And now, since "the woman" is the subject of the sentence, it can be relativized, as in (33).

---

[3]The structure in (31a) indicates the source for the raising process. As it stands, however, it is not acceptable, since most speakers of Malagasy will not accept a full sentence to occur between the main verb and its subject. Thus if no noun phrase is raised from the embedded sentence, the main clause must be removed to the right of the subject phrase yielding the unusual Verb + Subject + Object order (considering the embedded sentence to be the object of the verb "think") illustrated in (a) below.

(a)   *mihevitra*   *Rajaona*   *fa*   *nanasa*   *ny*   *lamba*   *ny*   *vehivavy*
     thinks   Rajaona   that   washed   the   clothes   the   woman
    John thinks that the woman washed the clothes.

(33)   *ny   vehivavy   izay   heverin-dRajaona   ho   nanasa*
         the   woman   that   thought-by-Rajaona   that   washed

         ny   lamba
         the   clothes

         The woman who John thought washed the clothes.

Notice in passing that when we raise a noun phrase from an embedded sentence, the subordinator *fa* changes to *ho* but otherwise the embedded sentence remains unchanged.[4]

Notice finally that the noun phrase we have raised to main clause object in Malagasy is originally the subject of the embedded verb. And in fact only subjects of embedded verbs may be raised. However, our original question was how to say *the clothes that John thought the woman washed*. Now looking at sentence (34) below, it is clear that *ny lamba* "the clothes" is not the subject of the embedded verb but rather the object.

(34)   *mihevitra   [fa   nanasa   ny   lamba   ny   vehivavy]*
         thinks   that   washed   the   clothes   the   woman

         Rajaona
         Rajaona

         Rajaona thinks that the woman washed the clothes.

At this point, the reader should be able, by successive application of the syntactic processes discussed so far, to form a Malagasy relative clause that translates *the clothes that John thought that the woman washed*. We shall present the answer immediately below, however, to make the conclusion of this last section clear.

To relativize on *ny lamba* "the clothes" in (34) above, we must reorganize the syntax of the sentence so that *ny lamba* is the main clause subject. Now, since *ny lamba* occurs embedded, we might hope to raise it to main clause object position and then passivize it to subject. But *ny lamba* cannot be directly raised because only subjects of embedded verbs can be so raised, and *ny lamba* is the object, not the subject of the embedded verb *nanasa* "washed." (Note that if we did directly raise *ny lamba* from (34), we would obtain a sentence that would be translated as *John thinks the clothes to have washed the woman*. That is, "the clothes" would be necessarily understood as the subject of "wash," and hence it would be the woman who got washed by the clothes!) However, we can easily make *ny lamba* into the subject of

---

[4]In English on the other hand, the identity of the embedded sentence is more severely affected. The tense marking on the verb is lost, and the verb takes an infinitival form ("to have washed the clothes" as opposed to "washed the clothes").

the embedded sentence by passivizing the embedded verb *nanasa* "washed." Then *ny lamba* can be raised to become the object of the main verb *mihevitra* "thinks," then it can be passivized to main clause subject, and finally it can be relativized, yielding (35).[5]

(35) ny   lamba   izay   heverin-dRajaona   ho
     the   clothes   that   thought-by-Rajaona   that

     nosasan'ny   vehivavy
     washed-by the   woman

> The clothes that were thought by John to have been washed by the woman (or more colloquially, "The clothes that John thought that the woman washed").

Clearly then the notion of 'subject' is not an unimportant one in Malagasy syntax, despite its occurrence in sentence final position. Rather, much of the major syntax of Malagasy is organized around ways to make different noun phrases into subjects. Thus we can now understand why the Malagasy voicing system and the raising process are much more developed and productive than the corresponding systems in English: they have a much greater functional role, since they make noun phrases accessible to major syntactic processes like relativization and question formation, and generally serve to place topics in subject position.

---

[5]We begin with sentence (a) below:

(a) *mihevitra* [*fa* *nanasa* *ny* *lamba* *ny* *vehivavy*] *Rajaona*
    thinks   that washed the clothes the woman   Rajaona
    John thinks that the woman washed the clothes.

Then we passivize the embedded verb:

(b) *mihevitra* [*fa* *nosasan'ny*   *vehivavy* *ny* *lamba*] *Rajaona*
    thinks   that washed-by-the woman   the clothes Rajaona
    John thinks that the clothes were washed by the woman.

Then we raise the subject of the embedded verb to become the object of the main verb:

(c) *mihevitra* *ny* *lamba* *ho* *nosasan'ny*   *vehivavy* *Rajaona*
    thinks   the clothes that washed-by-the woman   Rajaona
    John thinks the clothes to have been washed by the woman.

Then we passivize the main verb, making *ny lamba* "the clothes" the main clause subject:

(d) *heverin-dRajaona*   *ho* *nosasan'ny*   *vehivavy* *ny* *lamba*
    thought-by-Rajaona that washed-by-the woman   the clothes
    The clothes were thought by John to have been washed by the woman.

Now we may relativize on *ny lamba*:

(e) *ny* *lamba* *izay* *heverin-dRajaona*   *ho* *nosasan'ny*   *vehivavy*
    the clothes that thought-by-Rajaona that washed-by-the woman
    The clothes that were thought by John to have been washed by the woman.

The European learner of Malagasy who had perfected his knowledge of the sound system of the language and the various ways of forming words, phrases, and sentences would, as we indicated at the beginning of our discussion, still find himself unable to perform successfully most social acts requiring the use of speech in the type of peasant community in which we lived.

He would frequently draw many incorrect inferences from what people said and equally frequently fail to draw correct inferences. In addition he would frequently be misunderstood and find that his attempts at communication prompted reactions quite different from those he intended.

The general reason for such unsuccessful communication is that the norms of social interaction in Madagascar are different in many respects from those of European society. This point is easy to acknowledge in the abstract but difficult to understand in practice. Hence, in this section we will describe the differences in communication norms in terms of our personal experiences, which led us to adapt our speech habits to those of the Malagasy context.

To explain the types of misunderstandings that can occur, we shall first discuss several general conditions on the use of speech in a Malagasy peasant community and then illustrate how these conditions affect the interpretation of most socially normal everyday discourse.

4.1   The Information Structure of a Malagasy Peasant Community

The area in which we lived consists of many small villages scattered across a hilly, formerly volcanic area. Rice, the staple crop, is grown in the lower areas near the springs and small creeks; the villages themselves are located on the higher ground. An unpaved road, passable by car though sometimes cut off during the rainy season, links these villages to a somewhat larger road leading to the closest town (pop: 3,000–4,000).

In such communities new information, that is, information not known to the population at large, is properly described as a *scarce good*. Access to news from outside the community is difficult. Very few people are literate, and practically no one has a radio. Newspapers, magazines, and portable radios can be obtained in towns but must be paid for in cash—a commodity that is very limited in a subsistence or near-subsistence economy. Consequently information from outside the community is hard to obtain and must pass from person to person, community to community, by word of mouth. (Compare this situation with the deluge of new information that a middle-class American is subjected to everyday via newspapers, radio, and television.)

Furthermore, new information originating from within the community is also rare. Within a given village, everybody knows everybody else, and everybody knows most people in the closely neighboring villages. A typical household spends most of its day working in the fields and hence is in public view of everybody else. And as one's rice plot is normally within view of one's house, the people you live with are also the people you work with. Relatively few events occur on a day-to-day basis that are not publicly observable (although there are, of course, family squabbles). The most important unpredictable events to an agricultural people concern the weather, something again that is immediate public knowledge. In addition, within such communities there is very little specialization of labor. It is unusual for your neighbor to have a skill or occupation that you are not at least reasonably able in yourself, so it is unlikely that something would happen to him that wouldn't happen to you.

The regularity of day-to-day life is even more apparent on a larger time scale. The yearly cycle of events is largely determined by the rice planting, cultivating, and harvesting cycle. After the harvest there are about two months in which the ceremony season takes place, and during that time one does have the occasion to meet more people from outlying villages. However, even one's life cycle is, in general, predictable. A child is gradually initiated into the work cycle and when strong enough, assumes his or her full share. The child can expect to pursue that same work until he dies and can expect to live in the same locality where he was born, or at most move once to a newer village as land becomes scarce in his home village.

Consquently, any sort of new information is at a premium; and, someone who has, for example, been to market and found out something not generally known will find himself the center of interest until the information is divulged. So, in order to remain the center of attention, one imparts new information only piece by piece. As we shall see, eliciting what might appear to an outsider to be fairly trivial information is a lengthy and difficult process.

4.2 Collective vs. Individual Action

A second condition of Malagasy peasant life that governs much interpersonal behavior including speech behavior is the norm of collective responsibility for action. It would be *exceedingly* unusual in the communities we are discussing for an individual, as such, to initiate an important action and assume responsibility for it. There are two major 'units of responsibility' within a village: families, and the village "elders" (*ray-aman-dreny*, literally, "father-and-mother"). The concepts of family and of *ray-aman-dreny* are not independent and are central to understanding norms of personal action in Malagasy life.

A family is composed of the descendents of a given ancestor plus

those brought into the line of descent by marriage. Within a village, members of a given household belong to the same family. A normal household consists of parents plus their children, often ten to twelve in number. Grandparents usually live in separate houses and if they have no small children of their own will take to live with them the first born of one of their children. Within a village, members of the same family work their rice land in common, though each household may have possession of particular plots. The whole family, men, women, and children, participates in the cultivation of the rice plots. Certain work is usually done by women, such as the transplanting of the seedlings from the seed beds to the main beds; other work is done by men, such as preparing the main beds for planting; while other work is done in common, such as harvesting the main beds. The whole family, then, and no one single individual, is responsible for the rice crop.

FIGURE 3.3 *Tombs, Individual Oratory, and Collective Responsibility. On the left page, an orator delivering a kabary from the top of a tomb. Above, a work party building a tomb.*

As a given person may have married and separated more than once, more or less formally, individuals may have several possibilities for deciding from which principal ancestor they are descended. But in practice, family membership at any given moment is usually clear, since it imposes severe obligations in terms of mutual help in rice cultivation and upkeep of the family tomb. The family you belong to is determined by the tomb in which you will be buried. The tombs are massive stone vaults, partly above ground and partly below, containing various stone beds on which cadavers are laid out in expensive raw silk cloths during special ceremonies. These cloths and the general upkeep of a tomb are much more expensive than, for example, upkeep on one's house. (A house is normally made of sun-dried bricks with rice stalk roofs and is more easily built and destroyed than a family tomb.)

Psychologically the ancestors in one's tomb are very much a part of one's family. Every few years a family will have a major ceremony, called *famadihana*, "the turning (of the bones)." (*Famadihana* is the circumstantial noun from *mamadika*, "to turn.") At the *famadihana* the tombs are opened, the ancestors are brought out and rewrapped in new cloths. Cadavers that are reduced to a pile of bones are put in the collective ancestor cloth located in the rear of the tomb, the most sacred place within a tomb. While the ancestors are out of the tomb, much dancing and singing goes on. People may talk to their ancestors, inform them of recent happenings, perhaps confess for misdeeds they have done, and even give them a little rum. When the ancestors are returned to the tomb, new cadavers that were buried temporarily in shallow graves near the tomb (opening a tomb requires government permission and may only take place every few years) will also be taken into the tomb. This ceremony usually lasts a night and a day, requires marshalling together the entire extended family, and is in general an expensive and festive affair.

One of the major fears of a Malagasy is to die away from his family tomb and so not be able to be buried there. For example, when our villagers learned that men had been sent to the moon, the first question they expressed was "Where would they be buried if they died there?" The greatest shame a Malagasy can know is to be deprived of the right to be buried in the family tomb. This would mean that he would not be a member of the family and not be an ancestor. Even Malagasy who have left the country to work in a city feel a strong moral obligation to attend a family *famadihana* and are always returned to the family tomb for their burial.

The other major line of responsibility within a village is constituted by the *ray-aman-dreny*. People are *ray-aman-dreny* to the extent that they have offspring and hence will be ancestors. Any important *ray-aman-dreny* belongs to a family and has children and grandchildren. To be a couple without children is shameful. Marriages that do not produce children within the first year are under strong family pressure to dissolve. Normally upon marriage a woman moves to the village of her husband (though exceptions to this in our area were not uncommon). If she has children, she becomes part of the husband's family and is buried in his tomb. But if she has no children and withstands the pressure to leave her husband and return to her village, she will still not be buried in the tomb of the husband's family but rather in the tomb of her parents— the ultimate proof that she has not attained *ray-aman-dreny* status.

Members of a family (on the same side of the *ray-aman-dreny* line) are almost fully egalitarian. They share the same living quarters, working conditions, and possessions. It would be quite normal, for example, for a city cousin to return for a visit wearing European-style clothes (rather than the traditional togalike *lamba*). Upon arrival he might don a relative's traditional garb and shortly thereafter you would see his brothers and sisters wearing various pieces of his European clothing around the village.

Most actions then are taken by families or the *ray-aman-dreny* and not by individuals. This is true not only for the regular major activities like rice cultivation, but also for any sudden, unpredictable activity of any importance. For example, if a *ray-aman-dreny* dies suddenly, his family in his village and in the closely neighboring villages has the responsibility for the funeral. (This is the burial in the temporary grave near the family tomb and is not a major ceremony.) However, the other *ray-aman-dreny* of the deceased's village and their families will share in the preparations as well. No one individual assumes responsibility for effecting the entire undertaking. Women from many different households, whether of the deceased's family or not, will help in cooking the food for those who attend and will help out in other ways. A dozen men might easily contribute their effort to construct a coffin for the deceased. We once saw six different men participate in turn and sometimes jointly in the sawing of a *single* board for a coffin! Should it turn out upon the transferral of the body to the family tomb a year or two later that the coffin was not well constructed, no one individual would be to blame.

Under these conditions, then, very little is done to draw attention to any one person's particular abilities. For example children who might be exceptionally good at some task, for instance rice pounding, are *never* complimented for their abilities. They are normally described as *tsy mahay* "not able."

It is interesting to consider in this light, the situations that do force an individual to stand out from the rest. Few such situations arise in the natural Malagasy context, but one major one is the speech making that accompanies the opening of the family tomb at a *famadihana* or the formal request for a girl in marriage by the *ray-aman-dreny* of the boy's family. (These requests have the form of a debate or speech contest in which the boy's family loses, pays the brideprice, and leaves with the girl.)

The formal speeches on such occasions are called *kabary* and those who perform them *mpikabary* (from the verb *mikabary*). Being a *mpikabary* is a highly valued skill and requires a thorough knowledge of traditional lore, proverbs, and the structure of ceremonies and also requires exceptional ability to turn a good phrase. Within any community certain people are known to be good *mpikabary*. But giving a *kabary* and responding to your opponent (in the case of a marriage *kabary*) is an action that singles out the *mpikabary* as having special, personal abilities. And inwardly, of course, a good *mpikabary* is proud of his abilities and accomplishments. But outwardly the *mpikabary* is in the very awkward position of having to distinguish himself from his equals. So, in fact, such events are structured in such a way as to minimize his individuality. Thus the *mpikabary* will stand in a group with the other *ray-aman-dreny* of the family. His speeches will inevitably begin with a long and artful apology for his lack of ability. He will also stress that the words he uses are not his own and that he is merely the carrier of the words from the family and the ancestors. It is this last point, that he merely carries the words of others, that absolves him of the individual responsibility for his actions. Consider, for example, the following early lines from one *kabary* we recorded.

—Manao azafady aho, fa tsy tompon'ity ... tsy tompon-dalana fa mpanohy, tsy tompon-dia fa mpanaraka ... tsy tompon-teny fa *mpindrana.*

—I excuse myself, for (I) am not a master of this ... not an originator of paths but a continuer, not an originator of journeys but a follower ... not an originator of words but a *borrower.*

Other instances in which an individual is singled out from the group frequently occur in contact situations with Europeans. For example, one of our best informants was a young man from a neighboring village who made a four-hour trek to the town school every day. We thought to compensate him by providing him with a bicycle. But we quickly realized that this would do him a great disservice because it would be an object for him alone, and it could not easily be shared since most of the time he would be using it himself. This would have made him the object of jealousy, a dangerous emotion in an egalitarian community. In general it is not uncommon for Malagasy who work for Europeans to refuse gifts, despite an obvious need, simply to avoid the troubles that would ensue from their having an object that would distinguish them from their equals.

Perhaps a more common conflict of this sort, and one frequently misunderstood by Europeans, takes place in the context of the European-style school system in which the Malagasy participate (to a greater or lesser extent depending on the remoteness of the village from the school). It frequently happens, for example, that pupils copy each other's homework. The European teacher interprets this as "cheating." But the Malagasy pupil understands it quite differently. He has simply generalized his village ethic to the classroom. The teacher is a *ray-aman-dreny* and the pupils are all equals as non-*ray-aman-dreny*. If one pupil has finished an assignment, it would be as unnatural not to share it with others as it would be not to share any other temporary possession in the village, such as your city cousin's clothing.

4.3 Noncommittalism, Avoidance of Affront, and the Concept of Henatra

Another very important concept in understanding Malagasy social behavior is that of *henatra*, a root noun that translates as "shame." The predicate adjective formed from it is *menatra*, better translated as "be shamed" rather than merely "be ashamed," and the commonly heard causative form is *mahamenatra* "to cause shame." (The causative prefix before adjectives is *maha-* rather than *mamp-*, which is used before verbs.) One of the most commonly heard injunctions against a particular behavior in a Malagasy community is *mahamenatra izany* "That causes shame" or "That is shameful."

We shall consider here two types of activity that Malagasy easily recognize as causing shame. The first of these is overt committal to some future good. Actually this almost never happens. To commit oneself to a future good, overtly, and then have the future course of events turn out otherwise would cause excruciating shame. For example, a village Malagasy does not normally prepare for the birth of a child. Since it is common for children to die during birth, a prospective mother who bought baby clothes in anticipation of the birth runs the risk of bringing great *henatra* to all concerned. We once bought some baby clothes for the anticipated birth of a child of a friend of ours but had at least the sense not to give them to her beforehand. Unfortunately the baby died at birth, and our sadness was indeed heavily mixed with *henatra*.

The principle of noncommittalism to future goods extends as well to many European-introduced activities. One would, for example, never pay for work in advance. If the contractor fled before completing the work, one would be caught red-handed and red-faced. A personal example: on first arriving in Madagascar we set up a bank account and deposited some checks we had. On leaving the bank we realized that we had no receipt for our deposit and had a moment of panic. Suppose they "lost" the money. Had we deposited cash, we would have received a receipt. But since we deposited checks, the Malagasy bank had to wait until they cleared before they could be sure they actually had the money. Giving us a receipt would have, psychologically at least, committed them to the existence of our dollars before they had them.

The mentality of 'noncommittalism to future goods' leads to the tendency to leap to the worst possible conclusion—for this protects one from being deceived through hoping that any good might be forthcoming. Once, for example, while talking with some neighbors outside their house, we were startled by a sudden crash from the area where the rabbits were kept. Before we had recovered from the loud noise, the lady of the house blurted out, "The rabbits are all dead!" And indeed the correct interpretation of the noise turned out to be that a side of the rabbit pen had fallen over. But that the crash would kill any of the rabbits was unlikely and that it would kill all of them was absurd. Still, just to be on the safe side, our neighbor assumed the worst possible outcome.

Another example: on returning to the village one evening after a heavier than usual afternoon rain we were informed that a certain *ray-aman-dreny*'s dikes had collapsed and that his rice crop was *entirely ruined*. That night we pondered the catastrophe and wondered if there was some way we could help out. The next morning we went to investigate the plots in question and found the *ray-aman-dreny* patching up parts of some dikes that had been damaged. Some of the plots did have rice that was bent over, but the plots were mostly intact. So there was no tragedy, just a small loss at worst. However, it would be incorrect to infer that the Malagasy were inaccurate observers of the reported loss. Rather, since something bad had occurred, they portrayed it at its worst, lest in hoping for something better they be deceived and therefore shamed. Probably the single most inconceivable act for Malagasy peasants would be to brag, before the harvest, about what a great crop they were anticipating.

Another type of action that would bring shame to all participants would be to affront or confront someone directly. Any action that would put someone "on the spot," and so draw attention to an individual (especially oneself) would fall under this category. Thus in day-to-day interactions, individuals are very rarely held explicitly accountable for their actions. Suppose two people more or less agree to meet somewhere and go to market together (note that by the norm of noncommittalism it is unlikely that there would have ever been a fully explicit commitment to meet at a certain place at a certain time). Then suppose one of them doesn't show up. Although he might at a later time offer some explanation for his behavior, it is most unlikely that he would be called upon to do so. Or if a local pastor (whose pay is usually quite low) is found to have been dipping into the collection plate, he might find that under pressure from the *ray-aman-dreny* of the locality, higher church officials have decided to reassign him to another locality. However, it is most unlikely that he would actually be accused of stealing or would be forced to return the money.

Other types of sanctions are available against the transgressor of a norm or law. His family may simply avoid cooperating with him, and the norm of nonconfrontation prevents him from holding them accountable for lack of cooperation. At another time he may find himself the object of malicious, and very possibly totally untrue, gossip.

Overall the norm of nonconfrontation is certainly understandable to the European mind. What is peculiarly Malagasy is the array of actions that are counted as affronting. In rural Malagasy society any action that forces an individual to acknowledge individual responsibility for something or to commit himself explicitly to a future course of events is counted as a confrontation.

We should mention further that the norm of nonconfrontation does not apply equally to both sexes. Men, especially *ray-aman-dreny*, are expected to adhere to this norm much more thoroughly than women. Thus if a child misbehaves, its mother, or another woman of the village, can easily scold the child and hold it accountable for its actions. A man however, would more usually not do this, even if it meant delaying punishment for a considerable period, say until the mother returned from market. Once, for example, when the man who owned the house we lived in returned to the village to inspect some of his rice land he found that the white mud coating over the bricks on the house had been damaged by the village children who were using the wall to kick a ball against. He remained in the village for two days and occasionally suggested to the parents of the children that something ought to be done about it. But the suggestion was simply overlooked. On the third day he left and returned with his wife who vociferously lit into the first man (in fact, a *ray-aman-dreny*) she met upon entering the village.

As a general rule women do most of the buying and selling in markets (though men do certain heavy tasks like butchering and selling meat). Buying and selling in these communities normally involves bargaining, with one party refusing to pay an initial price, and the other party refusing to sell too cheap. Bargaining involves lots of small confrontations and definite decisions, and women, less subject to the norm of nonconfrontation, are the more natural buyers and sellers.

5 BEHAVIORAL NORMS AND SPEECH USAGE

The behavioral norms we have discussed have serious consequences for speech behavior. We mentioned previously that a European who could merely produce and understand sentences in Malagasy would very frequently misunderstand the intent of someone's speech and be frequently misunderstood himself. We shall consider two types of speech situations where a European speaking Malagasy would fail to make correct inferences.

5.1 The Everyday Exchange of Information

Most everyday conversations involve the exchange of information in one way or another. In middle-class Western society certain norms regarding such exchanges enable us to infer from what was said much more information than was made verbally explicit. In particular, we assume that our conversational partner will provide the information relevant to our needs if he has it, unless there are specific mitigating circumstances. Such circumstances are admittedly quite diverse, some may be quite general and others specific to the particular speech situation. For example, if we're talking with a lawyer about a client, a psychiatrist about a patient, or a priest about someone he confesses, we may expect that certain information will not be given freely. Or if the information we require of someone is particularly personal, he might not want to divulge it. Another possibility is that our partner might want to tease us, deceive us, or play some sort of joke on us. All of these factors limit access to information in Western society, but they are understood relative to the expectation that information will ordinarily be given freely. Thus if we perceive that someone is avoiding our questions or being intentionally vague, we then assume that either he doesn't have the information we need or that one or more of the special circumstances applies.

In Malagasy society, on the other hand, the basic norm concerning free exchange of information simply does not apply, so inferences Westerners would make concerning the absence of information in special circumstances are generally incorrect. Imagine the following situation in Western society: A neighbor of yours sees you and your son walking up the street by your house and asks "Hey, Ed. Wher're ya goin' so early?" And you answer, "Hi, just up to the hardware store. Gotta get some nails. We're building a treehouse."

It is safe to say that such an exchange would almost never occur among native rural Malagasy. Although it might be hard for the reader to appreciate, it would be totally bizarre for a Malagasy to volunteer all that information about the hardware store, the nails, building a treehouse, etc. A far more typical dialogue, when meeting a friend on a road or a path would be:

–Manao akory rangahy?	–How is it going, friend?
–Tsara ihany tompoko, ka manao ahaona ny vady-aman-janaka?	–Just fine sir, and how is the family?
–Tsara ihany fa misaotra, ka ho aiza moa?	–Just fine, thanks. Where are you headed?
–Atsy avaraparatra atsy tompoko. Ka ianareo moa, ho aiza?	–Just there a little to the North there. And where are you going?
–Izahay koa, dia mitsangan-tsangana ihany.	–We also, we're just out for a little walk.
–Eny ary, ka mandra-pihaona aloha.	–OK then, so long (lit.: until meeting).
–Eny, tain'Andriamanitra e.	–OK, may care be taken by God.

In the Malagasy dialogue, no real information was given. Even the fact that one person was going to the North contains nothing that is not obvious from context, for Malagasay always reckon position by the cardinal points (North, South, East, and West); and directions of roads, positioning of villages, etc. are known to a local Malagasy with the same ease as right and left are known to a Westerner. Notice also that the word for North is actually *avaratra*. The form *avaraparatra* is a reduplicated form. Reduplication, especially of verbs and adjectives, is very common in Malagasy and has the effect of attenuating in appropriate ways the meaning of the unreduplicated form. Thus to have answered *atsy avaratra atsy*, without reduplication, would have been slightly more specific. The reduplicated form of 'North' indicates that the person is going perhaps in a somewhat less northward direction than does the unreduplicated form. Notice as well that the verb *mitsangana* "to stroll" is also reduplicated in the dialogue as *mitsangantsangana* and means "to walk around a little." Otherwise the dialogue's greetings and closing are largely ritualized formulas. Performance of these greetings and closings is important in acknowledging your social relations. Different greetings are appropriate for different social classes of people. Failure to greet someone or to use the right greeting would indicate a break in social relations. But these social relations are always known to members of a community, so using the appropriate terms does not, once again, communicate new information, it just reaffirms known status relations.

But note that in the situation depicted above, while the Malagasy does not expect an informative answer to the question "Where are you going?" he would love to have one. For this would give him some new information that he could then pass on, and as we indicated in section 4.1, possession of new information is possession of a scarce good allowing the possessor to command the attention of others. Of course, when we first established ourselves in the community we always gave informative answers to such questions, much to the enormous delight and advantage of those with whom we spoke.

Once, for example, as one of the authors (Edward) was leaving the village by car, having picked up a number of covillagers, a lady from the next village asked him how his wife was. He responded that she was just a little under the weather. This elicited the surprise exclamation *Kai!* (since it was an informative answer), which he misinterpreted as the weak conjunction *ka...* which would have asked for a continuation of the discourse (like saying "and..." expectantly, with a rising intonation). So he continued by supplying more information, "She'll go to the spring and wash out some clothes later." This, of course, elicited an even stronger *Kai!* reaction, which again misinterpreted, prompted still further information, and so on. Finally it was necessary to cease giving further information, as Edward couldn't think of anything further to say. And much later, reflecting on this interchange, we realized that it must have had an almost surrealistic quality for the Malagasy who were listening—each surprise reaction eliciting even more intensely the very act that prompted the surprise reaction in the first place. It would be a bit as though scratching a little itch behind your ear served to intensify the itch, thus prompting more scratching, then more itching, and so on. What began as a trivial piece of everyday conversation turned into a grotesque parody.

Let us consider some other typical situations in which the free information norm of Western society is not followed, leading to incorrect inferences on the part of the European in a Malagasy context.

> A European enters a village where he is well known and asks some women in the courtyard for one of his friends. (If the European were not known, it is unlikely he would find anyone to talk with for no one would accept the responsibility for having introduced an unknown power into the village life. Maybe the man is a tax collector. Or maybe he has come to steal some hearts—it is widely believed that white men need blood and kill little children to take their hearts.) The women respond *Asa* (a single particle meaning "I don't know"). Then after some discussion the wife of the friend appears on the scene and says that the friend isn't there. You say you wonder when he'll return, to which she responds, "Well, if you don't come after dinner you won't catch him."

This use of a double negative would be interpreted as uncooperative in Western society. One might think the wife perhaps is being coy, but certainly is not giving as much information as she could. But, in fact, the wife is not being coy or uncooperative. She is merely adhering to the norm of noncommittalism. The more natural response here for a European would be, "He'll be here after dinner" or at least, depending on the knowledge of the speaker, "I expect him here after dinner." But such claims of course, commit the speaker to a future course of action. The weaker claim, "If you don't come after dinner, you won't catch him" does not commit the speaker to the claim that if you do come after dinner you will catch him. It merely rules out one case where your action of coming would be in vain and leaves the rest open. If you show up after dinner and he isn't there, you have no grounds for feeling that you had been given incorrect information. The wife can say in good conscience "He still hasn't returned."

> A family has been preparing for the marriage of their daughter for the past six months—negotiating with the boy's family, securing commitments for work and money from his extended family, registering the marriage in the local town government, making provisions for the ceremony, etc. It seems generally agreed that the marriage will probably take place on Thursday. On Tuesday you stop to inquire of the head of the family when the wedding will take place since you are to be one of the guests of honor and don't want to plan anything that would conflict with the wedding. His response is merely "Oh, pretty soon now." If you press him on the point by asking "Will it be on Thursday?"—which would be really gauche of you as this violates the nonconfrontation norm—he would likely respond with something like "Ah, Thursday, that would be a good day, we'll see, we'll see."

Again the Malagasy is not being uncooperative here. He is behaving in a natural way, and it would be most unnatural to commit himself to a particular date in advance. Imagine the shame if, at the last minute, something did happen.

> On returning to your village late one night, one of the *ray-aman-dreny* appears at your door. (It is most unusual to visit after dark, so you know something is up.) And you ask him, "What's new?" (*Inona no vaovao?*) to which he responds *Tsy misy* "Nothing" (lit.: "Not exist"). Then after some inconsequential discussion, it emerges that your neighbor who was expecting has had an unsuccessful labor, the child died, and the woman is in the town hospital. (For a country Malagasy, hospitals are generally regarded as places where you go to die, for they only take people to a hospital as a last resort).

However, the response "Nothing" to your original question was the only reasonable answer for the Malagasy to give. To come out directly with new, and unpleasant, information would violate convention and put the giver on the spot.

> You are taking some friends by car to a distant village. You come to a fork in the road and ask whether or not you go left there. The response is *Eny tompoko* "Yes, sir." As you start to bear left you hear a mildly excited cry *Eo avaratra eo, angamba* "There to the north perhaps." So you bear right.

Why did the Malagasy originally answer "yes" when asked about turning left? Because he doesn't have available, at least without reflection, the concepts of left and right. All directions are given in terms of the cardinal points. Even within a house if I want to ask you for something within easy reach of your left hand, I will still indicate the object as "the tobacco there to the East." But given that the Malagasy did not comprehend the term left, why did he still agree? Because agreement indicated social solidarity with the speaker. Disagreement would have been a confrontation and saying simply that he hadn't understood might have implied that you hadn't spoken appropriately. Normally when people perceive that there is a lack of understanding, they continue talking on the same topic until there is at least minimal communication. What was very awkward in the above situation was that a decision had to be reached quickly. There simply was no time to beat around the bush until the sentiments of your partner were clear.

Note as well that giving directions in terms of cardinal points rather than left and right serves to keep the speaker away from the center of attention. In general to reference objects and (as we shall see) people through oneself would draw attention to oneself, single oneself out from others, and would not then be a normal Malagasy behavior pattern.

Lastly then let us consider the ways human beings are referenced in everyday discourse.

A teenage boy from a few houses away pays you an informal visit. After a little discussion he mentions that *"Bosy's* mother is a little sick". Further discussion yields that he would like to take her some medicine, which you provide and he leaves.

But you are puzzled, since you had thought that he and Bosy were siblings. But had they been he surely would have referred to Bosy's mother as "my mother" or perhaps *Ravelo* (her name). So you infer that perhaps he and Bosy are not really blood siblings, perhaps she is some neighbor's daughter who is only living with the other family.

Your inference, however, would be incorrect. The woman in question was in fact the boy's mother. He didn't refer to her as *his* mother, though, as that would be to reference someone through himself, thus in a small way making himself the center of attention. Neither did he refer to her by her proper name, for that would be too direct a way to identify her and would draw attention to her. Rather he chose, quite naturally in the Malagasy context, to specify her identity through a third party. And even the third party is not, as might appear, unequivocally identified, for *Bosy* is a very common, almost generic, name used to refer to young girls. That is, even if a young girl's name is not *Bosy* I might refer to her as such in a context in which the reference is otherwise reasonably clear. Note further that to reference his mother as a parent of someone is respectful, since, as we have seen, having children places you in the *ray-aman-dreny* class. By contrast, to have referenced his mother as the spouse of X would not have had this slight advantage, although it would have preserved the general respect inherent in referencing someone through one's family affiliation.

Besides referencing through third parties, a great many other linguistic means are available for personal reference. Agent nouns are commonly used. Thus on a particular occasion a boy might be referred to as a *mpiandry omby* "cow watcher" (from the verb *miandry* "to watch, guard" and *omby* "cow"). Such names of course, are particularly adaptable to the activity that the person to whom you are referring happens to be performing at the time of reference. Similarly, most predicates, adjectives, adverbs, and demonstratives may be combined with *ny* "the" to form a referential phrase. Thus *ny omaly* "the yesterday" could easily be used to refer to "the person who was here yesterday" and *ny mbola tsy tonga* "the still not come" to those who hadn't yet arrived.

Further, existential constructions with no noun phrases often fulfill functions for which we use noun phrases in English. A simple example of an existential construction would be *misy mitomany* "exist cry," meaning "there is crying going on" or more naturally "someone is crying." (Both *misy* "exist" and *mitomany* "cry" are ordinary verbs. Existential constructions always begin with *misy* and are frequently followed by another verb.) However, suppose a brother of yours, well known to the village, comes looking for you. Someone who is coming to seek you out would most likely merely report *misy mitady* "exist looking for." There would be no need to say "exist looking for *you*" since the reference is clear from context, but neither is there mention of who is doing the looking.

In middle-class European or American society if someone who knew your brother well reported to you merely, "Someone was looking for you," you would be surprised to learn that the person was your brother and would likely infer that the person who reported the information did not have it firsthand and hence didn't actually know who was looking for you. But again, this would be an incorrect inference in the Malagasy situation.

5.2 Orders and Requests

The final case we shall consider concerns several linguistic aspects of ordering and requesting. Obviously giving someone an order is a confrontation experience, so when such is necessary we might expect the Malagasy to have recourse to means for "softening the blow." Such is in fact the case.

In English we give an order in the active voice, most usually omitting the addressee phrase "you." Thus we say "Wash those clothes": the verb "wash" is active (the passive would be "be washed [by]"). If the addressee phrase is present, it occurs as the subject and gives special emphasis as in "You wash those clothes right now!" When present, the subject phrase is the most prominent member of the sentence.

In Malagasy it is possible to form active imperatives by using the active form of the verb with the stress shifted to the right. Thus corresponding to "You are washing the clothes" *mánasa ny lamba ianao* (with stress marked on the first syllable of *manasa*), we have "(you) wash the clothes" *manasá ny lamba (ianao)*, where the addressee phrase *ianao* is usually omitted as in English but may occur for emphatic effect. But an active order in Malagasy is considered a highly brusque statement and a confrontation. It is used only in situations of stress or anger, and Europeans who frequently use active imperatives in Malagasy are often misinterpreted as being much more aggressive and authoritarian than they intend to be.

The normal form for an order is to put the verb in something other than the active voice, making the patient of the action or some circumstance of the action the subject phrase and hence the item on which attention is focused. The addressee phrase, again usually omitted, would occur as a passive agent or circumstantial agent if present. Thus the normal way to say "Wash the clothes" would be *Sasao (-nao) ny lamba* "be washed (by you) the clothes." The verb is passive in form, so attention is focused on the clothes and not the agent of the action (who is, of course, the addressee). Similarly if we want to say "Wash the clothes with this soap," it would be natural to form an imperative from the circumstantial form of the verb, making the instrument, the soap, the superficial subject. Thus *Anasao (-nao) ny lamba ity savony ity* "be washed by you the clothes this soap," or in more natural English "This soap is to be used by you to wash the clothes." Malagasy is in fact one of the relatively few languages in the world that has a well-developed system for forming nonactive imperatives. In English, for example, we simply could not say "be washed (by you) these clothes." The closest we get is "Let the clothes be washed (by you)," a construction archaic and elevated in tone that is not used freely.

Requests as well are often an occasion of considerable frustration on the part of the European in a Malagasy context. Needless to say by now, they are not given directly, for this would put the requestee on the spot and risk an affront to the requester if the request is denied. A normal request, even a fairly urgent one, usually takes place in stages. The requester approaches the requestee and engages him in conversation. Then he brings up the topic his request concerns but does not overtly make the request. The requestee is then free to ignore the topic and move to something else if he would prefer to not satisfy the request. He never has to confront the requester with a denial; he need not recognize the speech act as a request at all. Of course, the requester may persist and continually reintroduce a topic that concerns his needs, but if he is repeatedly ignored, he can still leave without feeling rejected, and hence shamed.

Once, for example, a group of boys, all known to us, came for an impromptu visit. We talked for perhaps twenty minutes, and finally the topic of a cut foot was brought up. Eventually one of the boys in the back of the group came forward and exhibited a severely bleeding foot. (Cut feet are common in this formerly volcanic area.) In this case not only was delaying the request normal but so was the arrival in the group. It would have been much more self-centered to arrive alone.

In fact, it is quite usual for a request to be made by someone other than the one who desires the service or object. For example, in the situation above, it was not the injured boy who directed our attention to the bleeding foot. It was his peer group that performed this act on his behalf. Such a procedure is so commonplace that even very young children are able to engage in this kind of interaction. Four-year-olds, for example, would frequently ask for a sweet for their younger siblings (and we were obliged, of course, to offer something to the older sibling as well).

Requests then are indirect in two ways: They are not made explicitly, and they are often made by a third party on someone else's behalf.

Recall in this connection the *mpikabary* in the formal speech situations who speaks for, or on behalf of, the entire family, including the ancestors. It is important to realize here that our characterization of the Malagasy request as indirect is ethnocentric on our part. What that means is indirect relative to our norms. But for the Malagasy, performing an 'indirect' request is simply to request. To force the behavior to be direct would make it into a social act with very different consequences. The 'indirectness' of Malagasy requests follows from the more general and pervasive norms of group, not individual, responsibility and nonconfrontation.

Thus, even in stress situations in which it is vital to have an answer to a request, it would not normally be possible to force a fully direct request. For example, towards the end of our stay in Madagascar a young man who we knew from the mission school in town but who lived in a village we did not know, arrived at our house with a very large sack of potatoes. It was rather obviously a gift for us, and one beyond the means of an ordinary household to offer. So we knew the boy must have come as a representative of a larger group, perhaps his entire village. And indeed, after having some tea together and chitchatting for perhaps a half an hour he began to approach the purpose of his visit, which was in essence that his village would consider it an honor for us to pay them a visit. And he was obviously commissioned to make the request since he was the only one from the village who knew us. He was further acutely embarrassed at being the sole representative to act on his village's behalf. We, however, had no desire to visit any new villages at that point in our stay so we continually skirted the topic of the visit in good Malagasy fashion. Had this been simply a casual request the hour's conversation with no committal on our part would have sufficed to discourage any further discussion of the matter. However, the boy was on the spot, obviously having to return to the village without his important gift and needing something to tell them in exchange. Finally, exasperated after an entire morning's conversation, he walked determinedly to our window and said, "There's the path (to the village) sir, there's the path." This was as close as he could bring himself to making a direct request. But we, of course, were still free to acknowledge that we indeed saw the path and knew where it went without having to acknowledge his request that we actually visit the village.

In general, request behavior in Madagascar is often misinterpreted by Europeans. A European's request often seems like a confrontation to the Malagasy and this engenders their hostility and lack of cooperation. And the Malagasy's request to the European often appears 'devious', perhaps even dishonest. Yet the Malagasy behavior here might be better termed considerate. Not only is asking a favor done indirectly, but so also is bestowing a favor. Thus a Malagasy may return a kindness by bringing a small gift of some sort. Offering a chicken, for example, is a highly valued way to express your appreciation to someone. Imagine, for example, a group of women arriving at your house, one of them with a chicken clucking and squirming under her *lamba*. You couldn't possibly remark upon the fact, or acknowledge the gift, until after much pleasant talk, serving tea, etc. Then finally one of the women would uncover the chicken and you would go through a reaction of surprise and appreciation.

Finally, regarding request behavior, the European may often find himself as having been understood to have made a request where in fact none was intended. For example, on one occasion, Edward, in making idle conversation with a neighbor, happened to remark on the large pile of sweet potatoes in front of the man's house. About twenty minutes later, having returned to our own house, we were surprised to see the man's son appear with a plate of two cooked sweet potatoes! On reflection, it was clear that our casual remark was interpreted as a request by our neighbor. So in adapting to this Malagasy norm, one must learn to both listen more attentively and to understate (by European standards) one's intentions.

5.3 Norms and Mitigating Circumstances

It would be incorrect to infer from our descriptions of Malagasy social behavior that the Malagasy are always uninformative, self-effacing, or that they never have confrontations. In the same way that in American society the norm of free exchange of information can be mitigated by other norms, like those of respecting the confidentiality relations between lawyer and client, priest and confessee, etc., so also we find that the Malagasy norms we have discussed may be mitigated in various ways. We have already seen, for example, that the norm of nonconfrontation applies less to women than to men.

Other general factors as well condition the application of these norms. Thus the directness of a request will vary with the magnitude of the request and the social relations that exist between the requester and the requestee. If the request is of small magnitude, as for a piece of tobacco, it is more likely to be made, all other things being equal, in a reasonably direct way. But if the request is major, as for a bride or for sizable assistance in a bone-turning ceremony, the request will certainly be indirect. Similarly, if the two parties are *havana* (a term that covers kinsmen and close acquaintances) the request is more likely to be direct. But if one of the parties is *vahiny* (outsider, stranger, foreigner), the request is almost certain to be indirect. If one of the parties is *vahiny* and the request is minor, or if the request is major and the parties are *havana*, the degree of directness will be adjusted to suit the particular circumstances, though always falling on the indirect side by European standards.

It is important to recognize the conditioning factors on speech norms, since the quality of observation a visitor, say a field worker, can make will be conditioned by the role he occupies in the local social structure. Had we, for example, merely lived in a town and visited different villages, we would never have been on a *havana* basis with anyone. We might easily then have mistaken the norms for interaction with *vahiny* as being the norms for everyone. Nor would we have observed the differential applications of the norms with respect to men and women, since most interactions between outsiders and a village are mediated by the men of the village. The nonconfrontation norm applies less to women than to men, but on a daily basis women interact mostly with their immediate family, their children, or other women. Only men formally represent the family or the village to others, thus only men perform the major *kabary* at marriages or bone-turning ceremonies.

It was important then for the quality of observation that we live in a village and become *havana* rather than remaining *vahiny*. This not only enabled us to observe the variable application of speech norms, it actually enabled us to observe elementary syntactic facts about the language that otherwise we would not have been in a position to note. Thus, in addition to the standard address terms (*ianao* "you" [sg] and *ianareo* "you" [pl]), we found that there were many other second-person address terms whose usage was socially very restricted. For example, *ise* is used only to address people with whom one is on very close terms. The restrictions are much more severe, for example, than the use of familiar address terms in European languages. It would be highly unusual for a Malagasy and a European to use this form between them. And other pronominal forms are even more highly restricted. Thus *indroky* is largely restricted in usage to a mother talking to her child. It would never be used between a Malagasy and a European. Most grammars of Malagasy don't even mention the restricted pronouns.

In general then, an alert field worker must be able to assess how those in the situation he is observing place him in their social structure. Only then can he judge what distortion his very presence introduces into the range of phenomena he will be trying to observe and understand.

SUGGESTIONS FOR FURTHER READING

Malagasy Grammar

Cousins, W.E. *A Concise Introduction to the Study of the Malagasy Language.* London: Antananarivo Press of the London Missionary Society, 1894.

A concise but excellent traditional grammar.

Malzac, R.P. *Grammaire Malgache.* Paris: Société D'éditions Géographiques, Maritimes et Coloniales, 1926.

Longer and more thorough than Cousins but no more insightful.

Keenan, E.L. "Relative Clause Formation in Malagasy." In *The Chicago Which Hunt*, edited by P. Peranteau, 1972: 169–189.

A detailed analysis of the highly characteristic way in which relative clauses are formed in Malagasy and several related Malayo-Polynesian languages.

———. "Remarkable Subjects in Malagasy," *Subject and Topic*, edited by C. Li. New York: Academic Press, 1976: 247–301.

An analysis of the notion 'subject of' in Malagasy.

Sociolinguistic Work on Malagasy

Keenan, E.O. "Norm-makers, Norm-breakers: Uses of Speech by Men and Women in a Malagasy Community." In *Explorations in the Ethnography of Speaking*, edited by R. Baumann and J. Sherzer. Cambridge, England: Cambridge University Press, 1974.

Discusses in particular the differential application of speech norms as applied to men and to women.

———. "On the Universality of Conversational Implicatures." *Language in Society*, no. 5, 1976: 67–80.

Discusses the sense in which the Gricean implicatures governing speech use apply differently in Malagasy society as compared with, for example, middle-class American society.

———. "Conversation and Oratory in Vakinankaratra, Madagascar." Ph. D. dissertation, University of Pennsylvania, 1974.

Discusses conversational norms, ritual oratory, and certain nonlinguistic aspects of ethnography.

General Anthropology of Madagascar

Bloch, M. *Placing the Dead: Tombs, Ancestral Villages, and Kinship Organization in Madagascar*. London: Seminar Press, 1971.

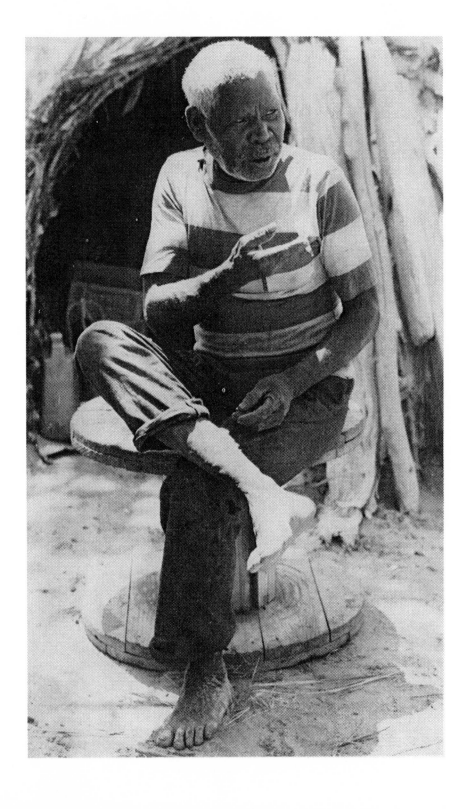

IV

How to Talk to Your Brother-in-Law in Guugu Yimidhirr

John B. Haviland

1 EMBEDDED SPEECH

When people exchange words, there is usually much more to be said than that they are simply "speaking to one another."

>"Howdy. My name's Maureen."

>>"Pleased to meet you. I'm Max."

>"How are you, Max?"

>>"Fine, thanks."

In this dialogue the protagonists are not merely talking; they are introducing themselves. (They are saying hello—even though the word "hello" does not occur.) It is the fact that we can recognize this dialogue as a conventionalized greeting—and not, say, as an interrogation or an interview—that allows us to interpret the question "How are you?" quite differently from the same question addressed, for instance, to

John Haviland, an American, is an anthropologist at the Australian National University, Canberra. He has studied traditional music and gossip in a Tzotzil (Mayan) Indian village in Mexico. His work on Guugu Yimidhirr speech practices has led him to dig more deeply, through bureaucratic leavings and people's memories, for the roots of modern Australian Aboriginal social life.

161

someone who has just fallen down a flight of stairs. The force of saying "My name's Maureen" as part of introducing oneself (which is partly to invite one's interlocutor to introduce him or herself in turn) is rather different from uttering the same words to *identify* oneself. ("Somebody named Maureen is wanted on the telephone." "My name's Maureen.")

Now compare the following conversation:

"How do you do? I am Dr. Maureen Smith."

> "I'm delighted to make your acquaintance, Dr. Smith. Allow me to introduce myself. My name is Gonzales, Max Gonzales."

"How are you, Mr. Gonzales?"

Although each sentence in the second dialogue has its counterpart in the first, we immediately see a difference in tone between the two conversations. The second dialogue portrays a more formal introduction than the first. For the moment we needn't try to say more exactly what the difference is. Partly it is a matter of different words—"meet you" and "make your acquaintance" are rather different turns of phrase. It is enough to see that even these sketchy hypothetical conversations are pregnant with information about their settings. (We might imagine the first dialogue occurring at an informal dancing party and the second at, say, a diplomatic cocktail party. We can even imagine how the protagonists might be dressed, how they are standing, and perhaps even how close together they are standing.) It is the settings that are more or less formal; the conversations are tailored to match them. People learn to speak as part of learning to live in the world. It is characteristic of speech that one fits one's words to the circumstances.

Often, in fact, a speaker's choice of words helps to create or change those very circumstances. Imagine two different responses Max might offer to Dr. Smith's polite query "How are you, Mr. Gonzales?"

(1) "I'm quite well, thank you."

and:

(2) "Call me Max."

The first is a polite reply to the conventionalized greeting that maintains the formal style. The second invites Dr. Smith to drop the formal tone—and notice that the invitation is itself a suggestion about how to talk, rather than an explicit remark about greater informality.

These brief conversations display some notable properties of speech. First, we see that speaking is *embedded* in human activity. J. L. Austin pointed out that much action is accomplished through speech or simply consists of speech. (One swears allegiance, or promises, by saying "I swear..." or "I promise..."; one gets married by saying "I do..."; and so on.) Examining the syntactic structure of sentences or the properties of words will be only a preliminary to an adequate study of the place of language in human life. Communicating information, or stating propositions, is only one sort of task that language accomplishes. Language also engenders and prompts, or prevents and hinders action. And a good deal of talk (including that in our hypothetical dialogue) establishes, reinforces, and changes social relationships between speakers.

Second, our examples demonstrate that speech mirrors features of the social context in which it occurs. When an occasion is formal, formal and stiff language is appropriate. Among specialists, specialized jargon emerges. Whether, in a given context, one says "damn!" or "darn!" "shit!" or "shucks!" is an *index*—a mark—of features of the situation. (Am I talking to maiden aunt, or roommate? Is this the church or the locker room? Did I bark my shin, or just bump my funny bone? Am I a seaman or a clergyman? And so on.) Politeness, formality, and propriety are features of human intercourse with reflexes in language. Correspondingly, impoliteness and impropriety also find linguistic expression. Speech can be antisocial and subversive, in form as well as in content. Speakers often turn conventions on their heads to surprise, to shock, and to snub. ("Hi, my name's Fred..." "...[silence]....")

These are matters that involve not only the properties of language as a code but also the nature of speech in a social situation. It is a person's knowledge of such matters that allows him or her to understand "How are you?" as a greeting and not a request for information; or to interpret "Whose junk is this all over the floor?" more as a command than a question. And it is ignorance of such matters in a different language community, or deliberate violation of the conventions in one's own, that allows one to commit stylistic, lexical, and social blunders in speech, despite adequate grammar. (*Host*: "Will you have more to eat?" *Foreign guest*: "No, thank you, I'm fed up." *Court Clerk*: "Do you solemnly swear to tell the truth, the whole truth, and nothing but the truth?" *Wiseacre*: "You bet your ass!") Looking at the ways that speech merges with social life in other communities can put into illuminating counterpoint our own language practices.

Aboriginal Australians are celebrated for their highly complex social organization, in which people reckon their relationships to one another largely in terms of kinship. Amidst a complicated calculus of social identities that divided everyone into kin or spouse's kin, into friends, neighbors, and strangers, or into elders and juniors, many groups of these original Australians observed elaborate etiquette, treating some classes of people with extreme respect and caution and enjoying unrestrained and often ribald relations with others. Not surprisingly, this social complexity is mirrored in correspondingly complex speech practices. In Australia, as elsewhere, respectful, restrained, formal speech differs markedly from ordinary talk, and again from joking, relaxed, or intentionally impolite and abusive language. For example, in the Guugu Yimidhirr language of Cooktown, in far North Queensland, the ordinary way to say "There is no food" is:

Mayi guya. (lit.: "food not.")

But to speak respectfully to one's father-in-law or brother-in-law, one must say instead:

Gudhubay ngangarra.

using special respectful equivalents in place of the ordinary words. Instead of *mayi*, one says *gudhubay* for "food"; instead of *guya* for "not," one says *ngangarra*. This chapter is about the special language of respect in Guugu Yimidhirr.

Throughout the discussion the reader should keep in mind two facts that we have uncovered about speech in our own society: first, that speech is part of action, that it performs work for its participants; and second, that speech adjusts itself to its surroundings—to the participants and to the social setting. Mechanisms of grammar—including the system of noun cases that we shall consider in the next section—along with the words or stems upon which such mechanisms act provide the tools for speech. However, it will be clear that no matter how much one knows about the formal properties of the language (for example, how to conjugate verbs or decline nouns) to speak Guugu Yimidhirr properly is to be embedded deeply in a particular social environment.

2   THE LANGUAGE OF COOKTOWN

On the eleventh of June, 1770, H.M. Bark *Endeavour*, with Lt. James Cook in command, struck a coral reef while exploring northwards along the east coast of Australia. The ship began to take water. After Cook directed his men to throw overboard extra weight in the form of guns, ballast, and rotting provisions, the ship again floated and slowly made its way to the mainland for repairs. Cook discovered a good harbor at the mouth of a river, and ultimately, by Friday the twenty-second, he brought the ship to shore where his men could examine and repair the damage. The river was named the Endeavour, and the spot where the *Endeavour* was beached became the site of the gold boom town Cooktown in North Queensland.

Cook first spied a strange animal "of a light mouse Colour and the full size of a Grey Hound, and shaped in every respect like one, with a long tail, which it carried like a Grey Hound; in short I should have taken it for a wild dog but for its walking or running, in which it jumped like a Hare or Deer."[1] On July 3 some of the Endeavour's crew scouting for a passage through the reef to the North and searching at the same time for food, came upon a party of natives, who scattered at their approach. On July 11, one month after the accident that had brought the *Endeavour* to shore, a small party of Aborigines appeared on the shore of the river and ultimately approached the ship. According to Cook's Journal:

> ... they were wholly naked, their Skins the Colour of Wood soot, and this seemed to be their Natural Colour. Their Hair was black, lank, and cropt short.... Some part of their Bodys had been painted with red, and one of them had his upper lip and breast painted with Streakes of white, which he called *Carbanda*. Their features were far from being disagreeable; their Voices were soft and Tunable, and they could easily repeat any word after us, but neither us nor Tupia could understand one word they said.[2]

Cook and his men were not long in learning from the natives that the strange animal that they had, by then, taken to shooting and eating, was called "Kangooroo or Kanguru." Cook, the botanist Joseph Banks, and members of the crew in fact collected more than sixty words from the "New Holland language" of the Endeavour River. These word lists from the Guugu Yimidhirr language still spoken around Cooktown were the first written records of an Australian language—just as Cook's men were the first Europeans ever to see a kangaroo. (In Guugu Yimidhirr *gangurru* is the name for a species of large, black kangaroo now rarely seen near the coast.)

Despite the fact that the *Endeavour* put to sea again in early August 1770 and that the Aboriginal inhabitants of that area were not again to be visited by white men in great numbers for nearly a century, they as well managed to learn a good deal from Cook about Europeans. On July 19 Cook reports that a party of Endeavour River natives visited the ship, evidently with a thought to sharing in the crew's meal of freshly caught sea turtle:

> Those that came on board were very desirous of having some of our Turtles, and took the liberty to haul 2 of them to the Gangway to put over the side; being disappointed in this they grew a little Troublesome, and were for throwing every thing overboard they could lay their hands upon. As we had no Victuals dress'd at this time, I offer'd them some bread to Eat, which they rejected with Scorn, as I believe they would have done anything else excepting Turtle....

---

[1] James Cook, *Captain Cook's Journal During His First Voyage Around the World Made in H.M. Bark* Endeavour, *1768–71*. Facsimile edition, State Library of South Australia, 1968, p. 281. (Also of relevance is John B. Haviland, "A Last Look at Cook's Guugu Yimidhirr Word List," *Oceania* XLIV 3 (1974): 216–32.)
[2] Cook, op. cit., p. 286.

After returning to shore the Aborigines remained "troublesome":

> ... [T]hey all went to a place where some of our people were washing, and where all our nets and a good deal of linen were laid out to dry; here with the greatest obstinacy they again set fire to the grass, which I and some others who were present could not prevent, until I was obliged to fire a Musquet load with small Shott at one of the Ring leaders, which sent them off"[3]

Friendly relations were soon again established, although the Natives showed the good sense, "whether through Jealousy or disregard," never to bring "any of their women along with them to the Ship," leaving them always "on the Opposite side of the River, where we had frequent Opportunities viewing them thro' our Glasses."[4]

After the *Endeavour* departed, the Guugu Yimidhirr–speaking natives of the area were spared more visits by white men in any numbers for the next hundred years. Some explorers came near in the 1840s, and in the previous two decades some ships had surveyed the area. But it was only the discovery of gold on the Palmer River in September 1873, inland from the spot where Cook had beached his ship, that brought Europeans (and later Chinese) in great hordes to the territory of the Guugu Yimidhirr and neighboring tribes. So numerous had the miners and prospectors become that in October 1873 the need was felt to open a port to supply them. A cutter was sent to land at Cook's original landing spot at the mouth of the Endeavour and to establish a camp. By early November there had been several major battles between the diggers bound for the gold fields and the Aboriginal natives of the area, almost certainly including Guugu Yimidhirr speakers or their close relatives. By February 1874, the height of the wet season, Cooktown was "a roaring, cosmopolitan, gold boom town, with hundreds of wood and iron buildings crowding both sides of two-mile-long Charlotte street, which ran from the wharves out to the beginning of the Palmer road, and dotting the bush on either side of it."[5] By 1876 Cooktown was a major seaport, surpassed only by Brisbane in the volume of its trade. The town had a population of over four thousand, of whom some two thousand were Chinese; and these figures do not include the estimated six thousand European and seventeen thousand Chinese miners in the gold fields.

Amidst this incredible invasion, the original inhabitants had little hope, indeed. According to the earliest reports, the policy of European gold hunters towards Aborigines was one of "dispersion"—a euphemism for massacre by rifle. No doubt some Aborigines found their way into

---

[3]Ibid., p. 289.
[4]Ibid., p. 319.
[5]Hector Holthouse, *River of Gold: The Story of the Palmer River Goldrush* (Sydney: Angus and Robertson, 1967), p. 53.

the new town, for G. C. Bolton reports that by 1885 Cooktown imposed on Aborigines a formal curfew after dark.[6] Travelers on Cape York toward the end of the 1880s who bothered to pay any attention to Aborigines reported wholesale slaughter, as well as kidnappings of women and children, and addiction to alcohol and opium.

There were also, inevitably, missionaries, following close on the heels of the gold diggers, who probably offered timely sanctuary to the local Cooktown Aborigines. In January 1886 a Lutheran missionary en route to New Guinea established a mission among Guugu Yimidhirr–speaking Aborigines at Cape Bedford, some thirty miles north of Cooktown. The next year the Reverend G. H. Schwarz arrived from Germany to take over the mission, which was christened Hope Valley, or Hopevale. And although the Palmer gold was exhausted after ten years and Cooktown itself largely abandoned after being destroyed by a cyclone in 1907 and never rebuilt, Schwarz remained at Hopevale, with his community of newly Lutheran Aborigines, until 1942 when the entire mission population was relocated because of World War II.

Before the European invasion, Guugu Yimidhirr was spoken in an area that extended inland from the mouth of the Endeavour to a place called Battle Camp (named after that first bloody encounter between a party of diggers heading for the Palmer and a large group of armed Aborigines). Dialects of the language were spoken to the north past Cape Bedford and the McIvor River to the present Starcke station and from there inland to the source of the Jack River. Most of the natives of these and surrounding regions were at the mercy of encroaching Europeans: first the gold seekers and fishermen who scoured the coast for beche-de-mer (a giant sea slug, much esteemed in dried form in Chinese cookery), and later the settlers. Hopevale and its sister mission to the south at Bloomfield River became receptacles for the Aborigines driven from elsewhere. (Neither mission site was of much use to settlers: Hopevale was described as "mainly on rock and sand"; and the site of the Bloomfield mission seemed, according to an early report, to have been selected by some "evil genius."[7]) Here was somewhere to take children who survived "dispersion," especially children of mixed white and Aboriginal ancestry who could not be suffered to grow up uncivilized. Children brought to the mission, usually without their families, were interned at the mission school at Cape Bedford. A few adults lived in camps on mission territory and seem to have been reliable aides to native police and local landowners in monitoring the movements of other Aborigines—especially those who worked on nearby properties—

---

[6]G. C. Bolton, *A Thousand Miles Away: A History of North Queensland to 1920* (Canberra: Australian National University Press, 1970) p. 96.
[7]C. D. Rowley, *The Destruction of Aboriginal Society* (Canberra: Australian National University Press, Pelican Books, 1970) p. 177.

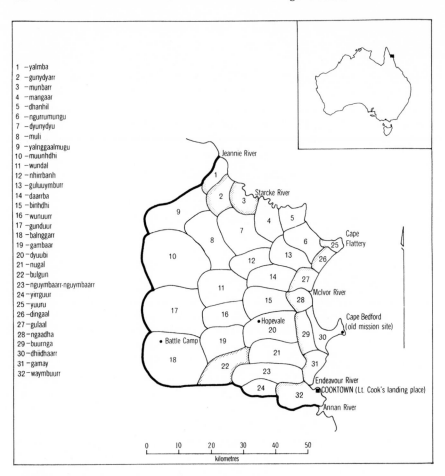

1 – yalmba
2 – gunydyarr
3 – munbarr
4 – mangaar
5 – dhanhil
6 – ngurrumungu
7 – dyunydyu
8 – muli
9 – yalnggaalmugu
10 – muunhdhi
11 – wundal
12 – nhirrbanh
13 – guluuymburr
14 – daarrba
15 – binhdhi
16 – wunuurr
17 – gunduur
18 – balnggarr
19 – gambaar
20 – dyuubi
21 – nugal
22 – bulgun
23 – nguymbaarr-nguymbaarr
24 – yirrguur
25 – yuuru
26 – dingaal
27 – gulaal
28 – ngaadha
29 – buurnga
30 – dhiidhaarr
31 – gamay
32 – waymbuurr

through the area. Hopevale, like other missions, was used to in-
stitutionalize, educate, and isolate Aborigines, who had by then become
dwellers on the fringes of towns and properties. Many people found
themselves transported to the far north from distant areas of
Queensland—one of the oldest inhabitants of the mission, now in his
eighties, was brought to Hopevale as a lad of six from Bowen, in the
south. In fact, of the native Guugu Yimidhirr speakers who were able to
lay ancestral claim to the area around Cooktown, rather few survived to
live under mission protection.

Nonetheless, Guugu Yimidhirr came to be the language of the
community. The Hopevale Lutheran "Order of Services," translated
into Guugu Yimidhirr by Reverend Schwarz and published in 1946, puts
the matter this way:

> It is an interesting experience that the Aboriginals on the Cape Bedford
> Reserve, though not all of them were members of the Cooktown tribe,

FIGURE 4.1 **The Traditional Territory of Guugu Yimidhirr–Speaking People**

The traditional territory of Guugu Yimidhirr–speaking people covered a wide area northwest of Cooktown in Northern Queensland. It was divided into thirty-two named locales (listed on the map), each with a dominant family group, and each with sacred places and favorite hunting spots. The shaded lines show major dialect areas. The dhalun-dhirr *("with the sea") dialect was spoken in locales 25–32. The* waguurr-ga *("of the outside") dialect was spoken in the remainder of the territory, except in locales 1, 2, 3, and 22, where individual dialect names have survived: Guugu Nyiiguudyi in 1, Guugu Nyalaadyi in 2, Guugu Yinaa in 3, and Guugu Diirrurru in 22.*

The map shows Lt. Cook's landing place at Cooktown on the Endeavour River and Battle Camp, scene of the first great battle between miners bound for the Palmer River gold fields and the aboriginal owners of the land. It shows the old mission site at Cape Bedford and its present location at Hopevale, where most of the surviving speakers of Guugu Yimidhirr and surrounding languages now live.

Traditionally marriages were contracted between individuals from widely separated locales. For example, one man from Dyunydyu *(7) married two sisters from* Balnggarr *(18) some fifty kilometers away. Guugu Yimidhirr people had extensive contacts with, and often married, speakers of neighboring languages—Gugu Yalandji to the South, the Barrow Point and Flinders Island languages to the North, and the so-called Guugu Warra and "Lama-Lama" languages to the West. The whole area formed a single large society, with the same basic kinship system, in which an individual spoke and understood several different languages in addition to his or her own native tongue.*

and though in the mission school they received all their instructions in the English language, among themselves always used the vernacular of the district, the Koko Yimidir dialect. They possess and read their English Bibles, and sing from the English Hymn Book, but their own tongue, the Koko Yimidir, speaks direct to their hearts, and their souls yearn to hear the Word of life in their native tongue, the Koko Yimidir.[8]

People have continued to come to Hopevale from other areas, but their own native or ancestral languages, if they still knew them when they arrived, have been largely submerged under the dominant local language.

Much remains to be learned about the recent history of the Hopevale Mission. Its residents clearly worked in large numbers cutting cane on sugar plantations farther down the coast. They have been, among other things, stockmen, sand miners, evangelists, seamen, professional boxers, and beche-de-mer fishermen. During World War II Reverend Schwarz was interned as a German alien, and the entire mission population was moved south to a large reserve inland from Rockhampton. There the colder climate decimated the Hopevale population. When,

---

[8]Board of the Lutheran Mission, Hope Valley, *Order of Service and Hymns* (Brisbane, Australia: Watson, Ferguson and Co., 1946) p. 2.

FIGURE 4.2   *Avoidance*

Fred Jacko (also shown in the photograph at the beginning of this chapter), the son of an important Guugu Yimidhirr leader from the Starcke River, and now in his fifties, is one of the few remaining people at Hopevale who still remembers and uses the respectful "brother-in-law" style of speaking. He uses the avoidance language here, for example, in conversation with another man who married a woman Fred classed as his granddaughter. In such a relationship, both men not only use the respectful vocabulary; they sit far apart, orient their bodies so as not to face one another, and avoid direct eye contact.

after the war, Hopevale was resettled (without Reverend Schwarz) inland from the original site at Cape Bedford, most of the old people who had once known life in the bush had not survived.

Hopevale is now a small community of six hundred permanent residents (and a dozen missionary staff). It is a community in most ways more substantial than nearby Cooktown, which Holthouse describes as "a shabby shell in which about five hundred contented people potter about, fish, and sip an occasional beer...."[9] The population is transitory. Many of the men work elsewhere; some nearby mine silica at Cape Flattery; others work in distant cities or towns. Some young

---

[9]Holthouse, op. cit., p. 209.

people, after finishing boarding school in the south, simply stay away, returning only to spend Christmas with family, at the beach near the old mission site, and singing some of those English hymns, now supplemented by a few Guugu Yimidhirr hymns written by an energetic Aboriginal minister.

Children still are taught in the white man's language, learning to read and write only in English. Although everyone speaks Guugu Yimidhirr, very few people are comfortable speaking *only* Guugu Yimidhirr. Instead, their language is full of English words and phrases, and detectable changes in Guugu Yimidhirr syntax and pronunciation are taking place. Much of the special linguistic knowledge about how to speak to a brother-in-law, or how to be especially polite (or impolite) is now lost, or confined to a handful of older people at Hopevale. The linguistic knowledge has faded, even though the social principles that motivated special speech remain matters of concern to Guugu Yimidhirr people. (The author apologizes in advance for saying so little about Guugu Yimidhirr women's speech, an omission that reflects serious gaps in his own knowledge and experience.) Perhaps the bits of information recorded here will contribute to some fate for Guugu Yimidhirr —whatever changes it may undergo—other than extermination.

3 THE GUUGU YIMIDHIRR LANGUAGE

Guugu Yimidhirr is in most respects a typical Australian language, sharing many features with the roughly two hundred other languages that faced the European takeover of Australia. For one thing, spoken Guugu Yimidhirr *sounds* like other Australian languages. It has only three vowels, *a*, *i*, and *u*, although long vowels (here written doubled) differ from short ones. For example, the word *bala* means "skinny" or "weak"; but the word *baalaa* denotes a kind of tree with a black, edible fruit. Guugu Yimidhirr also uses a number of sounds, called "laminals," produced with the blade of the tongue; the sounds represented as *dh* and *nh* are produced by pushing the tongue against the back of the front teeth so that it almost protrudes. (*Dh* sounds a bit like the *th* in *there*; *nh* sounds like an *n* pronounced with the tongue in the same position.) The sounds *dy* and *ny* result from putting the tongue against the roof of the mouth and sound something like the *j* of *judge* or the *ny* of *canyon*. There is also a difference between the "flap" or "trilled" *rr* and the single *r* which resembles the *r* of *rat*, with the tongue curled back. (The laminal sounds and the retroflex *r* are particularly common in Australian languages.) For the most part, the other sounds of Guugu Yimidhirr are pronounced much as their spellings suggest. The *ng* sound of Guugu Yimidhirr is like the *ng*'s of *singing* (and not like the *ng* of *finger*, which would be written in Guugu Yimidhirr with two *g*'s, as *ngg*). In Guugu

Yimidhirr a word can begin with *ng*: *ngaabaay* "head." Notice that there are no "fricative" sounds like English *s*, *z*, *f*, or *v*, and, finally, that there is no contrast in Guugu Yimidhirr between voiced and unvoiced consonants: *b* sometimes sounds like *p*, or *d* like *t*.

Guugu Yimidhirr also resembles other Australian languages in having a highly developed system of noun morphology. The specific form a noun takes in a sentence delimits the role of the corresponding person or thing in the event described. The system is extremely elaborate, allowing a Guugu Yimidhirr speaker to pack a good deal of meaning into a simple ending on a noun. The overall system and its detailed elaborations are worth our attention in this chapter, for such productive devices are among the verbal resources Guugu Yimidhirr provides to its speakers for accomplishing verbal tasks, or for endowing speech with a character appropriate to specific social situations.

3.1 Guugu Yimidhirr Pronouns

Let us transpose our original dialogue into a Guugu Yimidhirr setting. How does one introduce oneself in Guugu Yimidhirr? Or, to imagine a more likely situation—since most speakers of Guugu Yimidhirr know one another in the first place—how does one perform a greeting, or "say hello," at the Hopevale Mission?

> *Wanhdharra, dhawuunh? Nyundu ganaa?*
>
> Howdy, friend. Are you well?
>
> *Ngayu ganaa. Nyundu ganaa?*
>
> I'm fine. Are you well?

The word *wanhdharra* (which means "how") is a normal greeting for friends, corresponding to "howdy" or "what's up?" or "how are you?" *Dhawuunh* means "friend." Another informal greeting is:

> *Wanhdharraga?*
>
> How are ya?

in which the suffix *-ga* conveys still more informality. The word *ganaa* means "all right, well, fine, okay."

The pronouns of a language are called "pro-nouns" because they are said to *stand for* nouns. When we say:

George likes fried grasshoppers, but Mary abhors them.

we have used the pronoun *them* to stand for the full noun phrase *fried grasshoppers*; this device allows us to avoid repetition without sacrificing clarity. (We know that it is fried grasshoppers that Mary abhors.) And pronominalization allows us to replace extremely long and complex noun phrases with single monosyllables. For example:

The head dogcatcher's one-eyed son went out to look for the spotted black-and-white cocker spaniel that George lost at the creek. Did he find it?

But there is another sort of pronoun that does not, in any straightforward sense, stand for a full noun phrase and that illustrates a basic sense in which all languages are embedded in the speech contexts of their use. When a Guugu Yimidhirr speaker says to his friend:

Nyundu ganaa?
> Are you well?

he uses the pronoun *nyundu* "you" not as a replacement for some full noun phrase, but rather as a pointer that denotes the friend, that is, the person to whom he addresses his words. In a similar way, there is no longer noun phrase which the pronoun *ngayu* stands for. (*Ngayu* denotes the speaker, but "I am sick" does not mean the same thing as "The speaker is sick.") All languages must have this kind of word (called *a deictic* pronoun or *shifter*) in order to situate utterances in their typical contexts, such as when two people speak to one another about their own affairs or about the circumstances in which they find themselves. (Words like *this*, *here*, and *now* depend in the same way on the contexts of their occurrence and have shifting reference.)

The pronouns of Guugu Yimidhirr are somewhat different from English pronouns. We have seen *ngayu* "I" and *nyundu* "you." Here are a few more:

Nyulu Billy ganaa?
> Is Billy OK?

Nyulu ganaa.
> He's OK.

Nyulu Mary ganaa galmba?
> Is Mary OK too?

Nyulu galmba ganaa.
> She too is fine.

> *galmba*   also, too

Nyulu can mean both "he" and "she"; it can also mean "it" when it replaces, for example, a noun like *gudaa* "dog."

> *Nhanu gudaa ganaa?*
>> Is your dog OK?

> *Nyulu gaari ganaa. Nyulu biini.*
>> It's not OK. It died.

>> *nhanu*   your (Second person singular possessive)
>> *gaari*   not
>> *biinii* die

(Each new word will be glossed as it appears in the examples that follow. For words you have seen before but whose meanings you can't remember, you should consult the full glossary at the end of the chapter.) However, unlike English, Guugu Yimidhirr has no pronoun that can stand for an inanimate noun, a thing.

> *Nhanu galga wanhdhaa?*
>> Where is your spear?

> *Gadabadhi.*
>> (It) broke.

>> *galga*   spear
>> *wanhdhaa*   where?
>> *gadabal*   break, be broken

One cannot say here:

> **Nyulu gadabadhi.*

because *nyulu* can only be used to replace a noun that denotes some animate entity, not a spear. Here, then, the Guugu Yimidhirr system of pronouns has only one word, *nyulu*, where English has three: "he," "she," and "it." But Guugu Yimidhirr also distinguishes between certain sorts of nouns that can be replaced by a pronoun and others that cannot.
  Notice that a sentence like:

> *Nyulu Billy ganaa.*

would be translated, word for word, "He Billy is OK." That is, the word *nyulu* is not simply standing for the noun *Billy* but actually occurs together with it. We might think of this doubling up of pronoun and noun as a device both to highlight the topic of the remark and to tell us, among other things, that Billy is a person (or at least an animate being) because an inanimate thing could not generate the word *nyulu*.

Where English has different pronouns for singular and plural, Guugu Yimidhirr distinguishes a further set of forms; it has pronouns that denote exactly two people, called "dual" forms.

> *Nyundu dhadaa?*
>> Are you going to go?
>
> *Yuu, ngayu dhadaa.*
>> Yes, I'm going to go.
>
> *Ngayu galmba dhadaa.*
>> I too am going to go.
>
> *Ma, ngali dhadaa gulbuuygu.*
>> Come, we'll go together (the two of us).
>
>> *dhadaa* go
>> *gulbuuygu* together

Ngali means "you and I"—that is, it includes just the speaker and the hearer. Another pronoun, *ngaliinh*, is called an 'exclusive' form because it indicates the speaker and one other person who is *not* the hearer. It thus means "he/she and I (but not you)." *Yubaal* means "you two," and *bula* "the two of them." Notice how one says "X and Y" for animate things:

> *Dharramali bula Wurrbal*
>> Thunder and Fog

Thunder and Fog are mythical beings, here conceived as animate. Inanimate things are conjoined by simply putting them together with no overt equivalent for "and."

> *yugu nambal*
>> stick(s) and stone(s)

Table 4.1 shows all the different 'personal pronouns' in Guugu Yimidhirr.

A pronoun like *ngayu*, as we have seen, is a kind of pointer that each speaker can use to talk about himself or herself. However the precise *form* of the pronoun tells us something about its syntactic function in a sentence. One way of putting this is to say that the form of the pronoun

TABLE 4.1   *Guugu Yimidhirr Personal Pronouns*

1st person (inclusive)	1st person (exclusive)	2nd person	3rd person	
ngayu		nyundu	nyulu	**singular**
ngali	ngaliinh	yubaal	bula	**dual**
nganhdhaan		yurra	dhana	**plural**

ngayu depends on the role of the speaker in the action or event he or she is describing.

> *Ngayu ganaa.*
>> I'm well.
>
> *Ngayu dhadaa.*
>> I'm going to go.

In both these sentences, *ngayu* is the subject: it represents the person who is well, or the person who is going.

> *Ngayu Billy nhaadhi.*
>> I saw Billy.
>>
>>> *nhaadhi*   saw

In this sentence, the same form, *ngayu*, represents the fact that *I* am the one who saw Billy. We see that *ngayu* corresponds exactly to the English word "I"; it refers to the speaker, and it is the form appropriate to the subject of a sentence. This subject form of a pronoun is often called the "nominative" form. Similarly, the word *nyundu* is the nominative form of the second-person singular pronoun (the one that refers to the hearer).

> *Nyundu ganaa.*
>> You are OK.
>
> *Nyundu dhadaa.*
>> You are going to go.
>
> *Nyundu Billy nhaadhi.*
>> You saw Billy.

Now, how do I say that the person with whom I am speaking saw *me*? First let's recall how we say this in English.

You saw Billy.

I saw Billy.

You saw me.

Notice first the order of the parts in these sentences. The subject (the person who did the seeing) comes first, followed by the verb, and then by the object (the person who was seen). Second, notice that when the subject is in the first person (i.e., is the speaker) the form of the pronoun is nominative—"I." But when there is a first-person object, the form of the pronoun is "me"; in English this is the "objective" or "accusative" form of the pronoun. (Similarly there are accusative forms of "he" and "she"; and what are the accusative forms of "you" and "it"? These are, of course, extremely elementary facts about English.) The situation in Guugu Yimidhirr is similar.

Nyundu Billy nhaadhi.
You saw Billy.

Ngayu Billy nhaadhi.
I saw Billy.

Nyundu nganhi nhaadhi.
You saw me.

Notice that the typical order here is different from English: instead of the order Subject–Verb–Object, Guugu Yimidhirr has the order Subject–Object–Verb. Moreover, we can see that the Guugu Yimidhirr first-person singular pronoun also has an accusative form; *nganhi* corresponds to *me.* You can see some of the other accusative forms in the following sentences.

Ngayu nhina nhaadhi.
I saw you.

Nyulu nganhi nhaadhi.
He saw me.

Ngayu nhangu daamay.
I speared him.

daamal spear

First we can see that Guugu Yimidhirr is more systematic than English about distinguishing nominative from accusative forms. In the sentences:

You saw it.

It saw you.

only the order of the words determines what (or who) saw what (or whom). But in Guugu Yimidhirr each pronoun has an accusative form distinct from its nominative form.

Nyundu nhangu nhaadhi.
>   You saw him.

Nyulu nhina nhaadhi.
>   He saw you.

One corollary of this specificity of forms is that the precise order of words in a Guugu Yimidhirr sentence is rather variable. Although

TABLE 4.2   *Nominative and Accusative Forms of Guugu Yimidhirr Personal Pronouns*

1st person (inclusive)	(exclusive)	2nd person	3rd person	
ngayu		nyundu	nyulu	**singular nom.**
nganhi		nhina	nhangu	**acc.**
ngali	ngaliinh	yubaal	bula	**dual nom.**
ngalingan/ ngaliin	ngalinhun	yubalin	bulangan/ bulaan	**acc.**
nganhdhaan		yurra	dhana	**plural nom.**
nganhdhanun		yurrangan/ yurraan	dhanangan/ dhanaan	**acc.**

Note: The alternate accusative forms are dialectal variants.

ordinarily a sentence follows Subject–Object–Verb order, this is by no means always the case.

Billy ngayu nhaadhi.
I saw Billy.

Nhina nhaadhi ngayu.
I saw you.

Nhaadhi nhangu nyundu.
You saw him.

There can be no confusion about who did what to whom since each pronoun is unambiguously marked as either subject (nominative form) or object (accusative form). Table 4.2 shows the accusative forms of Guugu Yimidhirr personal pronouns.

(The reader might try to formulate a concise statement of the shape of alternate accusative forms for dual and plural pronouns. Which pronouns have alternate forms, and how are they formed? Notice that some non-singular pronouns end with consonants and others with vowels.)

3.2 The Dative Case and Possession

So far we have distinguished several different relationships that a person (denoted by a pronoun) can have to the action or event depicted in a sentence. In sentences with intransitive verbs there is a subject; in those with transitive verbs there is a subject (who is typically the actor) and an object. A third sort of sentence, typically one that describes some sort of giving, has an actor (the person who gives), an object (the thing given), and a beneficiary (or indirect object: the person to whom the object is given). In English, the indirect object form of a pronoun is like the object form, and it often occurs with the preposition *to*.

He gave me water.
He gave water to me.

I brought you food.
I brought food to you.

In Guugu Yimidhirr there are distinct indirect object (or 'dative') forms of the first- and second-person singular pronouns.

Nyulu ngadhu buurraay wudhi.
He gave me water.

Ngayu nhanu mayi maandi.

　　I brought you food.

> *buurraay*　water
> *wudhi*　gave
> *mayi*　food, vegetable food
> *maandii*　bring
> *maandi*　brought (past tense of *maandii*)

For the other persons and numbers, the dative and accusative forms are the same.

Nyundu nhangu mayi wudhi.

　　You gave him food.

Dhana ngaliin mayi maandi.

　　They brought us two food.

When a noun is the indirect object of a transitive verb, then it combines with a special ending or suffix to give its dative form. The suffix is *-bi* if the noun ends in a consonant and *-wi* if it ends in a vowel.

Ngayu Billy-wi mayi wudhi.

　　I gave food to Billy.

Nyulu dyin-guurr-bi minha maandi.

　　He brought meat to his sister.

> *dyin-gurr*　younger sister
> *minha*　meat

(Notice that the word *dyin-gurr* "sister" changes to *dyin-guurr-* when the suffix *-bi* is added. Most noun endings in Guugu Yimidhirr cause such lengthening on words of two syllables if the word ends with a consonant other than *n*. Be on the lookout for lengthening in the later examples.)

　　The dative form is used in another, clearly related meaning, which we have already seen in the phrase *nhanu gudaa* "your dog": it expresses what might be called ordinary possession.

buurraay ngadhu

　　my water

mayi nhanu

　　your food

nhangu ganggal
>   his/her child

ngaliin bayan
>   our house (of the two of us)

>   *ganggal*   child
>   *bayan*   house

Similarly, noun possessors require the dative suffix.

yarrga-wi galga
>   the boy's spear

ganggaal-bi mayi
>   the child's food

>   *yarrga*   boy
>   *galga*   spear

Dative forms of nouns and pronouns are used to express sentences that in English would use the verb "have."

Bayan nhangu wunaa.
>   He has a house. (lit.: his house exists.)

Mayi gabiirr-bi guya.
>   The girl has no food.

>   *wunaa*   exist
>   *gabiirr*   girl
>   *guya*   lacking, nonexistent, not

Table 4.3 summarizes the different dative forms for nouns and pronouns.
   All languages have shifters, including personal pronouns, that connect speech to the world by pointing at objects (or places or moments); demonstratives like *this* and *that* (and *here* and *now*) have this character. One particular act we perform frequently in speech is to give something its name, or to identify it.

Yiyi ngadhu bayan.
>   This is my house.

Nhayun bama ngadhu biiba.
>   That man is my father.

TABLE 4.3 *Dative Case Marking*

---

1. Personal Pronouns

    (a) First and second singular have distinct forms:

1st person sing.		**2nd person sing.**		
ngayu	"I"	nyundu	"you"	**nominative**
nganhi		nhina		**accusative**
ngadhu		nhanu		**dative**

    (b) For all other personal pronouns, the dative form is the same as the accusative form (see Table 4.2).

. . . .

2. Nouns

    (a) If the noun ends in a consonant, add *-bi*. (The second syllable of a two-syllable word ending in a consonant other than *-n* is lengthened.)

dyin-gurr	younger sister	*dyin-guurr-bi*	to the sister, the sister's
yarraman	horse	*yarraman-bi*	to the horse, the horse's

    (b) If the noun ends in a vowel, add *-wi*.

yarrga	boy	*yarrga-wi*	to the boy, the boy's

Yiyi yugu.

   This is (called) "yugu" (wood).

> *yiyi*   this, here
> *bama*   person (especially Aboriginal person)
> *nhayun*   that, there
> *biiba*   father
> *yugu*   wood

Notice that in Guugu Yimidhirr there is no separate word corresponding to the English word *is*. In equational sentences (of the form "X is Y") Guugu Yimidhirr simply puts X and Y together.

3.3 Subjects and Objects

Let's look again at the nominative pronouns. These forms are used in two different sorts of context: as subjects of intransitive verbs:

Ngayu ganaa.

   I'm well.

Ngayu dhadaa.
> I'm going to go.

and as subjects of transitive verbs:

Ngayu Billy nhaadhi.
> I saw Billy.

Ngayu nhanu mayi maandii.
> I'll bring you food.

Since these two 'functions' both employ the nominative forms, and since in both cases the pronoun serves as the 'subject' of the verb, on what grounds may one distinguish the two cases at all? For one thing, not all Guugu Yimidhirr pronouns have a single form that can occupy both sorts of position. Consider the interrogative pronoun *wanhu.*

Wanhu gaga-dhirr?
> Who is sick?

Wanhu dhadaara?
> Who is going?

> *gaga-dhirr*   sick

These intransitive sentences are correct, but it is impossible to say:

*Wanhu nhanu mayi wudhi?
> (Who gave you food?)

Instead, Guugu Yimidhirr has an entirely different word, *wanhdhu,* that serves precisely as the subject of transitive verbs.

Wanhdhu nhanu mayi wudhi?
> Who gave you food?

Wanhdhu Billy nhaadhi?
> Who saw Billy?

And although a transitive verb cannot have *wanhu* as its subject, it *can* have *wanhu* as its object.

Nyundu wanhu nhaadhi?
> Whom did you see?

If we diagram the pronoun forms that can serve in various capacities—as subjects and objects in intransitive and transitive sentences—we see two patterns. (Refer to Table 4.4.) In one case, the same form (*ngayu*) is used for subjects of both intransitive and transitive verbs, and a special accusative form is used for the objects of transitive verbs. In the other case, the same form serves as the subject of intransitive verbs and object of transitive verbs, and a special form (*wanhdhu*) is required as the subject of transitive verbs. The first pattern, with a nominative case for subjects and an accusative case for objects, is common throughout the world and predominates in the well-known languages of Europe. (Russian is a typical nominative/accusative language—see Chapter III in the companion volume. English once had this pattern for all nominal expressions and, as we have seen, retains it for pronouns.) The second pattern, in which the form used for intransitive subjects and transitive objects is often called the "absolutive" form and the special form for transitive subjects the "ergative," is considerably less frequent; although languages that display this pattern in some parts of their grammatical systems are widely distributed, occurring in every continent. In Guugu Yimidhirr both patterns coexist in the marking on nouns and pronouns; for in Guugu Yimidhirr nouns and a few pronouns follow the absolutive/ergative pattern, while personal pronouns follow the nominative/accusative pattern. (Some American Indian languages show the same split between an ergative/absolutive pattern for nouns and a nominative/accusative pattern for pronouns. Georgian, a language of the Caucasus, has an ergative pattern with perfective sentences but not with those in other tenses or aspects. A similar split holds in Yucatec, which like other Mayan languages—including Jacaltec [see Chapter I]—exhibits an ergative/absolutive pattern not by noun suffixes but in the system of pronominal cross-reference on verbs.)

Let's examine the ergative/absolutive pattern more closely. The greetings now complete, our hypothetical conversation continues.

Ngayu gaga-dhirr.
I'm not feeling well.

TABLE 4.4 Two Patterns of Subject/Object Marking

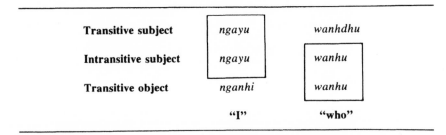

Transitive subject	ngayu	wanhdhu
Intransitive subject	ngayu	wanhu
Transitive object	nganhi	wanhu
	"I"	"who"

Ngaanii? Nyundu buli?

   Why? Did you fall down?

Ngayu gaari buli. Nganhi dhuurrngay.

   I didn't fall down. I was pushed.

> *ngaanii*   why?
> *bulii*   fall down

In this last sentence *dhuurrngay* is the past tense of the transitive verb *dhuurrngal* "push." And as we know *nganhi* is the accusative (or object) form of the first-person singular pronoun. Thus this sentence means, word for word, "me pushed"—roughly comparable to the English passive sentence "I was pushed." Another translation with an indefinite subject is possible: "Somebody pushed me." In Guugu Yimidhirr such a sentence with no overt subject is quite ordinary; the subject simply does not appear, and there is nothing special about the form of either object or verb.

The natural response now is to ask "*Who* did the pushing? *Who* pushed you?" (a question the reader should be able to construct from the words he or she already knows.) The special ergative form *wanhdhu* has precisely the properties needed to query the actor, the subject of the verb *dhuurrngay*, the pusher.

Wanhdhu nhina dhuurrngay?

   Who pushed you?

Just as Guugu Yimidhirr allows transitive sentences with no overt subject, so too does it allow transitive sentences with no explicit object. Thus one can ask simply:

Wanhdhu dhuurrngay?

   Who pushed?

Here, of course, the object is understood to be *nhina* "you"; prior conversation has already established who was pushed. (How do you think one might ask "Who got pushed?" Hint: use the "absolutive" form of the pronoun for "who.")

The first speaker, prodded by his interlocutor's questions, now reveals who the culprit was:

Billy-ngun nganhi dhuurrngay.

   Billy pushed me.

Here all the parts of the sentence are familiar except the special ending *-ngun* on *Billy*. This is an ergative suffix that marks the proper noun *Billy* as the subject of *dhuurrngay*.

A noun with the *-ngun* suffix is functionally parallel to the form *wanhdhu*, and the unsuffixed noun is like the absolutive form *wanhu*. This is clear from the following sentences:

> *Billy dhadaa.*
>> Billy is going to go.
>
> *Ngayu Billy nhaadhi.*
>> I saw Billy.
>
> *Billy-ngun nganhi nhadhi.*
>> Billy saw me.

As we can see from Table 4.5, the noun *Billy* follows the ergative/ absolutive pattern of *wanhdhu/wanhu* rather than the nominative/ accusative pattern of personal pronouns. In fact, all nouns in Guugu Yimidhirr follow the ergative/absolutive pattern. The unsuffixed form occurs when a noun is the subject of an intransitive verb or the object of a transitive verb; when a noun is the subject of a transitive verb, an ergative suffix is attached to it.

> *Yarrga-ngun nganhi gunday.*
>> The boy hit me.
>
> *Yugu-ngun bayan dumbi.*
>> The tree broke the house. (i.e., it fell and crushed it.)

TABLE 4.5   *Two Patterns of Subject/Object Marking: Personal Pronouns vs. Interrogative Pronouns and Nouns*

Transitive subject	*ngayu*	(nomi- native)	*wanhdhu*	(erga- tive)	*Billy-ngun*
Intransitive subject	*ngayu*		*wanhu*	(absolu- tive)	*Billy*
Transitive object	*nganhi*	(accu- sative)	*wanhu*		*Billy*
	"I"		"who"		"Billy"

Yarraman-ngun nhina dhuurrngay.

The horse pushed you.

Gudaa-ngun yarrga dyinday.

The dog bit the boy.

> *gundal*   hit, kill
> *dumbil*   break
> *yarraman* horse
> *dyindal*   bite, peck

Guugu Yimidhirr grammar here poses a puzzle for us: Why is there one pattern for pronouns but a different pattern for nouns? To find part of the answer requires that we examine more closely the sentence roles that different case markings distinguish (as such systems of special pronominal forms or of special noun endings are usually called). The nominative/accusative pattern marks subjects differently from objects; the ergative/absolutive patterns lump together intransitive subjects and transitive objects and distinguish these from transitive subjects. We can abbreviate these different sentence functions as follows: S means intransitive subject, O means transitive object, and A (for actor or agent) means transitive subject. Nouns in these different functions can have quite different roles in the actions described, depending on the meanings of the words involved.

Consider, first, the subjects of intransitive verbs (nouns in function S). An intransitive sentence by definition makes some statement about a single principal noun phrase.

The little dog laughed.

> (Tells us what the little dog did.)

The stone rolled away.

> (Tells us what happened to the stone.)

The plot thickened.

> (. . . or to the plot.)

The funny little man split into a thousand pieces.

> (. . . or to the funny little man.)

In intransitive sentences, the subject is sometimes the actor (the one who laughs, say), sometimes the patient (the one that rolls or splits), and sometimes merely the neutral receptacle for some predicated property (color, existence, etc.) Sometimes the subject is part actor and part patient, both inititiating action and undergoing its effects. Contrast:

The bird flew out the window.

> (Subject is both agent and patient.)

The Frisbee flew out the window.

> (Subject is patient only.)

or:

The child skipped.

The record skipped.

Thus a noun in *S* function can have one or more of a variety of roles in the event or action depicted in a sentence.

In a transitive sentence, on the other hand, there are typically two major noun phrases. The subject (function *A*) is usually an actor who does something; the object (function *O*) is the thing to which something is done, the patient.

The cat put the rat on the mat.

> (Tells us what the cat did to the rat.)

The funny little man split the queen into a thousand pieces.

> (Tells us how Rumplestiltskin repaid his tormentor.)

In most cases the actor will be animate, capable of independent initiative. The sentence will emphasize the actor's operation on the patient, whose own potential activity (if any) is thus deemphasized. (The rat isn't just *on* the mat; the cat put it there. She didn't just split; he split her.) Of course, not all transitive sentences, at least in English, fit this pattern, but this is the *typical* form of a transitive sentence.

The entities of the world thus fall into two natural categories. Some things—inanimate objects, stones, trees, food, etc.—are natural patients or objects, often acted upon but infrequently themselves actors. Other things—typically human beings, but also animals (occasionally machines, etc.)—are likely potential actors, capable of initiating and carrying out operations on other things.

For nouns that denote things in the first category, the absolutive/ergative patterning has a certain naturalness. Consider the following sentences:

The tree fell.

I felled the tree.

In both sentences more or less the same thing happens to the tree: it falls. In the first "tree" is the subject of the intransitive verb "fall"; in the second it is the object of the transitive verb "fell." The word *yugu* "tree" has the same absolute form in both the corresponding Guugu Yimidhirr sentences:

Yugu buli.

Ngayu yugu bandi.

   bandil   chop, fell

Many languages have verb pairs, like "fall" and "fell," that hold constant the relationship of the intransitive subject and the transitive object. Think of such English verbs as "roll" (intransitive) and "roll" (transitive—i.e., "cause to roll, set rolling"), "open" ("come to be open") and "open" ("cause to be open"), or even "die" and "kill." (Can you think of other such verb pairs? Can you think of any intransitive/transitive pairs that do *not* hold constant the relationship between *S* and *O* functions? See Chapter II for a discussion of this aspect of the grammar of Maninka verbs.) Guugu Yimidhirr also has a productive system of deriving from intransitive verbs corresponding "causative" transitive verbs, meaning "cause to X" where X is the intransitive verb.

Yugu buli.

   The tree fell.

Ngayu yugu bulii-mani.

   I made the tree fall.

Nambal duday.

   The rock rolled away.

Yarrga-ngun nambal dudaay-mani.

   The boy rolled the rock away.

   nambal   rock (also means "money")
   dudaa   run, roll

Nouns that denote inanimate, concrete things are natural subjects for the intransitive members of such verb pairs (which mean "something happened to ____") and similarly are natural objects for the corresponding transitive verbs (which mean "____ caused something to happen to ____").

Nouns that denote these "natural patients" *can* be subjects of transitive verbs as well. (That is, inanimate things can cause other things to happen, although they cannot properly be said to "act"). But it is precisely to such nouns that the special ergative ending attaches, in the *A* function.

Yugu-ngun bayan dumbi.

> The tree crushed the house (i.e., by falling on it).

Galga-ngun nganhi daamay.

> The spear speared me (i.e., it was thrown at me).

The unsuffixed absolutive form of such nouns thus coincides with their normal patient or object status (in functions *S* and *O*); the ergative form marks the atypical situations in which such nouns are in the *A* function.

On the other hand, the nominative/accusative pattern of case marking seems especially appropriate for first- and second-person pronouns. These words denote entities that clearly belong to the class of potential or likely actors: the people actually present, taking part in a conversation. Speaker and hearer are certainly *qualified* actors (being human, conscious, and active), whose own doings are salient topics for speech.

Ngayu buli.

> I fell down.

Nyundu duday.

> You ran away.

Ngali mayi budal.

> We two will eat food.

> > *budal*   eat

Personal pronouns in Guugu Yimidhirr exhibit normal nominative form when they act as subjects, in both *S* and *A* functions. It is on those occasions when they are robbed of activity—when they are the patients of the actions of others—that special accusative forms appear.

Nganhi daamay.
> Somebody speared me.

Dyaarba-ngun nhina dudaay-mani.

> The snake chased you (i.e., made you run).

> > *dyaarba*   snake

It is thus the expected, normal situation when a pronoun is in the *A* function and an inanimate thing is in the *O* function.

Ngayu galga dumbi.

> I broke the spear.

In such a case the pronoun is nominative and the noun is in absolute form. A reversal of the expected roles (when the inanimate thing acts on me) engenders special forms of both pronoun and noun.

>*Galga-ngun nganhi daamay.*
>>The spear speared me.

What becomes of nouns that denote likely or potential actors: nouns for humans, or for animals? As nouns, such words in Guugu Yimidhirr receive ergative/absolutive case marking. But it is these nouns that typically occur *together with* third-person pronouns, inflected on the nominative/accusative pattern. Let's look more closely at this situation.

We have already seen sentences in which a noun and a pronoun occur together.

>*Nyulu Billy ganaa.*
>>Billy is OK. (lit., He Billy is OK.)

The subject of this intransitive sentence is *Billy*, a proper noun. The pronoun *nyulu* adjoined to it is seemingly redundant, although we have seen that it shows that Billy is an animate being (since the pronoun *nyulu* cannot stand for an inanimate noun.)

In fact, Guugu Yimidhirr as a rule adjoins a third-person pronoun to an animate (especially a human) noun in S, O, or A function. This is especially likely to happen in a sentence that introduces the noun as a new topic of conversation—when it initiates a discourse in which the noun figures prominently.

>*Nyulu Billy-ngun nganhi dhuurngay.*
>>Billy pushed me.

>*Nyulu Billy gaday.*
>>Billy came.

>*Ngayu nhangu Billy gunday.*
>>I hit Billy.

(Each of these sentences gives special prominence to the noun phrase represented by *Billy* plus the adjoined pronoun.) In other words, in the case of a human noun, *both* the ergative/absolutive noun pattern and the nominative/accusative pronoun pattern co-occur, and they unambiguously distinguish between the three possible sentence functions. Table 4.6 presents these three functions diagrammatically.

Here we see the motivation behind the fact that only animate, and usually only human, nouns can be replaced by third-person pronouns.

TABLE 4.6 *Animate Noun with Adjoined Third-Person Pronoun*

"Billy" as:

A—Transitive subject	"Billy pushed me."	Nyulu	Billy-ngun (ergative)	nganhi dhuurrngay.
S—Intransitive subject	"Billy came."	Nyulu (nominative)	Billy	gaday.
O—Transitive object	"I hit Billy."	Ngayu nhangu (accusative)	Billy (absolutive)	gunday.

pronoun   "Billy" noun

These are exactly the nouns that denote members of the category of potential actors. It is, therefore, not surprising that these are also the nouns that can occur together with (or be replaced by) personal pronouns, which as we have seen are inflected on a pattern appropriate to potential actors. As we might predict, inanimate nouns do not allow the adjoined third-person pronoun in either subject or object position.

Yugu-ngun nganhi gunday.
>The stick hit me.
>(Not: **Nyulu yugu-ngun . . .*, if *nyulu* is to refer to the stick.)

Ngayu galga dumbi.
>I broke the spear.
>(Not: **Ngayu nhangu galga . . .*, if *nhangu* is to refer to *galga*.)

When a pronoun does appear in a sentence, we know that it must refer to something animate, probably a person, and not to an inanimate object.

Ngayu Billy nhaadhi, nhangu gunday.
>I saw Billy and I hit **him**.

(Notice how the two parts of this sentence are chained together so that the noun object of the first clause appears in the second clause as an accusative pronoun. And notice further that the subject is not repeated in the second clause.) But:

Ngayu yugu nhaadhi, nhangu gunday.

cannot mean "I saw a stick, and I hit *it* (the stick)." (Why not?) Instead it must mean "I saw a stick, and I hit *him* (i.e., someone already mentioned)."

In much the same way, a sentence like:

Nyulu galga-ngun nganhi daamay.

cannot mean "The spear (lit: it the spear) speared me" because *nyulu* cannot refer to the spear. Instead, *nyulu* must refer to some person (whose identity is understood from what has gone before in the conversation). In this case, the ergative ending on *galga* signifies not the transitive subject, actor, or first cause, but rather the *instrument* by which the action was carried out. Thus, the sentence means:

He speared me *with a spear.*

In such a sentence the ergative suffix is doing a different (though clearly related) sort of job in the sentence, still marking something instrumental in bringing the action about, but not marking the active agent.

As a result, a single sentence can have two noun phrases with ergative marking, one for the agent and the other for the instrument.

[*Nyulu Billy-ngun*]   [*yugu-ngun*]   *nganhi*   *gunday.*
Agent   Instrument   Object   Verb
        Billy hit me with a stick.

3.4 Animate and Inanimate Nouns, Alienable and Inalienable Possession

The contrast between animate and inanimate nouns thus affects both the interpretation of an ergative suffix (animate nouns are generally interpreted as actors and inanimate nouns as instruments, if they have ergative endings), and the possibilities of pronominalization (animate nouns can be replaced by or adjoined to third-person pronouns, but inanimate nouns cannot). In fact, the distinction between animate and inanimate nouns figures in other areas of the language as well, and it intersects with a difference between two kinds of possession. We have seen that dative forms of nouns and pronouns express ordinary possession.

Yiyi ngadhu yarraman.
        This is my horse.

Yiyi yarrga-wi galga.
        This is the boy's spear.

Ordinary possession is a transitory, often socially constituted, relationship between a thing and a person or being that has control over it (rights to its use, its disposal, etc.). Several features characterize ordinary possession: first, generally only human beings (and very occasionally animals) are able to exercise this sort of control over their possessions. (In our society it is also possible to talk, in an extended sense, of institutions possessing things: "the Chase Manhattan Bank's oilfields," "the Army's stock of antipersonnel weapons," etc. In English there are also certain abstract nouns that both inanimate and animate things can "possess"; for example, we can say both "the villain's demise" and "the forest's destruction.") But a rock cannot have a house in the same sense that, say, a man can (although, of course, there can be a house *for* a rock). In a similar way, I cannot give food to a tree in the same sense that I can give food to a child (to have, to eat, etc.) Only potential recipients can be ordinary possessors; that is, precisely those nouns that allow adjoined pronouns in Guugu Yimidhirr (nouns denoting humans or other animate beings) are potential indirect objects or possessors. Only these nouns can take the dative ending *-bi/-wi* in this possessive sense.

There is, of course, another sort of possession in regard to which things as well as people can be possessors. This is the relationship between a thing and its parts. We can talk about "the man's foot" and "the foot of the mountain"; or "the back of the man" and "the back of the house." Such a part-whole relationship is often called "inalienable possession," since a part cannot be separated from its whole in the same way that an ordinary possession can be separated from its owner.

In English, possession can be represented by at least two different constructions:

X's Y

and:

Y of X

Thus, we have:

the parson's bulletproof vest

and:

the bulletproof vest of the parson

In many cases, the choice between one construction or the other seems more or less indifferent:

the house's hilltop location
    the location of the house on a hilltop
a woman's position in her family
    the position of a woman in her family
the car's acceleration
    the acceleration of the car

When we talk about parts, however, there seems to be a difference between animate and inanimate possessors. Thus we can say "the man's head" but not "*the line's head" (rather: "the head of the line"), or "the horse's mouth" but not "*the cave's mouth." In fact, inanimate nouns often allow an entirely different construction to express the part/whole relationship.

*the refrigerator's door (questionable)

the door of the refrigerator (correct, but somewhat awkward)

the refrigerator door

In the last example, whole and part are simply put together with no overt mark of the possessive. This structure is frequently, but by no means always, successful;

the top of the tree
the tree top
the foot of the tree
*the tree foot.

Here, then, English distinguishes, within the category of inalienable possession, between animate and inanimate nouns, with animate nouns using the X's Y or Y of X constructions, and with inanimate nouns using only the Y of X or the more restricted X Y constructions.

Another interesting, if less conspicuous, reflex of the interrelated distinctions of animate/inanimate and alienable/inalienable possession in English appears in sentences like:

I patted George on the head.

which seems a somewhat more natural way of saying:

I patted George's head.

(This latter sentence seems, somewhat oddly, to suggest that I could pat George's head without patting him in the bargain.) But the sentence:

I patted George's watch.

is not equivalent to the very dubious sentence:

?I patted George on the watch.

Seemingly only parts (of the body, of some larger whole) allow a construction like:

Verb X *in/on the* Y

where X is the whole and Y is the part. Such an expression will be equivalent to one of the form:

Verb X's Y

when what happens to the part also happens, in some sense, to the whole. Thus, the verb in question affects the possibility of the *in the/on the* formulation. For example, we can say:

I ran over George's big toe.

but:

?I ran over George on/in the big toe.

seems doubtful, because, though I may have run over his *toe*, I didn't actually run *him* over. But the fact that the whole as well as the part must be affected by the action seems to disallow this sort of construction with inanimate entities and their parts. So, for example, though one can say:

I dented the door of the car.

and, although when I dent the door I at the same time dent the car, it does not seem possible to say:

?I dented the car in/on the door.

Although the details are complex, in English, the division between animate and inanimate possessors crosscuts the division between alienable and inalienable possession, with varying constructional possibilities for each case.

The same distinctions operate in Guugu Yimidhirr, although the syntactic realization of the facts is somewhat different. First, as we have seen, inanimate nouns cannot be recipients (indirect objects) and therefore are not possessors in the ordinary sense, with the *-bi/-wi* suffix. In Guugu Yimidhirr inalienable possession requires no special case marking, nothing that corresponds to the dative marking of ordinary possession. The part and the 'possessor' merely appear together as a compound noun phrase, both nouns in the case appropriate to the function of the entire phrase in the sentence. (Recall the English example "the refrigerator door.") This construction is possible with inanimate nouns:

Yugu ngarraa munhi.

The tree('s) bark is black. (lit.: tree skin black)

ngarraa skin
munhi black

And it works equally well with animate nouns:

>   (*Nyulu*) *yarrga mangal munhi.*
>
>>   The boy's hand is black. (lit.: he boy hand black)
>
>>   *mangal*   hand

In this sentence both *yarrga* and *mangal* appear in unmarked absolutive form. Contrast this sentence with another that displays ordinary possession, with a dative case ending:

>   (*Nhangu*) *yarrga-wi bayan munhi.*
>
>>   The boy's house is black.

(What accounts for the difference between *nyulu* in the first sentence and *nhangu* in the second?) Similarly, if a body part is the object of a transitive verb, both part and possessor appear in the case appropriate to an object.

>   *Nyundu yarrga dhamal wagi.*
>
>>   You cut the boy's foot.
>
>   *Nyundu nganhi dhamal wagi.*
>
>>   You cut my foot.
>
>>   *dhamal*   foot
>>   *wagil*   cut

(What is the case of *nganhi* and why?) Contrast these sentences with the following:

>   *Nyundu yarrga-wi ngamu nhaadhi.*
>
>>   You saw the boy's mother.
>
>   *Nyundu ngadhu ngamu nhaadhi.*
>
>>   You saw my mother.
>
>>   *ngamu*   mother

We see that Guugu Yimidhirr uses the *-bi/-wi* suffix, with animate possessors, for ordinary possession. For both animate and inanimate nouns Guugu Yimidhirr represents the part/whole relationship by simply putting whole and part together, in the form [X Y] (plus case). The situation is diagrammed in Table 4.7.

Can you now translate the following sentences? (Check in the

TABLE 4.7 *Possession in Guugu Yimidhirr*

	Animate nouns	Inanimate nouns
Ordinary possession	*X -bi/-wi Y* *yarrga-wi ngamu* the boy's mother	
Inalienable possession	*XY* *yarrga mangal* the boy's hand	*XY* *yugu ngarraa* the tree('s) bark

glossary at the end of the chapter for words you do not recognize or whose meanings you don't remember.)

Nyulu gabiirr-ngun yarrga-wi ngamu mangal wagi.

Ngayu nhanu biiba dhamal daamay.

Nyulu nhina dhamal galga-ngun daamay.

When a body part is called upon to act as the subject of a transitive verb, both part and possessor receive the case appropriate to sentence function *A* (ergative for nouns, nominative for pronouns), hence;

Nyulu yarrga-ngun mangaal-ngun nganhi gunday.
>The boy's hand hit me. (i.e., the boy hit me with his hand.)

(Notice the two different interpretations of the *-ngun* suffix.)

Ngayu nhina dhuurrngay dhamaal-ngun.
>I pushed you with my foot.

The same sort of thing happens when a body part is the object of a transitive verb.

Nyundu nganhi dhamal wagi.
>You cut my foot.

Here *dhamal* is in absolute form, appropriate to a noun in *O* function; and *nganhi* is the appropriate accusative object form of the first-person pronoun.

3.5 Further Elaborations of the Case System

Guugu Yimidhirr performs rather complex work with case endings, not simply distinguishing the syntactic functions of *S*, *A*, and *O*. We have already seen that the ergative suffix *-ngun* can signify either actor or instrument, depending on the noun in question. There are also different ergative endings that suggest action remote in time. Instead of simply:

> *Nyulu gabiirr-ngun nganhi wagi nambaal-ngun.*
> The girl cut me with a rock.

one can say:

> *Nyulu gabiirr-nda nganhi wagi nambaal-nda.*
> The girl cut me with a rock some time ago.

using the "remote" ergative suffix *-nda*. Guugu Yimidhirr thus accomplishes with case endings what English expresses with an adverbial expression or a special verb tense.

Let's consider the nuances of meaning connected with the Guugu Yimidhirr dative case. We have seen that an inanimate thing cannot be, in any ordinary sense, a possessor. Nor can it be a beneficiary, an indirect object. Instead, the *-bi/-wi* ending attached to inanimate nouns has a locational sense, encompassing both motion towards an object and rest when it reaches it.

> *Ngayu dhaday nambaal-bi.*
> I went to the rock.

> *Ngayu mayi maandi nambaal-bi.*
> I took food to (i.e., up to) the rock.

> *Ngayu dagaadhi nambaal-bi.*
> I sat on the rock.

> > *dagaadhi*   sat

The inanimate counterpart to an animate indirect object is thus seen to be a location instead of a beneficiary. Whether motion or rest is involved depends largely on the verb in question.

> *Ngamu ngadhu bayan-bi nhin-gaalnggal.*
> My mother is sitting in/at the house.

Ngamu ngadhu bayan-bi dhadaara.

> My mother is going to the house.

> *nhin-gal*   sit, be located

We can provisionally represent the noun cases we have met. (See Table 4.8.)

A separate ending *-nganh* indicates motion away from a place. (This is called the "ablative" case.)

Ngayu ngulgu gaday yuwaal-nganh.

> Yesterday I came from the beach.

Ngadhu ngamu dhaday bayan-nganh.

> My mother went from the house.

Nyulu yarrga-ngun galga nangguurr-nganh maandi.

> The boy took the spear from the camp.

> *ngulgu*   yesterday
> *gadaa*   come
> *yuwaal*   beach
> *nanggurr*   camp

The ablative case also has a related temporal and causal sense (shared, incidentally, by the English preposition "from").

Ngayu mayi-nganh nangguurr-bi dhadaa.

> I will go to camp after eating. (lit.: from food. Compare: This office will be closed from Friday.)

TABLE 4.8 *Guugu Yimidhirr Cases—1*

Case	Ending	Meaning with animate nouns	Meaning with inanimate nouns
Absolutive	zero ending	S, or O	S, or O
Ergative	*-ngun*; *-nda* (remote)	A	A or Instrument
Dative	*-bi/-wi*	Indirect object, possessor	Location, motion towards

Nyulu biini muganh-nganh.

> He died from the cold.

> *muganh*   cold

It is clear that the two meanings of the *-bi/-wi* suffix divide along the same lines that distinguish the agent and instrument interpretations of the ergative suffix. Just as an inanimate noun cannot in any ordinary sense be a possessor, a human being is not normally a location. We can see this most clearly with personal pronouns. It is at least odd to say:

> ?George is at me.

and there seems to be a difference between the sort of motion/location expressed in:

> George came to the house.

and

> George came to me.

—at least if by "me" one means my person and not just, say, my body.

English seems to make a related distinction between animate and inanimate destinations (or "end points for motion"). All of the following sentences are possible:

> I sent the package to John.
> I sent the package to England.
> I brought the food to Mary.
> I brought the food to the picnic.

Both animate and inanimate destinations here seem to be treated in the same way. The verbs *bring* and *send* allow another word order, but only when the "destination" is animate:

> I sent John the package.
> *I sent England the package.
> I brought Mary the food.
> *I brought the picnic the food.

When we talk of sending a package to John or bringing food to Mary, neither John nor Mary is simply a place; instead we understand them to be *recipients.* Inanimate places or events cannot usually be recipients in the same sense, and they cannot then immediately follow verbs like *bring* and *send* as destinations. In a sentence like:

James Bond sent London a cable.

the word *London* stands for a good deal more than an inanimate location. And consider what makes a sentence like:

The President sent China thirty tons of surplus wheat.

more acceptable than one like:

*The university sent the top of Mt. Everest an expedition.

In Guugu Yimidhirr dative inflection can only be used with animate nouns to represent situations in which they are not merely destinations, but are directly affected by the actions involved, usually as recipients.

Guugu Yimidhirr uses an entirely different case, called 'adessive', to signify being in or coming into the conscious presence of an animate being. The case ending is *-gal.*

> *George ngadhun-gal nhin-gaalnggal.*
>
>> George is staying (lit.: sitting) with me. (i.e., in my company, under my care.)
>
> *George ngaliin-gal gaday.*
>
>> George came to (stay with, see) us two.

With verbs of speaking, the *-gal* suffix marks the person with whom one talks.

> *Nyulu ngadhun-gal yirrgaalga.*
>
>> He is talking to me.
>
>> *yirrgaa*   talk, speak

Similarly, leaving someone's presence is rendered by the 'abessive' suffix *-ga.*

> *George nhangun-ga gaday.*
>
>> George came from (e.g., visiting) him.

(These pronominal forms are based on the dative pronoun, plus *-n-* for all singular pronouns, plus the appropriate case ending.)

Motion away from a place is marked with the ablative case, and motion away from a person is marked with the abessive case in a combined sentence like the following:

Nyulu duday dhanaan-ga nangguurr-nganh.

He ran away from them, from the camp.

The *-ga* suffix also represents the reverse of the dative. Where the dative marks the beneficiary, recipient, or possessor, the abessive marks the origin, source, or former possessor of an object.

Ngayu yarraman biibaa-ga maani.

I took the horse from (my) father.

This sense extends even to inanimate nouns. Compare:

Nyulu yugu yalmba-nganh maani.

He took the tree from the sand hill. (i.e., he chopped it there and brought it away.)

Nyulu yugu yalmbaa-ga maani.

He took a tree of the sand hill. (i.e., a tree of the type that comes from the sand hill.)

yalmba   sand hill

(You will see that the suffix *-nganh* does not cause words that end in a vowel to lengthen, although the suffix *-ga* does. Several other case suffixes cause both vowel- and consonant-final words to lengthen.)

Table 4.9 summarizes these interrelated case usages. With these four cases an animate noun represents a possessor or a conscious presence; an inanimate noun represents a location.

Three final examples will demonstrate the range and power of the Guugu Yimidhirr case system. There is a suffix *-ngu* that can express the goal or purpose of an action or the intended function for an object.

Ngayu gaday mayii-ngu.

I came for food.

Nyulu bayan balgay gudaa-ngu.

He made a house for the dog.

Yiyi galga guudyuu-ngu.

This is a spear for fish.

balgal   make, do, wash
guudyu   fish

TABLE 4.9   *Locational Cases in Guugu Yimidhirr*

Case	Suffix	Meaning with animate nouns	Meaning with inanimate nouns
Dative	*-bi/-wi*	possessor, beneficiary	location, motion towards
Ablative	*-nganh*	from possession of	motion away from
Adessive	*-gal*	in or into presence of	—
Abessive	*-ga*	from presence or possession of	from place of origin

This 'purposive' case also allows a Guugu Yimidhirr speaker to incorporate into a sentence a noun that is not, syntactically, subject or object, but that is involved in some way in the action or event depicted.

Nyulu wanggaar nhin-gaalnggal ngaliin-ngu.

> He is waiting for us outside. (lit.: he above is sitting for us.)

> *wanggaar*   above

This device occurs particularly frequently when an idea that we might express in English with a transitive verb is rendered in Guugu Yimidhirr by an adjective or other intransitive construction that does not admit a direct object. For example, instead of using a transitive verb like "fear," Guugu Yimidhirr uses the adjective *yinil* "fearful, afraid," with the object that inspires fear marked by *-ngu*.

Nyulu Billy yinil dyaarbaa-ngu.

> Billy is afraid of snakes.

In much the same way Guugu Yimidhirr expresses desire by means of the word *wawu* "soul, breath, insides" plus the derivational formative *-dhirr* (which means "with"). The object of one's desire carries the purposive ending.

Ngayu wawu-dhirr mayii-ngu.

> I want food. (lit.: I am with-soul for-food.)

TABLE 4.10 *Composite View of Guugu Yimidhirr Cases*

				Meaning	
Case	Personal pronoun form	Noun suffix		animate referents	inanimate referents
Nominative	*ngayu, nyundu, nyulu,* etc.	—		S, A (personal pronouns only)	—
Accusative	*nganhi, nhina, nhangu,* etc.	—		O (personal pronouns only)	—
Absolutive	—	zero		S, O (nouns but not pronouns)	S, O
Ergative	—	*-ngun/ -nda* (remote)		A (nouns, but not pronouns)	A, Instrument

I—syntactic cases

Group	Case				
II—locational cases	Dative	ngadhu, nhanu, nhangu, etc.	-bil-wi	possessor, beneficiary	location, motion towards
	Ablative	Dative form + -nganh	-nganh	from possession of	motion away from
	Adessive	Dative form + -gal	-gal	in or into presence of	—
	Abessive	Dative form + -ga	-ga	from possession or presence of	from place of origin
III—additional cases	Purposive	Dative form + -ngu	-ngu	goal, purpose, intended effect	
	Comitative	—	-dhirr	accompaniment	
	Privative	—	-mul	lack	

The ending *-dhirr* transforms a noun into an adjectivelike word that means "with _____" or "having _____". Thus one can say:

Ngayu gambuul-dhirr.

> I'm full, satisfied. (lit.: I am with stomach. This can also mean "pregnant.")

> *gambul*   stomach

Here are some further examples:

Ngadhu dhawuunh gaday yarraman-dhirr.

> My friend came by horse.

Ngayu dingga-dhirr.

> I'm hungry.

(In modern Guugu Yimidhirr there is no word **dingga* for "hunger" and only the compound exists.) This 'comitative' suffix is, in fact, part of the name Guugu Yimidhirr. *Guugu* means "word" or "language." *Yimidhirr* comes from the demonstrative root *yi* (which occurs in some forms as *yim-* or *yimi-*) and means literally "this-with": that is, "this way, in this way." Hence, Guugu Yimidhirr means "speaking this way" or "this kind of talk"—a literally descriptive label for the language.

Complementing the comitative suffix *-dhirr* is a 'privative' suffix *-mul* that means "without."

Nyundu wawu-dhirr buurraay-ngu?

> Do you want water?

Ngayu wawu-mul.

> I don't want (any).

Or consider the following short conversation. (Can you understand it?)

Ngayu dingga-dhirr. Ngayu wawu-dhirr mayii-ngu.

> Ngadhu mayi guya. Ngayu mayi-mul.

Ma, ngali dhadaa bayan-bi mayii-ngu.

Personal pronouns occur with locational and purposive cases as well. Pronouns use the same suffixes as nouns, attached to the dative form of the pronoun (with an added *-n* on singular pronouns). For example, the dative form of *ngayu* "I" is *ngadhu*. One says:

Nyulu ngadhu-n-gal dhadaa.

He's going to (be with) me.

Billy ngadhu-n-ga gaday.

Billy came from (being with) me.

(What are the cases involved here?)

We can summarize the Guugu Yimidhirr cases we have met in a single composite chart. The first four cases in Table 4.10 interact to delimit the syntactic functions of nouns and pronouns as subjects and objects. Cases of the second group elaborate on further entities involved in the action or event depicted in a sentence—providing locational and dative complements or introducing auxiliary personnel. These cases also maintain a systematic distinction between animate and inanimate things, with distinct meanings when applied to nouns from different categories. The last cases further expand the expressive potential of simple noun endings—introducing goals, purposes, and accompaniments to action by simple morphological mechanisms. Hopefully even this much abbreviated treatment conveys a picture of the richness of the system.

4   THE SOCIAL CONTEXT OF SPEECH IN TRADITIONAL GUUGU YIMIDHIRR SOCIETY

The common Western theory of language, in a tradition that derives from Aristotle, holds preeminent a language's logical structure: its capacity for conveying information or expressing propositions. However, when Aboriginal Australians theorize and talk about language, they concentrate on its social aspects. Language does not exist and utterances do not occur in a social vacuum. Speech between two people both expresses and helps to maintain the relationship between them. In Guugu Yimidhirr words are not simply linguistic units. They belong to people (their rightful users), and they have striking social properties, rendering them appropriate or inappropriate to different circumstances. Moreover, the way one Guugu Yimidhirr speaker chooses to speak to another creates in large part the relationship they establish. The relationship, once set up, itself has consequences for future linguistic interaction.

Both aspects of language—its systematic and logical properties on the one hand and its social applications on the other—feed one another. For to use language for social ends, speakers must master its grammar: Guugu Yimidhirr speakers, whether speaking in ordinary language or in the respectful language, which we shall examine in this section, must employ the system of case marking, along with all the other syntactic devices of the language. (Although the respectful style uses special words, it combines these words with the same case suffixes that we have learned.) At the same time, the conditions under which a language is spoken and the uses to which it is put in turn motivate the form it takes—a tool reflects its tasks. The Guugu Yimidhirr respectful style makes do with a very small number of distinct roots; it therefore pushes a formal mechanism like the case system to its expressive limits—to construct specific messages from restricted lexical raw material.

Here are two examples that anticipate later discussion. In everyday Guugu Yimidhirr, the noun *ganggal* means "child," and the adjective *muli* means "barren, infertile." But in respectful speech neither word may be used; *ganggal* has the respectful equivalent *duula* "child." But there is no single respectful word equivalent for *muli*. Instead, to convey the same idea in respectful speech, a Guugu Yimidhirr speaker says *duula-mul.* (Recall that *-mul* is the privative case suffix. What is the literal meaning of this expression?) In a similar way, there is no respectful word for *nambi* "grave, casket." To express this idea to a tabooed relative, one must use two respectful words together with the *-bi/-wi* suffix:

wuurrii   ground, earth (equivalent to the everyday word *bubu*)

dhuwun   below (equivalent to the everyday word *bada*)

wuurrii-wi dhuwun   grave (lit.: under the earth, equivalent to the everyday word *nambi*)

Throughout Aboriginal Australia words are endowed with a special potency. In most areas a name becomes taboo when its bearer dies; often the prohibition extends to other words that sound like the names of the deceased. Frequently, when an ordinary word must be dropped from speech, people borrow the equivalent word from a neighboring dialect or language—a practice that accounts in part for the relatively large amount of shared vocabulary between Australian languages. A person's everyday vocabulary thus becomes a repository of social history, carrying the imprint of recent deaths.

Special language also frequently marks ritual. Kenneth Hale describes an "upside down" version of the Aboriginal language Walbiri, used during male initiation, in which words are replaced by their opposites—one says "It's hot" to mean "It's cold." Special occasions engender special kinds of talk.[10]

So too do special people: among many Aboriginal groups special "mother-in-law" languages are used in conversation between kinsmen

---

[10]An article by Hale describing an Australian initiation language is found in Steinberg and Jakobovits, eds., 1971. See "Suggestions for Further Reading" at the end of the chapter for full reference.

who are taboo to each other and who must avoid and treat each other with special respect and care. Typically, throughout Aboriginal Australia a man was obliged to behave with extreme deference to his wife's mother or simply to avoid contact with her altogether. The mother-in-law was, then, the prototypical person to inspire the use of special avoidance language. The lexicon of respect in Guugu Yimidhirr might be called a "brother-in-law" language, because traditionally among the Guugu Yimidhirr–speaking people a man was not allowed to speak *at all* to his mother-in-law. He used the special language with brothers-in-law, with father-in-law, and with certain other kin. (It does not seem to have been necessary for a woman to use the special language with her in-laws, although she showed deference to her father-in-law. That a woman could be freer with her in-laws than could a man with his perhaps reflects the fact that a woman, on marriage, entered into close contact with her husband's family; whereas a man, after marriage, could to a greater extent avoid his wife's relatives. It may be, too, that women did not in general employ the special vocabulary, much as elsewhere in Australia women were denied access to special ritual language and knowledge.)

It may seem bizarre to have to use special words with specific kinsmen, but there are less exotic parallels in our own experience. Frequently we have to rephrase our thoughts, substituting one expression (or even a gesture) for another to avoid offending people within earshot.

> Where have you been?
> I went outside to take a . . . uh, to relieve myself.

> I saw Dick and Jane in the bushes.
> What were they doing?
> (Gesture) . . .

And although we may find it hard to imagine spearing a man for speaking impolitely around his mother-in-law, it would be perfectly imaginable, if somewhat foolish, even in our own society, for a gentleman to offer to defend his lady's sensibilities from the unrepeatable remarks of some ill-mannered oaf. Even a hardened seaman may well blush with sincere shame or embarrassment when his ordinary turn of phrase accidentally reaches his mother's loving ears. Proverbs notwithstanding, words *can* harm. They certainly arouse powerful emotions and can move people to action. ("Them's fighting words, pardner!")

Guugu Yimidhirr speakers tailor talk to circumstances. Thus an important feature of a Guugu Yimidhirr word, whatever its meaning or grammatical properties, is its compatibility with particular social situations and its appropriateness for conversation with particular people.

FIGURE 4.3   Relaxed Amicability

A gami *(grandfather) and his* gaminhdharr *(classificatory grandchild)
together scrape the roots of an ironbark tree, the first step in preparing tar
for making spears. The two men enjoy a close, relaxed relationship, with no
restrictions on physical proximity, face-to-face interaction, joking, or
obscene language.*

But speech does not merely fit the social situation in which it occurs.
The character of talk between two individuals symbolizes their whole
relationship. With his mother-in-law a Guugu Yimidhirr man is *guugu-
mul* "without words, speechless"—a diagnostic symptom of the restraint
and avoidance that characterizes all his dealings with her. On the other
hand, between two men who stand in the relationship of grandfather to
grandson there are unrestrained, often ribald relations; accordingly, their
talk together is typically a kind of obscene verbal joking called *guya-
gurral* (literally, "saying nothing," i.e., "speaking nonsense.")

In this section we shall be concerned first with the partitioning of the
traditional Guugu Yimidhirr social universe; second, with the elaborations of Guugu Yimidhirr vocabulary that create a special vocabulary of
respect; and finally, with the correspondences between social relationships and kinds of speech.

4.1 Kinship and Geography

The Guugu Yimidhirr social universe is composed entirely of kin. Like many people throughout the world who live in limited, relatively small groups, Guugu Yimidhirr speakers apply classificatory principles to extend kinship to everyone with whom they come into contact. One's family, of course, can be reckoned so as to extend a long way—from remote cousins and great-uncles, to half-kin and step-kin. In the Cape York Peninsula people employ a further classificatory device: every individual belongs to one of two great groups, or *moieties*, each of which has a representative animal as its symbol (its 'totem'). One moiety has *waandaar* "white cockatoo," the other *ngurraar* "black cockatoo." One moiety is my own and my father's; the other belongs to my mother and her brothers and sisters. In my moiety are also my siblings. In the other moiety I find my wife or husband. And so on. Moiety membership is a feature that goes well beyond tribal or lingistic boundaries, so that a person from a distant area, whose language one cannot understand, nonetheless has a moiety affiliation. Through such affiliation it is possible to assign a stranger to a likely and appropriate kin category. If I am from white-cockatoo moiety and you are someone about my age from the same moiety, even if we are strangers, we may agree to call one another "brother" or "sister."

The system of moieties generalizes on local genealogical relationships to categorize every member of the social world. It divides the world into two sorts of people: members of "my moiety" and members of "their moiety." If we distinguish further between generations (starting with one's grandparents' generation and going to one's grandchildren's generation—a total of five generations including one's own), and between men and women, we will have a system that divides the whole society into twenty discrete categories, as shown in Table 4.11. For example, in the box marked X go men of my moiety of my parents' generation. (This category includes my own father.) A person in the category marked Y is a woman of the other moiety of my parents' generation. (My closest relative in this category would be my own mother.)

The Guugu Yimidhirr system of labelling relatives makes many more discriminations than does this simple chart, and it also omits distinctions that appear here. For example, in Guugu Yimidhirr there is only a single term for both males and females of the +2 generation at the upper left of the chart: *gami*. This term corresponds to the category of "same moiety person of grandparents' generation." It is the term one would apply to, among others, one's father's father. (Can you imagine a woman to whom the term might also apply?) And, within the category of zero-generation males of my own moiety, Guugu Yimidhirr distinguishes *yaba* "older brother" from *garga* "younger brother." Table 4.12 schematizes, in

TABLE 4.11   *Moiety Categorization*

	My moiety		Their moiety	
	Male	Female	Male	Female
+2 gen.				
+1 gen.	X			Y
0 gen.				
−1 gen.				
−2 gen.				

highly simplified form, part of the Guugu Yimidhirr kinship terminology as seen from a man's perspective. (An important difference in the kin terms used by men and women is this: a man calls his own children *yumurr*, but a woman calls her son *dyuway* and her daughter *nguudhurr*. This is because a man's children belong to his own moiety, but a woman's children belong to the opposite moiety, that of her husband.)

Where a single box in Table 4.12 has two entries there is a

TABLE 4.12   *Simplified Partial Guugu Yimidhirr Kinship Terminology*

	My moiety		Their moiety	
	M	F	M	F
+2	gami		ngadhi	babi
+1	mugagay biiba	biimuur	mugur	ngamu
0	yaba garga	gaanhaal dyin-gurr	gaanyil, dunhu, etc.	dyiiral
−1	yumurr		dyuway	nguudhurr
−2	gaminhdharr		ngadhinil	

Note: Shaded kin categories are potential in-laws, people who might become a man's *dhabul* relatives.

distinction of relative age (e.g., older/younger brother; older/younger sister.) I call my father and his younger brothers *biiba*, but there is a different term, *mugagay*, reserved for my father's oldest brother. Each term has a genealogical meaning; for example, *biimuur* means "father's younger sister" (a Guugu Yimidhirr speaker might give "auntie" as an English equivalent). But by a classificatory extension, the term is also appropriate for an unrelated woman of my own moiety of the appropriate age, just as *biiba* may be applied to other men of the same moiety and generation as my own father.

A Guugu Yimidhirr man traditionally was supposed to marry a woman from the opposite moiety. One's *biiba* "father" married one's *ngamu* "mother" from the other side. Similarly, a *mugur* marries a *biimuur*; their daughter will be a woman in the category of *dyiiral*—a word that means "wife." It is clear that such a woman is precisely an appropriate bride for a man: she is of the right age, and she belongs to the right moiety. This sort of reasoning underlies the typical Guugu Yimidhirr formulation of what makes a good marriage. One should marry *muguur-nganh* (what is the case ending?): "from a *mugur*"—but "not too close": that is, a) not from a closely related *mugur* (not from a real mother's brother, for example), and b) hopefully from a distant area of the territory, which was subdivided into named locales.

Certain of a man's relatives were *dhabul* "sacred, forbidden, taboo" to him. Chief among these was his wife's mother, his *biwul*, whose presence he strictly avoided. He also avoided, but nevertheless could still have some dealings with, his wife's father, his *ngadhiina*, and his wife's brothers, called among other terms *gaanyil*. (A man was not obliged to avoid his wife's younger sisters, whom he also called by the term *dyiiral* "wife"; in a sense they were like wives to him, and he could joke with them freely, in ordinary Guugu Yimidhirr, just as he could with his actual wife.) The reader is invited to verify, by examining Table 4.12, that kin in the shaded categories are precisely those who might become a man's *dhabul* relatives through marriage: they are the parents and brothers of a woman a man might marry, his *potential* in-laws (or "affines"). The structural point is important, for although a man was obliged to use the special "brother-in-law" language with his actual wife's kin, he *could* use it as a special sign of respect with any of these *potential* in-laws: for example, with *biimuur* who is a kind of potential mother-in-law. (It is worth repeating that women were less likely to use special respectful vocabulary with their fathers- and mothers-in-law than were men, possibly because as members of their husband's group after marriage, they were in somewhat closer contact with their in-laws than were men with theirs.)

At the opposite extreme, certain kinsmen enjoyed extraordinary freedom and familiarity in their dealings with one another. A classificatory *gami* (same moiety grandparent) of the same sex was the prototypical joking partner whom one could tease, insult, and goad, in both word and gesture. A *gami* and his *gaminhdharr* (same moiety grandchild) were permitted a license completely beyond the bounds of behavior appropriate between ordinary acquaintances, let alone between *dhabul* relatives.

In the Guugu Yimidhirr area it might be more appropriate to speak of a "father tongue" than a "mother tongue." For just as moiety membership came from the father, so too did one adopt as one's own the language spoken by one's father. Traditionally in the Guugu Yimidhirr area there were more than forty named tribal areas, each with distinctive ways of talking and idiosyncratic words for common objects and actions. (Although the dialects are all mutually intelligible, even the pronouns vary: inland Guugu Yimidhirr speakers say *nganhdhaan* for the first-person plural nominative pronoun "we"; speakers from coastal areas use *ngana* instead.) As one's mother might well come from a distant area and thus speak a different version of Guugu Yimidhirr (perhaps a different language altogether if she came from another tribe) it frequently happened that a child grew up laying claim to his or her father's language but also speaking, or at least knowing, a good many words from his or her mother's language as well. Occasional contacts with more distant groups multiplied the words from other languages a person was likely to know, so that many Guugu Yimidhirr speakers were accomplished polyglots. It is important here to realize that it is the norm in Guugu Yimidhirr society for things to have alternate names. Everyone is likely to know two or three different ways of identifying common objects: their *own* word and some other people's words as well. The device of substituting a respectful word for an everyday word when speaking with tabooed relatives is, therefore, similar to using someone else's word in place of one's own.

Here, then, are two outstanding features of traditional Guugu Yimidhirr society. On the one hand it was entirely subdivided into kin. Each person had a particular kin relationship with every other person in the community. Even a stranger from outside one's own area could be assigned a categorical status as some sort of a relative, once certain (perhaps hypothetical) kin connections had been worked out. Accordingly, one's personal relationships with everyone else were influenced by kin categories: every *biimuur* was to be treated with restraint; every *gami* was a potential joking partner. And this was true even of a stranger: if he turned out to be a classificatory *gami* (someone in the same category as my father's father), I could joke with him; if she were a distant *biimuur*, I would watch my tongue. On the other hand, despite the interpersonal regularity created by this wide-ranging kinship system, the Guugu Yimidhirr area was linguistically heterogeneous, with many alternate ways of talking circulating throughout the area. It was in this context that the special "brother-in-law" language existed.

4.2 The Structure of the Guugu Yimidhirr Vocabulary of Respect

Guugu Yimidhirr speakers use the English word "deep" to describe the words of the respectful style, which is called *guugu dhabul*. Ordinary Guugu Yimidhirr words are to be used *mundaal-gal*—literally, "with the rest of them," i.e., with people who are not *dhabul*. In fact, as we have seen, the very name *guugu yimidhirr* means "this kind of word/this kind of language"—it is a label that describes itself. *Guugu yimidhirr* or *guugu nganhdhanun* "our language" are terms one uses to contrast the local language with other Australian languages spoken farther away—*guugu dhanangan* "their language" or *guugu ngarrbal* "strange language."

The *dhabul* style is also described as *dani-manaarnaya* "being soft or slow." To speak respectfully is to avoid the strident tones and rapid speech that characterize ordinary conversation; one speaks to a brother-in-law or a father-in-law in a deliberately subdued voice, drawing out words and dropping into a near whisper. At the same time it is impolite to attempt physical proximity with one's in-laws; instead one *diili yirrgaalga* or *wurriin yirrgaalga*—that is, speaks "sideways" or "crosswise," neither facing one's interlocutor nor, if it can be avoided, addressing him or her directly. (In areas to the north of Cooktown it was said that a man would avoid speaking to his father-in-law by addressing his dog instead!) This indirection contrasts with ordinary Guugu Yimidhirr, which is said to be *dhumbuurrgu* "straight out."

The brother-in-law vocabulary is not in itself a full language separate from ordinary Guugu Yimidhirr. Instead it consists of a relatively small set of special words considered to be appropriate for highly polite and respectful speech. Since there were a number of alternate words for common items, the existence of a separate set of respectful words must have seemed perfectly reasonable. A Guugu Yimidhirr man once spoke of several different words he knew for "echidna" (a porcupinelike Australian animal):

Balin-ga is porcupine. That's my word. I got another word, too: *nhalngarr*. You can use that word to brother-in-law and father-in-law. Some of these people call it *barradhal*. Well, I understand that *guugu* but that's not my word. That's their word—people who come from up Cape Flattery way.

Here the everyday word *balin-ga* has a single brother-in-law equivalent.

More frequently several different everyday words are replaced in formal brother-in-law speech by a single respectful word that spans the meaning of the whole set. For example, the verb *balil* is the respectful word for the everyday *dhadaa* "go." Thus, to say to one's brother-in-law that:

Balin-ga dhaday.

The porcupine went away.

one must say, instead:

Nhalngarr bali.

But *balil* is also the brother-in-law equivalent of a number of other everyday verbs: *gaynydyarr* "crawl," *biilil* "paddle (in a boat)," *dhaarmbil* "float, sail, drift," *yaalgal* "limp," *daabal* "wade," etc. None of these everyday words can be used with a brother-in-law. But rather than have a separate respectful equivalent for each of these words, *balil* is used in brother-in-law speech as the equivalent for any of them. A word like *dhaarmbil* could be rendered more precisely in brother-in-law language by adding further qualification; and here the case system comes into play, for the same case endings are used in brother-in-law language as in everyday Guugu Yimidhirr. The brother-in-law equivalent for *buurraay* "water" is *wabirr*. A more specific way to say *dhaarmbil* in the respectful style is, thus, *balil wabiirr-bi* (can you supply a literal gloss?) *Yaalgal* "limp" may be better rendered as *dyirrun balil*. (*Dyirrun* is the brother-in-law equivalent of *warra* "bad.") And so on. The principle resembles that described by R. M. W. Dixon for the mother-in-law language spoken by the Dyirbal people (south of Cairns), where the limited lexical resources of the respectful style are pushed to their limits to accommodate everything it would be possible to say in everyday language. The brother-in-law vocabulary itself is kept to a minimum, and syntactic and derivational devices are used heavily to express specific and detailed ideas.

TABLE 4.13   *Brother-in-law Equivalents for Everyday Vocabulary*

	Everyday word	**Brother-in-law equivalent**
one-to-one	balin-ga ⟶	nhalngarr "echidna"
many-to-one	dhadaa "go"	balil "go"
	dhaarmbil "float, sail, drift"	(*balil wabiirr-bi* "go in water")
	yaalgal "limp"	(*dyirrun balil* "go badly")
	gaynydyarr "crawl"	etc.
	biilil "paddle"	
	daabal "wade"	

Of course, the special brother-in-law vocabulary in Guugu Yimidhirr is used in somewhat restricted circumstances. Consider how one says "wife" in brother-in-law speech. One way is to use the word *munamuna*. In brother-in-law *muna* means "breast, milk"; reduplicated it simply means "woman." The narrowly defined context surely helps clarify the meaning, for in conversation with his wife's kin a man's use of the word "woman" as a replacement for "wife" is a fairly transparent euphemism. Another equivalent for "wife" in brother-in-law is the expression *yurrangan yambaal*. *Yurrangan* is the possessive (dative) form of *yurra* "you (all)." *Yambaal* is the respectful equivalent of the everyday word *bama* "person." Hence, *yurrangan yambaal* means, literally, "your person"—again, surely a reasonable way for a man to speak about his wife in conversation with the people who gave her to him.

Since the correspondences between everyday and brother-in-law words are generally many to one, they provide evidence for superordinate categories in the Guugu Yimidhirr scheme of things. For example, in everyday Guugu Yimidhirr there are at least ten names for different types of kangaroo and wallaby, but there is no overall generic term for "kangaroo." Purely on the basis of the ordinary terminology, there seems to be no Guugu Yimidhirr category of kangaroo but only a set of discrete kangaroo varieties. But the brother-in-law vocabulary groups all ten varieties under a single respectful word, *daarraalngan*. The category thus exists even though it is labelled only in the brother-in-law language. (See Table 4.14.)

The connections between single brother-in-law words and sets of everyday terms are sometimes less obvious. For instance, the single brother-in-law word *dyinu* encompasses a range of everyday words that form an apparent category comprising parts of the body with protruding bones and joints on the one hand (e.g., hip, chin, knee, elbow, wrist, anklebone, heelbone, armpit, crotch, and ribs), and certain small animals (including wild pheasant, water rat, worm, native cat, and some lizards) on the other. Whatever these items have in common, they are all referred to by the word *dyinu* in brother-in-law language. Other sets of everyday words collapse into single brother-in-law equivalents according to a clearer logic: the brother-in-law word *balnggirr* stands in for words denoting leg, lap, shin, hip, pelvis, and calf; whereas the lowest parts of the human body are rendered in brother-in-law by a different word, *buyiibuyii*, which replaces everyday words for foot, footprint, corn (on foot), shoes, ankle, heel, and toes.

Some everyday words, if they are pronounced in the proper slow and respectful manner, do not require replacement in conversation with a brother-in-law. The sentence:

Mayi guya.

There is no food.

becomes in brother-in-law style:

Gudhubay ngangarra.

The more specific sentence:

Mayi badhuurr guya.
> There is no zamia-nut food.

becomes simply:

Gudhubay badhuurr ngangarra.

The everyday word *badhuurr* remains unchanged in brother-in-law speech, even though the other words in the sentence are replaced by polite equivalents. Many words, particularly names for species of plant and animal, are like *badhuurr* in this respect.

Other words do a kind of double service in brother-in-law language: they serve as their own equivalents, but they also replace other everyday words that cannot be used with brother-in-law. Words from distant dialects frequently behave this way, as if an everyday word from someplace else is sufficiently polite for use with a brother-in-law simply by virtue of its being alien. So, for example, the coastal word *babaar* "spear thrower, womera" is a polite brother-in-law equivalent for the inland everyday word *milbiirr* (which also means "womera"). When variant everyday words have found their ways into Guugu Yimidhirr from outlying dialects and languages, seemingly only the local everyday words stand in need of a special brother-in-law replacement.

A more interesting example of an everyday word that does double service in brother-in-law is the everyday second-person plural pronoun *yurra*. The singular pronouns *ngayu* "I" and *nyulu* "he, she"—and their respective case forms—survive in brother-in-law with no change from their everyday forms.

Ngayu bada dhaday.
> I went down yonder. (Everyday)

>> *bada*   down, yonder

Ngayu dhuwun bali.
> (Brother-in-law equivalent.)

>> *dhuwun*   down, yonder (Brother-in-law)

Ngayu nhangu nhaadhi.
> I saw him. (Everyday)

Ngayu nhangu midungadhi.

> (Brother-in-law equivalent)

> *midungal* see (Brother-in-law)

However, the second-person singular pronoun is replaced in brother-in-law speech by the plural pronoun *yurra*. The question:

Nyundu buurraay waami?

> Did you find water? (Everyday)

> *waamil* find

becomes, in brother-in-law style:

Yurra wabirr yudurrin?

> *yudurr* find (Brother-in-law)

A speaker uses a second-person pronoun to refer to his interlocutor. When the speaker must treat the interlocutor with deference and respect, he may do so in part by means of various linguistic devices. He may use circumlocution or stylized indirection. Recall formal English style: "Will your Lordship have another slice of raisin toast?" "Allow me to escort Madame to the door." Many languages use kin terms in order to refer to the hearer without making a direct reference. (Thus, our parody of tribal language: "I invite my white brother to enter the wikiup.") Another device is formally akin to the Guugu Yimidhirr brother-in-law use of *yurra*: French uses a plural pronoun *vous* as the polite form of a singular second-person pronoun *tu*, suggesting perhaps that a plural form that literally makes more of the hearer is more deferential than a singular form. That the same device for showing respect should have been developed in such widely separated regions (and a number of other Indo-European languages do the same sort of thing) attests both to the universality of the problem—expressing deference in speech—and to the naturalness of the solution.

Finally, there are in Guugu Yimidhirr some everyday words that have no equivalent whatsoever in the formal brother-in-law style. These are words that denote things about which one cannot speak with a father-in-law and brother-in-law. Of such words Guugu Yimidhirr speakers say: "You can't say those words against your mother-in-law." They include the everyday words for various sexual organs and sexual acts. To use such words within earshot of one's in-laws would be to curse them, to be deliberately insulting. Plainly, sexual relations—of which the forbidden words are all metonymic reminders—are sensitive issues between a man and his wife's parents and brothers; and the sensitivity is mirrored in the content of speech between them.

TABLE 4.14   Everyday and Brother-in-law Vocabulary: Types of Correspondence

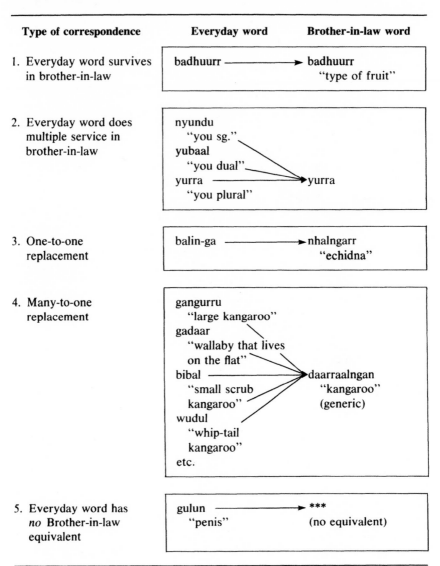

Type of correspondence	Everyday word	Brother-in-law word
1. Everyday word survives in brother-in-law	badhuurr ⟶	badhuurr "type of fruit"
2. Everyday word does multiple service in brother-in-law	nyundu "you sg." yubaal "you dual" yurra "you plural"	yurra
3. One-to-one replacement	balin-ga ⟶	nhalngarr "echidna"
4. Many-to-one replacement	gangurru "large kangaroo" gadaar "wallaby that lives on the flat" bibal "small scrub kangaroo" wudul "whip-tail kangaroo" etc.	daarraalngan "kangaroo" (generic)
5. Everyday word has *no* Brother-in-law equivalent	gulun "penis" ⟶	*** (no equivalent)

Thus, two sorts of features of everyday words seem to motivate the special brother-in-law vocabulary. On the one hand, an everyday word (having to do, for example, with sexual matters) may because of its meaning require at least a special brother-in-law word, different from the everyday; or it may be excised completely from speech with tabooed relatives. On the other hand, some everyday words seem to require alternate brother-in-law forms simply because they are *familiar* or *ordinary*; and in this case even an everyday word from a neighboring dialect or language may have the required properties as a respectful equivalent. These various possibilities are schematized in Table 4.14.

4.3   Respect (and Disrespect)

Let's look a bit more closely at the sort of respect due a man's in-laws. First, notice that there are at least two crosscutting dimensions of respect and avoidance. One has to do with kinship: a man is obliged to treat with respect certain people with whom he is related through his wife—in-laws (with the notable exception of a man's wife's sisters) become *dhabul*. Second, the fact that a man cannot speak *at all* to his mother-in-law suggests that special restraint operates across sexes: the relationship between a man and his wife's mother is more delicate than that between him and his wife's father or brothers. This cross-sex restraint will be discussed later.

Furthermore, as we can easily discern in our own behavior, there is more than one way to act deferentially. In Guugu Yimidhirr society more is involved in proper behavior with a brother-in-law or father-in-law than simply speaking with the special brother-in-law words, although the tenor of speech between tabooed kin is symptomatic of the tone of all their interactions.

First, as we have seen, brother-in-law utterances are soft and slow, contrasting strongly with ordinary Guugu Yimidhirr. When one's father-in-law comes around, this is how one should act:

Keep away! Don't talk hard! Stay quiet! If your mother-in-law comes, she can't talk. But your father-in-law can speak up. *Nhanu dyiiraal-gal yirrgaalga nyulu.* (He'll speak to your wife.) But *nhanun-gal gaari* (not with you). Your wife will ask him what he wants. But you can't say, "*Ngaanaa?*" (What?).

Notice that the quality of a relationship between a man and his wife's father is described specifically in terms of speech (or, more accurately, in terms of the absence of or limits on speech between them). Simply asking what someone wants, with the abrupt but quite ordinary word *ngaanaa* here exemplifies in microcosm all that must not take place between a man and his wife's parents.

Speaking loudly and rapidly is associated not only with familiarity and informality but also with anger and scolding. One speaks softly to a brother-in-law and, accordingly, one doesn't "fight him."

I can't fight him. If I do he just won't talk. He won't joke or tease or get angry. And I won't growl at him. If he gets angry with me I won't answer. I'll just walk away.

Again, the nature of the relationship (respectful, deferential, polite) is expressed in terms of permissible speech interaction (slow, soft, restrained).

Brother-in-law words have about them a character that suggests to Guugu Yimidhirr speakers situations that contrast markedly with those situations appropriate for everyday words.

> You could use [everyday words] if you talked to any person-*gal*. You can talk, laugh, anything.

(Notice here the case ending appended to an English word; "any person-*gal*" is the adessive case form of "any person"—meaning, then, "(talk) with any person.") So, for example:

> You can use *mayi banggamu* (potato) to any common person, to *gami* or to *dhawuunh* (friend). But not with *ngadhiina* (father-in-law). But "*dhirrguul-dhirr*"—you can use that *guugu* with father-in-law."

Here the ordinary word *banggamu* suggests joking, familiar contexts; it suggests speech with friends or with the prototype of the familiar kinsman, the *gami*.

Relatives who were obliged to avoid each other typically adopted physical postures and arranged themselves spatially so as to minimize mutual interaction. (See Figure 4.2.) Elsewhere in Australia it is reported that a man will walk well out of his way to avoid possible meetings with his mother-in-law. In Guugu Yimidhirr society a man and his mother-in-law did not sit in one another's presence, did not look at each other, approach one another, or stand face to face. They both *diili nhingaalnggal* and *diili yirrgaalga* (sat and talked sideways). In former times there were also severe restrictions on the sharing of food and possessions between a man and his parents-in-law.

Physical and spatial avoidance has an exact linguistic parallel. Transfer of information between a man and his taboo relatives was mediated and indirect. Speaking with brother-in-law words, a man directed messages to his in-laws via his wife. In return, the wife's father, speaking either in brother-in-law or everyday words, gave his daughter messages for his son-in-law. Indirect address in speech thus corresponds to sitting sideways, avoiding eye contact, and so on.

> I can't talk to my mother-in-law. But I got my children. And *ngadhu dyiiral* (my wife) can talk to her own mother. But I can't. She might be over there, but I'm facing away from her. My kids can talk—she is their *gami*. But I sit over here, behind the fence.

In the olden days a man who spoke in everyday language to his mother-in-law would have been speared to death for his offense. But such drastic sanctions applied to breaches of etiquette seem only to supplement deep-seated inner feelings of restraint about those relationships that called into play brother-in-law language and associated avoidance behavior. As we have seen, when confronted with insult or inappropriately rough or joking speech, people would often withdraw in silence from the presence of their tabooed relatives. A child who spoke impolitely in the wrong company would be made to feel *muyan* "shame." It is from *muyan* that one cannot bring oneself to speak in everyday language to a *dhabul* relative, to look at, still less to *touch* him or her.

> *Nyundu mangal gaari garrbal. Muyan.* (You can't grab her hand. It would be shameful.) If I were to touch my mother-in-law, hiii, *muyan!* Then I might go and wash my hand in water.

The spectre of having to wash away the touch of a mother-in-law's hand suggested a further image:

> *Biwul gaga.* (Mother-in-law is poison.)

Why? Because:

> You married her daughter; and so real shame, real *muyan!*

A man avoided his actual wife's relatives. But he was also expected to be restrained and polite—and he might use brother-in-law words as a special sign of respect—with his actual and classificatory father's sisters, mother's brothers, and mother's brother's sons, people we have seen to be his *potential* in-laws. Whether or not one used brother-in-law language with these people, one had always to behave in a decorous manner, without joking or cursing and refraining from anger—restrictions that plainly parallel, in somewhat reduced form, the stricter prohibitions on interaction with real in-laws.

Furthermore, a man was expected to monitor his behavior with his elder sisters and, to some extent, with his mother. Here again is evidence for a restraint between the sexes independent of *dhabul* relationships. A man could share food with his sister, but he could not sit or stand facing her or even close to her. (A Guugu Yimidhirr friend once introduced the author to his elder sister and induced him to shake her hand, all without moving from the far end of the room and by only glancing sideways at her.) Although one used everyday vocabulary, it was important to prune from one's speech with such people all "bad words," that is, words with vulgar overtones.

That there are such "bad words" further elaborates the continuum from familiar to polite vocabulary. We have distinguished between 1) everyday words that can themselves be used in speech with taboo relatives, 2) sensitive everyday words that, for one reason or another, require brother-in-law replacements, and 3) words whose referents simply cannot be labelled at all in polite brother-in-law speech. Words of the last sort are often called "swearing words"; they are used in extremely rude curses in the everyday language. Saying *mangal gulun* (literally, "hand penis")—usually with an accompanying gesture—is a very impolite way to call someone greedy.

Other so-called bad words, however, refer to seemingly innocuous items. They have impolite connotations that are activated merely by the presence of people who must be treated with care (whether or not one used the special brother-in-law vocabulary with them). For example, a man should not say *warrbi* "axe" to his sister because to her it might suggest "penis." He should not say *nambal* "stone" because she might interpret instead "testicles." He should not say *warrigan* "hole" because it suggests "vagina." And so on. These are not merely symbolic or metaphorical associations; the impolite connotations seem to inhere in the words themselves. It is not that one cannot talk about axes or holes with one's sister, but only that one cannot use these particular words. Instead of saying *warrbi*, a man might use the more polite word *guliirra*, which also means "axe." Or in modern times he could simply use the English word "axe";

> *Ngadhu **axe** wanhdhaa?*
>
> Where is my axe?

Neither word would offend his sister, although neither would be sufficiently polite for speaking to his father-in-law or brother-in-law. With them he would use the brother-in-law word *gadiil-baga*, said to be the "deepest" or most polite word for "axe." The range of politeness associated with individual Guugu Yimidhirr words is more elaborated than a simple distinction between everyday and brother-in-law language would suggest.

The range of conventional social relationships is correspondingly complex. There is ordinary, relaxed amicability between friends and family members, and there is strict avoidance between a man and his mother-in-law. Between a *gami* and a *gaminhdharr* there is an obscene joking relationship. Between these extremes are various forms of politeness and restraint, sometimes tempered by special circumstances or genealogical distance. One man spoke of visiting in the hospital a remote relative who fell into a *dhabul* category. He felt ashamed to speak openly to the sick person, who, in turn, sought sympathy and initiated direct conversation. Also, a man might joke in a suggestive manner with potential wives (for example, with his wife's sisters) but be obliged to speak circumspectly with his own sister, who could never be

TABLE 4.15 *Social Relationships, Speech Categories, and Lexical Alternatives*

Social Relationship: kin-category	Dhabul		Non-*Dhabul*		
sex	opposite sex	same sex	opposite sex	same sex	Unrestricted (e.g., with wife or potential wife; or joking relationship with *gami*)
Type of speech interaction:	no speech	respectful "brother-in-law" words	polite	everyday	joking or vulgar language
Lexical alternative:					
"axe"	***	*gadil-baga*	*guliirra*	*warrbi*	
"food"	***	*gudhubay*	*mayi*		
"penis"	***				*gulun*

his sexual partner and who might be offended by an incautious utterance.

Such a highly structured social universe, as we have seen, implies a set of speech styles, levels, or *registers* appropriate to different sorts of interaction: informal, deliberately obscene, restrained and polite, or deferential and respectful. Formally these registers comprise different sets of words that have the character appropriate to one tone or another. People may often manipulate registers to a particular purpose: choosing a brother-in-law word to convey an extra hint of deference where an everyday word would do; or deliberately violating normal rules of speech politeness to insult, startle, or to undermine a relationship. What is important is that in every case, in more or less highly codified ways, people's speech is partly determined by and partly itself a determinant of the relationship between speakers. The existence of discrete registers is a symptom of the different sorts of interaction that occasion speech in the community.

5   LANGUAGE IN THE MODERN GUUGU YIMIDHIRR COMMUNITY

In traditional times the Guugu Yimidhirr kinship system probably worked smoothly. Reckoning by moiety membership and genealogical relationships presumably produced few discontinuities, and people doubtless married correctly most of the time according to what older Hopevale residents call "the law." Nowadays kinship remains an important part of the conceptual apparatus for dividing up the world, but there are frequently crossed ties and "crooked" relationships. For many older people these confusions are distressing since often one doesn't know what kin term to apply to someone else.

> *Walu dhula-gadhaadhi, walu gumbiin.*
> It seems all twisted, like a vine.

Frequently, because of the high rate of intermarriage between people of part-Aboriginal and part-European descent, modern marriages violate old rules. And in the present day there are no elders to spear offending parties or to drive them from the community. Instead, Guugu Yimidhirr speakers continually adjust their usage so as to bring their relationships with others under appropriate kin categories.

The habits of language we have discussed in the previous section were largely dependent on social habits. As kin categories became confused, as old-style standards of proper behavior gave way to Lutheran precepts, as groups of people were forcibly relocated or "dispersed," as dialects were thrown together or died, many of the traditional speech practices that drew meaning from lapsed social arrangements in turn disappeared from Guugu Yimidhirr society. Nowadays, few people remember, and still fewer can use, words of the respectful brother-in-law style. Older people brought up at Hopevale before the relocation during World War II still experienced practices of avoidance and the corresponding speech behavior. Though such practices have fallen into disuse, they have left deep impressions. As one old man says:

> These young people here at the Mission talk to their mothers-in-law. They fight and scold and curse. But we older people *just can't* . . . .

Older people carefully monitor their interactions with tabooed relatives, even though they may speak everyday Guugu Yimidhirr, and even though they do not fear physical punishment for breaches of etiquette. But elaborate avoidance is anachronistic in the society in which Guugu Yimidhirr speakers now live. The name of a deceased person cannot be tabooed in the face of a Lutheran funeral; nor can one speak brother-in-law words to a brother-in-law who comes from a distant Queensland town, and who doesn't even know everyday Guugu Yimidhirr.

It is not only speech habits that are changing. Guugu Yimidhirr is undergoing syntactic changes as well, partly as a result of external influences and partly from internal motivation.

The major outside force is English. Ordinary language around Hopevale is a confirmed mix of English and Guugu Yimidhirr. Young people have difficulty eliminating English words from their speech; quite often they revert to an English laced with Guugu Yimidhirr pronouns (which, as the reader will recall, are organized on slightly different principles from English pronouns).

> **Ngali** *got no* **mayi**.
> We (two) have no food.

Occasionally, Guugu Yimidhirr speakers attach Guugu Yimidhirr formatives to English words.

> *Nyundu* **mother-in-law-gal** *gaari yirrgii*.
> Don't speak to your mother-in-law.

Though this situation may change in the future, Hopevale people go to school only in English; they read and write only in English, and they attend church services conducted for the most part in English.

(The first German missionaries at Hopevale translated a good deal of evangelical material into a peculiar sort of Guugu Yimidhirr—one that, for example, almost entirely omits ergative inflection. Only older people can read the idiosyncratic spellings that Reverend Schwarz used. This missionary version of the language is now enshrined as a kind of semiofficial church language—one appropriate to Bible stories but distinctly odd in terms of the actual spoken language.)

Even when they speak only in Guugu Yimidhirr, younger people use forms that older speakers regard as incorrect. Modern speech smooths over exceptions and syntactic irregularities of the past language. A good example involves verb forms.

Guugu Yimidhirr verbs display as much morphological elaboration as do Guugu Yimidhirr nouns. A single verb ending can convey a good deal of specialized meaning. There are familiar contrasts of tense.

>*Nyulu mayi buday.*
>>He ate food.

>*Nyulu mayi budal.*
>>He eats food; or, he'll eat food by and by.

There are also reduplicated forms that signify action in progress.

>*Nyulu mayi budaaral.*
>>He's eating food.

>*Nyulu mayi budaaray.*
>>He was eating food.

There are verb forms that command.

>*Mayi budala!*
>>Eat food!

>*Gaari dhadii!*
>>Don't go!

>*Mayi budaarala!*
>>Keep eating food!

There are special endings that express desire or intention.

>*Ngali dhadanhu.*
>>We want to go, ought to go, intend to go.

And there are even special precautionary endings that issue warnings or try to head off undesirable consequences.

>*Ngayu buliya.*
>>I might fall.

Nhina gundaya.

> You might get hit.

Gaari dhadii, nyundu bulii-gamu.

> Don't go, otherwise you might fall.

Nyulu duday biiba-ngun gundayigu.

> He ran before his father could hit him.

Guugu Yimidhirr verbs fall into several natural groups, or conjugations. Verbs of one large group have a final -*l* in the "present" tense (which can be translated into English in several ways).

Ngayu buligi gundal.

> I'll hit the bullock. (Or "I hit the bullock.")

Nyulu mayi wagil.

> He'll cut the food. (Or "He cuts the food.")

These *l*-final verbs form an imperative in -*la*.

Gundala!

> Hit it!

Wagila!

> Cut it!

The vast majority of these *l*-final verbs are transitive.
Verbs of another major conjugation end in long vowels.

Ngali dhadaa.

> We (two) will go.

Nyulu Billy gadaa.

> Billy will come.

The imperative form of these verbs has -*ii* instead of the final long vowel.

Dhadii!

> Go!

Gaari bulii!

> Don't fall!

Most of these vowel-final verbs are intransitive.

In the speech of older Guugu Yimidhirr speakers there are a few verbs in each conjugation that do not conform to the normal pattern with regard to transitivity. That is, there are some intransitive *l*-final verbs, such as *wurrgal* "suffer."

> *Nyulu wurrgaalgal.*
>> He is suffering.
>
> *Gaari wurrgala!*
>> Don't suffer!

And there are some vowel-final verbs, like *banydyii* "wait for," that are transitive.

> *Ngayu nhina banydyii.*
>> I'll wait for you.
>
> *Nganhi banydyii!*
>> Wait for me!

Older speakers of Guugu Yimidhirr insist that these are the correct forms. In both cases, however, younger people seem to be in some doubt; they seem to have reanalysed these verbs so as to interpret the transitive *banydyii* as actually an *l*-final verb, and the intransitive *wurrgal* as actually vowel-final. One hears such forms as:

> *Gaari wurrgii!*
>> Don't suffer!
>
> *Nyulu wurrgaalga.*
>> He is suffering.

(These forms would only be possible for vowel-final verbs). Or:

> *Banydyila nhangu!*
>> Wait for him!
>
> *Nyulu banydyiilndyil nganhi.*
>> He is waiting for me.

Older speakers reject such forms as corrupt and incorrect, although they frequently occur in speech.

Here the language seems to be shifting in the direction of greater regularity, where the form of a verb corresponds exactly to its transitivity. Such changes undoubtedly take place constantly in all languages; although in the past, when many variant dialects and languages coexisted in the same wide community, Guugu Yimidhirr might have resisted more vigorously against such shifts, accommodating more irregularity as a means of maintaining its integrity against other forms of speech.

Despite the reduced use of Guugu Yimidhirr and the gradual disappearance of both the brother-in-law vocabulary and associated social institutions, speech in the Hopevale/Cooktown community remains a primary sociological index. A person's choice of words from a larger repertoire is as much a function of social facts as it was in traditional times. Here is a crude example to illustrate the principle. In the Hopevale Mission store, which is staffed both by Aboriginal Guugu Yimidhirr speakers and white missionary personnel (who do not speak Guugu Yimidhirr), one decides whether to order an item in English or in Guugu Yimidhirr partly on practical grounds (one does not speak to the white store manager in a language he doesn't understand) and partly on social grounds. For often people order in English from a Guugu Yimidhirr–speaking shop assistant whenever the manager is present, even when he is not attending them. His presence creates, as it were, an English context, whether or not he himself is part of the dialogue. Speaking Guugu Yimidhirr in front of the store manager is, by contrast, a conscious means to exclude him from the conversation.

Guugu Yimidhirr is a language with limited range in the modern world. Young people at Hopevale say that although they can speak Guugu Yimidhirr, they cannot write it and have little interest in trying to do so. Others lament the passing of skills and knowledge (including knowledge of language) possessed by previous generations but now largely lost. Still others regard Guugu Yimidhirr as an exclusive possession, certainly not to be shared with white men, but not even to be squandered on Aborigines from other areas or on young people whose lives will carry them away from the mission. In the company of non-Aborigines, many Hopevale residents who are uncertain of their English lapse into silence; others deprecate their language and claim to know little of it. These phenomena, taken together, suggest that in the Cooktown/Hopevale area, Guugu Yimidhirr is still an index, still a mark, setting its speakers apart from other people. Choosing to speak Guugu Yimidhirr instead of English can be an unambiguous signal. (In front of the Cooktown policeman it can mean: "Let's keep him out of this conversation." With an Aboriginal evangelist or in a gathering of the men's society it can mean, "Let's get together on this, speak our true minds, bare our hearts.")

Although the linguistic registers are different—different languages instead of discrete special-purpose vocabularies—these phenomena formally parallel the use of brother-in-law language to signal a deferential kin relationship, or the deliberate use of insulting or vulgar language as part of a special sort of friendship. In each case, some feature of an interaction is mirrored in the character of the speech that accompanies it; or, just as often, some feature of speech sets the tone of an interaction as it develops.

Speech is *inherently* indexical; to speak at all is to choose a register (even if only a word, or a tone of voice) that will index the moment. Such phenomena have been widely described. In Java people speak in a high, a low, or a middle variety of Javanese according to the relative status of the protagonists. (A high-status person speaks down to a low-status person by using the low language, and vice versa.) Throughout Asia languages have elaborate systems of honorifics to elevate the addressee. (See the following chapter on Japanese.) Respect for a Samoan chief is shown in part by respectful vocabulary used when common people speak to or about him. Such devices are widespread, although the details doubtless vary from one speech community to another. In every case, speech is connected with a set of situations and social relationships—sometimes binding people and constraining their interactions, sometimes marking and reinforcing social facts, but often facilitating communication, lubricating sore points, and serving as the medium by which people forge new relationships and ideas.

SUGGESTIONS FOR FURTHER READING

Those students who wish to pursue Australian languages in more detail should begin with R.M.W. Dixon's *The Dyirbal Language of North Queensland*, which surveys the major features of Australian languages (including sound systems and ergative inflection), and which provides a comprehensive look at this language of the Cairns rain-forest region. Readers with a knowledge of introductory linguistics will find especially useful Dixon's account of the relationship between noun and pronoun morphology and the syntax of clauses and complex sentences. Further descriptions of the semantics of a mother-in-law language and an initiation language are in articles by Dixon and Kenneth Hale in the Steinberg and Jakobovits reader in semantics. A good place to start further inquiry into speech as part of and equivalent to action is J. L. Austin's *How to Do Things with Words*, or Searle's *Speech Acts*. Chapter IV in the companion volume gives a look at another sort of language spoken widely in Cape York, even by some Hopevale residents, called Cape York Creole.

A good deal has been written about Aboriginal Australians. Robert Tonkinson's *The Jigalong Mob* describes a traditional group who have recently come under Mission conditions. But before plunging more deeply into ethnography and learning about the "dream time," students are well advised to read C. D. Rowley's *The Destruction of Aboriginal*

Society to locate contemporary Aborigines firmly in the Australian reality.

Austin, J. L.. *How to Do Things with Words*. Cambridge, Mass.: Harvard University Press, 1962.

Crowley, Terry, and Rigsby, Bruce. "Cape York Creole." In *Languages and Their Status*, edited by Timothy Shopen. Cambridge, Mass.: Winthrop Publishers, 1979.

Dixon, R.M.W. *The Dyirbal Language of North Queensland*. Cambridge, England: Cambridge University Press, 1972.

Rowley, Charles D. *The Destruction of Aboriginal Society*. Canberra: Australian National University, Pelican Books, 1970.

Steinberg, D. D., and Jakobovits, L. A., eds. *Semantics: An Interdisciplinary Reader in Philosophy, Linguistics, and Psychology*. Cambridge, England: Cambridge University Press, 1971.

Searle, John R. *Speech Acts: An Essay in the Philosophy of Language*. New York: Cambridge University Press, 1969.

Tonkinson, Robert. *The Jigalong Mob: Aboriginal Victors of the Desert Crusade*. Menlo Park, California: Cummings Publishing Co., 1974.

GLOSSARY

The glossary lists all the Guugu Yimidhirr words that appear in this chapter together with their English equivalents. Nouns appear in absolutive form, and verbs appear in unreduplicated present-tense form, unless otherwise indicated.

baalaa fruit tree species
babaar womera (Coastal word)
babi mother's mother
bada down, yonder
badhuurr zamia-nut palm
bala skinny, weak
balgal to make, to wash
balil to go (Brother-in-law style)
balin-ga echidna
balnggirr leg (Brother-in-law style)
bama person
bandil to chop, to fell
banggamu potato
banydyii to wait for
bayan house
bibal small scrub kangaroo
biiba father
biilil to paddle

biimuur   father's sister
biinii   to die
biwul   wife's mother
bubu   earth, ground
budal   to eat
bula   the two of them (Third-person dual nominative)
bulaan   them two (Third-person dual accusative/dative)
bulangan   them two (Third-person dual accusative/dative)
buligi   bullock
bulii   to fall down
buurraay   water
buyiibuyii   foot (Brother-in-law style)

daabal   to wade
daamal   to spear
daarraalngan   kangaroo (Generic, Brother-in-law style)
dagaadhi   sat down
dani   slow, soft
dhaarmbil   to float
dhabul   sacred, forbidden, taboo
dhadaa   to go
dhamal   foot
dhana   they (Third-person plural nominative)
dhanaan   them/their (Third-person plural accusative/dative)
dhanangan   them/their (Third-person plural accusative/dative)
dharramali   Thunder (Mythical character)
dhawuunh   friend
dhirguul-dhirr   potato (Brother-in-law style)
dhula   flood, confused
dhula-gadaadhi   twisted
dhumbuurrgu   straight, direct
dhuurrngal   to push
dhuway   son (of woman)
dhuwun   down, yonder (Brother-in-law style)
diili   sideways
dingga-dhirr   hungry
dudaa   to run
duula   child (Brother-in-law style)
dunhu   husband, sister's husband
dumbil   to break
dyaarbaa   snake
dyiiral   wife
dyindal   to bite, to peck
dyin-gurr   younger sister
dyinu   small animal, joint (Brother-in-law style)
dyirrun   bad (Brother-in-law style)

gaanhaal   elder sister
gaanyil   wife's brother

gaari not
gabiirr girl
gadaa to come
gadaar type of wallaby
gadabal to break, be broken
gadiil-baga axe (Brother-in-law style)
gaga sick, poison, salty
gaga-dhirr sick
galga spear
galmba also, too
gambul stomach
gami father's father, or mother's mother
gaminhdharr son's child
ganaa okay, all right, well
ganggal child
gangurru kangaroo species
garga younger brother
garrbal to grab
gaynydyarr to crawl
gudaa dog
gudhubay food (Brother-in-law style)
gulbuuygu together
guliirra axe (Polite)
gulun penis
gumbiin string, rope
gundal to hit, to kill
gurral to say
guudyu fish
guugu word, language
guya not, absent, nonexistent

ma now! come! (Exclamation)
maandii to bring
manaa to cause to _____(Causative verb)
mangal hand
mayi food, vegetable food
midungadhi saw (Brother-in-law style)
milbiirr womera
minha meat, edible animal
mugagay father's older sibling
muganh cold
mugur mother's brother
muli barren, infertile, childless
muna breast, milk, woman (Brother-in-law style)
mundal the rest, the others
munhi black
muyan shame

nambal rock, money

nambi   grave, casket

nanggurr   camp

ngaabaay   head

ngaanaa   what?

ngaanii   why?

ngadhi   mother's father

ngadhinil   daughter's child

ngadhiina   wife's father

ngadhu   to me, mine (First-person singular dative)

ngali   you and I (First-person dual inclusive nominative)

ngaliin   you and me (First-person dual inclusive accusative/dative)

ngaliinh   he/she and I (First-person dual exclusive nominative)

ngalingan   you and me (First-person dual inclusive accusative/dative)

ngalinhun   him/her and me (First-person dual exclusive accusative/dative)

ngamu   mother

ngana   we (First-person plural nominative, Coastal form)

ngangarra   not, nonexistent (Brother-in-law style)

nganhdhaan   we (First-person plural nominative)

nganhdhanun   us (First-person plural accusative/dative)

nganhi   me (First-person singular accusative)

ngarraa   skin, bark

ngarrbal   strange, alien

ngayu   I (First-person singular nominative)

ngulgu   yesterday

ngurrraar   black cockatoo

nguudhurr   daughter (of woman)

nhaadhi   saw (Past tense of *nhaamaa* "to see")

nhalngarr   echidna (Brother-in-law style)

nhangu   him/her (Third-person singular accusative/dative)

nhanu   your (Second-person singular dative)

nhayun   that, there

nhin-gal   to be, to sit

nhina   you (Second-person singular accusative)

nyulu   he/she (Third-person singular nominative)

nyundu   you (Second-person singular nominative)

waamil   to find

waandaar   white cockatoo

wabirr   water (Brother-in-law style)

wagil   to cut

walu   like, resembling; side, temple

wanggaar   above

wanhdhaa   where?

wanhdharra   how, howdy

wanhdhu   who (Ergative)

wanhu   who (Absolutive)

warra   bad

warrbi   axe

warrigan   hole

wawu   soul, breath
wawu-dhirr   want, desirous of
wudul   whip-tail kangaroo
wudhi   gave (Past tense of *wumaa* "to give")
wunaa   to exist, to lie down
wurrbal   Fog (Mythical character)
wurrgal   to suffer
wurriin   crosswise
wuurrii   earth, ground (Brother-in-law style)

yaalgal   to limp
yaba   older brother
yalmba   sand hill
yambaal   person (Brother-in-law style)
yarraman   horse
yarrga   boy
yimidhirr   this way
yinil   fearful, afraid
yirrgaa   to speak, to talk
yiyi   this, here
yubaal   you two (Second-person dual nominative)
yubalin   you two (Second-person dual accusative/dative)
yudurr   to find (Brother-in-law style)
yugu   wood, stick, fire
yumurr   child (of man)
yurra   you all (Second-person plural nominative)
yurraan   you/your (Second-person plural accusative/dative)
yurrangan   you/your (Second-person plural accusative/dative)
yuu   yes
yuwaal   beach

V

Japanese
A Story of Language and People

Kyoko Inoue

INTRODUCTION

Japan, located in the northwestern corner of the Pacific Ocean, is an island country consisting of four major islands, *Honshuu, Kyuushuu, Shikoku* and *Hokkaidoo*, and numerous minor islands. In area it is smaller than France but larger than the British Isles—Honshuu alone is slightly larger than England, Wales, and Scotland combined. It has a long coastline extending from north to south. Compared with the east coast of the North American continent, the northern tip of Hokkaidoo is at about the latitude of Montreal, Canada, and the southern tip of Kyuushuu is at about that of Savannah, Georgia. The southernmost Ryuukyuu Islands extend as far south as the southern tip of Florida.

Japan is a mountainous country with great stretches of volcanic ranges. The mountains are lush with vegetation, and rivers come down from the mountains forming cascades. Rugged coastlines, towering volcanoes and lush vegetation make Japan's landscape varied and beautiful.

Japanese is spoken by over one hundred ten million people almost all of whom are Japanese citizens. Among the world's languages it ranks

Kyoko Inoue is a Japanese who teaches linguistics and Japanese at the University of Illinois at Chicago Circle. Throughout her extensive bicultural and bilingual experience in the United States and Japan she has pursued her interest in the analysis of English and Japanese within their respective cultural frameworks.

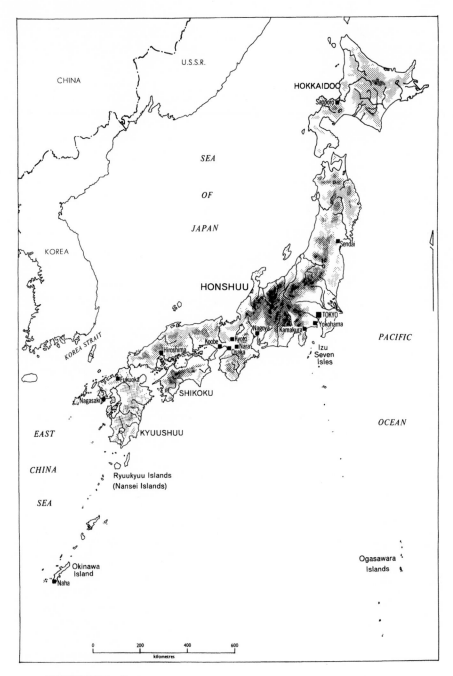

FIGURE 5.1   Japan

eighth in number of speakers. It has a written tradition of nearly two thousand years.

The structure and use of a language grows out of the experience and innovation of the people who speak it. The discussion that follows is threefold: it presents an outline of the cultural history of Japan, a discussion of the structure of the Japanese language, and a consideration of its relation to cultural and natural environment. Its purpose is to help the reader gain an understanding of the ongoing cultural experience of which the language and its writing system are a part.[1]

1   A HISTORY OF JAPAN

1.1   The Early Years—Contact with China and the Evolution of the Writing System

It is believed that the islands of Japan were inhabited as far back as ten thousand years ago. The first grain-raising agricultural revolution occurred in western Japan during the *Yayoi* period, 200 B.C.–300 A.D. The Yayoi people are believed to have been Mongoloid in race, related to their neighbors in Korea and China. However, it is speculated that during or after the Yayoi period there were several waves of people migrating to the islands of Japan, contributing to the variety of facial types found among the present-day Japanese, among them the *Ainu*, a Caucasoid people with light skin color, wavy hair, and heavy body hair.

At the end of the Yayoi period and throughout the Tomb period, which followed it, there were tribal communities competing for power and military dominance. By the beginning of the fifth century A.D. a group known as the *Yamato* had gained a position of supremacy in central Japan. Legend has it that the leader of the Yamato court descended from the Sun Goddess and was in turn the ancestor to the imperial family of Japan. Nature and ancestor worship of the Yamato comprised the roots of the Japanese religion *Shintoism*.

The early influence of Chinese civilization, including that in the Japanese writing system, is a legacy of ancient Japan that has had a profound effect throughout history. Interest in things Chinese took root in the first century A.D. when the scholars from Korea first taught

---

[1]Japanese utterances are analyzed in terms of moras. Each mora consists of either consonant plus vowel, or vowel alone, or mora nasal, or mora obstruent, and it functions as the unit of length in the language. *Honshuu* is four moras, *ho-n-shu-u*, and *Hokkaidoo* is six moras, *ho-k-ka-i-do-o*. Pronounce them rather evenly so that each mora will receive approximately the same duration. It should be noted, however, that there are four proper nouns appearing in this discussion which are given in the conventional spelling, although it does not adequately reflect the number of moras they have in their widely known usages. These are "Tokyo," which is pronounced *To-o-kyo-o*; "Kyoto," pronounced *Kyo-o-to*; "Osaka," pronounced *O-o-sa-ka*; and "Shinto," pronounced *Shi-n-to-o*.

Confucianism to the Japanese. Then in 552 A.D., as it is officially dated, Buddhism was introduced to the Yamato court, located in the vicinity of Nara, thus initiating three hundred years of active cultural exchange between China and Japan.

From this time on Japanese borrowed much vocabulary from Chinese, not only in the Buddhist terminology (some of which came directly from Sanskrit and Pali), but also in the areas of governmental bureaucracy, arts and architecture, music, medicine, agriculture, the system of weights and measurements, animals, plants, clothing and foods—indeed throughout the entire language. Although it is difficult to distinguish many of those loanwords, which have become completely assimilated into Japanese over centuries, nearly one-half of the contemporary Japanese vocabulary is Sino-Japanese, including many words that have been created by the Japanese based on the old Chinese etymologies. Table 5–1 shows a few attested examples from ancient times.

The Japanese writing system today is a hybrid system of several thousand Chinese characters and two syllabaries, *Katakana* and *Hiragana*. Katakana and Hiragana are two different versions of simplified characters, some of them deriving from the same character and others from different ones. There are forty-six symbols in each syllabary.

In trying to adopt Chinese characters to write Japanese, the ancient Chinese and Korean scholars were faced with the fact that Chinese and

TABLE 5.1   *Vocabulary Borrowed from Chinese*

Chinese		Japanese	Meaning
hak		*haka*	"grave"
kin		*kinu*	"silk"
kun		*kuni*	"state"
ma		*uma*	"horse"
muk		*mugi*	"wheat"
sung		*sugi*	"cryptomeria"
tak		*togu*	"to sharpen"
we		*e*	"picture"
ambā	*(from*	*ama*	"nun"
pâtra	*Sanskrit*	*hachi*	"bowl"
sâkya	*via Chinese)*	*Shaka*	"Buddha"
thera	*(Pali via Chinese)*	*tera*	"temple"

FIGURE 5.2 A Calligraphy Lesson at Primary School

Japanese are fundamentally different languages. Chinese is an isolating language, while Japanese is agglutinating. That is, in Chinese each word tends to have an immutable form, but in Japanese a word can have a number of shapes and be made of various morphemes that combine to represent different meanings. For instance, in Chinese, the verb "to eat" is /chī/, the same word irrespective of time reference. Chinese has no tense marking on verbs. In Japanese, *taberu* "(I) eat" is a composite of two morphemes, *tabe-* "to eat" and *-ru*, the nonpast tense marker; *tabeta* "(I) ate" is a composite of *tabe-* "to eat" and *-ta*, the past tense marker; and *tabehajimeta* "(I) began to eat" is a composite of *tabe-* "to eat," *hajime-* "to begin," and *-ta*, the past tense marker. This presented a problem for the scholars trying to write Japanese accurately with Chinese characters.

They adopted the characters representing the content words—nouns, verbs, adjectives, and adverbs—and simply assigned them

Japanese readings. For example, they took the character which meant "man" and which was pronounced /jen/ in Chinese and assigned to it the Japanese word for "man," /hito/. This was straightforward enough, but in addition they borrowed characters strictly for their sounds to represent various grammatical functions that were not in the grammar of Chinese. For example, an important small Japanese word, the topicalizer

ha, was represented by 波, which means "wave" in Chinese but has the sound /ha/.

To demonstrate this process, we shall see how one might conceivably write an English sentence using Chinese characters. Here is an example:

(1)   The students are drinking beer.

First, we shall take all the words which have equivalents in Chinese, and arrange them according to the English word order.

(2)   學生   是   飲   麥酒
      sywé sheng   *shr̀*   *yǐn*   *mài jyou*
      student   are   drink   beer

This, however, is highly unsatisfactory, for there is no definite article, *the*, nor the plural *s* of "students," nor the *-ing* of "drinking."

One way to correct these deficiencies is to find the characters that are similar in sound to the missing elements. We will introduce the Chinese characters for /de/ "the one . . . that," /sì/ "stream," and /yíng/ "welcome," not for their meaning but because they sound like the English elements not yet represented:

(3)   的   學生   氾   是   飲   迎   麥酒
      DE   *sywé sheng*   *SÌ*   *shr̀*   *yǐn*   *YÍNG*   *mài jyou*
      The   student   s   are   drink-   ing   beer

Notice, sentence (3) no longer makes any sense in Chinese.

There is a minor problem here. Chinese has an immutable form of copula "to be" pronounced /shr̀/ and written 是. What we have done here is to simply take it and match it with "are." But what about the other forms of the copula in English (*am, is, was, were*, etc.)? One conceivable solution might be to always use 是 and hope that the reader would read it appropriately in each context. Another solution might be to combine it with characters that would correspond to the sounds of the respective form, for example adding 兒 /êrh/ "son" for its sound value only, so that the representation of "are" would be 是兒. And the third alternative is to simply disregard 是, and use a different character for each copula, e.g., only 兒 would stand for "are."

The first important Japanese literary work, called *Man'yooshuu*, which is a collection of over four thousand poems compiled around the year 760 A.D., is written entirely in Chinese characters using a conglomeration of these various orthographic devices. What makes it particularly difficult to read them today is the fact that the ancient system, especially of adopting characters for their sounds, was in no way unified. Reading those poems is rather like trying to solve a series of rebuses.

Over a period of time, when writing characters to represent various functional elements, the Japanese people began to use the ones that were simpler in shape. These characters were then abbreviated into forms that were no longer recognizable as characters. For example, the topicalizer 波 /ha/ was simplified into 伋, 达, and finally to the present shape は. The topicalizer is now pronounced /wa/ instead of /ha/. The character 波 remained in the Japanese writing system representing the word "wave" pronounced /nami/. It also occurs in compound expressions such as "wave length" 波長 and retains its Chinese pronunciation /ha/ (the full expression is pronounced /hachoo/). Another important small word, the genitive marker 乃 /no/ gradually changed into 乃, 刀, and finally to the present shape の. Thus a set of symbols were developed, which we now call Hiragana.

A second syllabary which is called Katakana comes from the Buddhist monks' practice while reading Chinese script of making marks alongside the text to aid in understanding the sentence construction and memorizing new words. They divised a shorthand system to mark word-order differences between Chinese and Japanese and also used characters and the newly developed Hiragana for glosses (translations). Eventually, they began to devise their own angular and more simplified symbols. Take, for example, the character 阿 which is pronounced /a/—one element or radical of this character 阝 was taken to represent the sound /a/. This was simplified into ア, ア, and finally, to the present shape 7. Another example would be the symbol for /ku/ which comes from 久, changed to 久, 夕, and finally to the present shape, 勺.

In the contemporary writing system, the two syllabaries serve different functions. Hiragana is used to write various function words and verbal endings so that a Japanese sentence typically has both characters and Hiragana. Katakana is used to write western loanwords and is also used for emphasis in a way similar to the use of italics in English.

We might add that in recent years, various proposals have been made to improve this cumbersome writing system—from the most radical proposal to abolish characters completely and use only *kana* (syllabary writing) or adopt the Roman alphabet, to a more moderate proposal to limit the number of characters in use. The former approach would have the disadvantage of failing to distinguish the many homophones of contemporary Japanese, words with different meanings that sound exactly the same.

A moderate reform has been undertaken since World War II. Today, there is a list authorized by the Ministry of Education that includes 1,850 characters to be used in newspapers and popular reading materials. Furthermore, many of them have been simplified to a considerable degree. It is interesting to note that the People's Republic of China has also been engaged recently in a similar reform. But since no effort has been made at coordination, many of the characters in Chinese and Japanese now look very different. For instance, the traditional character 發 "to dispatch" (pronounced /hatsu/ in Japanese) is 発 in Japanese, and 发 in Chinese. The traditional character 勞 "to toil" (pronounced /roo/ in Japanese) is 労 in Japanese, and 劳 in Chinese. The two writing systems have been slowly drifting apart during the past fifteen hundred years, and this recent reform is a decisive step toward making them distinctly different.

Beginning in the ninth century A.D., Japan gradually withdrew from heavy reliance on the Chinese culture, although the prestige of all things Chinese remained great. In 838, she sent her twelfth and last embassy to the T'ang Dynasty of China, and for the next three hundred years, the Japanese concentrated on assimilating their borrowings from China—the political system of bureaucratic central government, the religious and ethical concepts of Buddhism and Confucianism, and the writing system—to fit their owr tastes and way of life. Instead of the bureaucratic civil servants of a central government overseeing the country, the Japanese gradually developed strong provincial aristocrats in the tradition of family loyalty and hereditary rights. They also syncretized Buddhism and Shintoism and created a uniquely Japanese religious tradition, which continues in modern times.

Among the court aristocrats of the Fujiwara family in Kyoto, the capital of Japan, there was a flowering of the first distinctly Japanese literary tradition, especially among the court ladies. The most famous work is a lengthy novel called *The Tale of Genji*, the love adventures of an imaginary figure, Prince Genji, written by Lady Murasaki in the early eleventh century. As it was customary for the court ladies not to be allowed to learn Chinese or Chinese characters, Lady Murasaki wrote in Hiragana, called then *onna-de* "woman's hand." During this period various levels of speech, and the distinction between men's and women's speech began to develop.

1.2 The Middle Ages—The Rise and Fall of a Feudal Society

Japan's Middle Ages began in the twelfth century and continued until the middle of the nineteenth century. During the first half of this period, the "dark ages," several military dictatorships rose and fell. The first was the *Kamakura Bakufu* (*bakufu* means "military headquarters"), established by the Minamoto family in Kamakura, two hundred miles east of Kyoto, after they defeated the Taira family of the western part of Japan in 1185. Then came the *Ashikaga Bakufu*, founded by Ashikaga Takauji, who defeated the imperial army, forced the emperor to flee, enthroned a new emperor in Kyoto in 1336, and established a rule which lasted two hundred years until new political struggles brought another period of flux.

The dark ages of political confusion and turbulence was a richly rewarding period of Japanese culture. The tastes of the new ruling class, *bushi* (the warriors, commonly known as *samurai* in the West), produced sophisticated poetry and a whole new style of prose writing— heroic tales of battles marked by chivalry. A marvelous technique of scroll painting developed portraying the famous battles of the day. There was once again new influence from Chinese Buddhism. The sects that emphasized salvation through faith found appeal among townsfolk and peasantry; and Zen Buddhism, with its emphasis on meditation and self-discipline, found appeal among the warrior class. In fact, under the patronage of the feudal lords, Zen monks made a major contribution in developing the arts. *Noo* drama, a highly stylized theatrical art, monochrone brush painting, flower arrangement, and the tea ceremony—the arts that Japan was to be identified with in later years—were all developed by Zen monks during the Ashikaga period.

The fourteenth through sixteenth centuries are noteworthy in one other respect. Japan engaged actively in international trade, first importing and exporting goods from China and Southeast Asia, and eventually meeting with the European merchant-adventurers who had entered East Asian waters. In 1542, Portuguese traders arrived on Kyuushuu with firearms. Seven years later, St. Francis Xavier, a Portuguese Jesuit, arrived; thus began the first Christian missionary movement in Japan. Sakai, the modern Osaka, became the commercial and industrial center, free from the tight control of feudal lords. There came about a money economy of considerable strength.

There are also some noteworthy developments pertaining to the Japanese language. For instance, there was a proliferation of personal pronouns of the first and second persons representing various levels of speech, which reflected the complex social stratification of the emerging feudal society. The Portuguese missionaries compiled various dictionaries and grammars of Japanese using the Roman alphabet and thus recorded more accurately than ever before the pronunciation of the sixteenth- and seventeenth-century spoken Japanese. The Portuguese traders and missionaries also introduced hundreds of new words into Japanese, half of them ecclesiastical. Table 5.2 gives some examples.

In 1603, Tokugawa Ieyasu gained control of all Japan and assumed the title of *shoogun* "commander," and established the *Edo Bakufu* in Edo, the modern Tokyo. This began the second half of Japan's feudal

TABLE 5.2   Vocabulary Borrowed from Portuguese

Portuguese	Japanese	Meaning
Christão	*Kirishitan*	"Christian"
confissão	*konhisan*	"confession"
graça	*garasa*	"grace"
oratio (Latin)	*orasho*	"prayer"
padre	*bateren*	"priest"
batão	*botan*	"button"
carta	*karuta*	"playing cards"
copo	*koppu*	"cup, tumbler"
raxa	*rasha*	"woolen cloth"
sabão	*shabon*	"soap"
tempero	*tenpura*	"deep-fried batter-coated fish and vegetables"
tutanaga	*totan*	"zinc"

era of political stability and national unity, which lasted for the next two and a half centuries.

Tokugawa Ieyasu, having witnessed the succession of political disruptions that could be caused by the death of a leader, was obsessed with the idea of building a political system that would survive after his passing. To accomplish this, he developed a highly bureaucratic central administration emphasizing collective responsibility rather than personalized leadership; collective responsibility allowed for the continuation of generations of Tokugawa dominance and is still an important characteristic of Japanese society. He continued to maintain the facade of the imperial rule from Kyoto, while he gained the control of the entire country from Edo by maneuvering to keep the power of the feudal lords in check. The emperor of Japan remained a figurehead until the end of the Tokugawa regime. He also adopted the social theories of Confucianism and created and maintained a hierarchy of four hereditary social classes—the warrior-administrator, the peasant, the artisan, and the merchant. This was a significant step backward from the first half of the feudal period when people of the middle and lower classes could rise to political power.

From the mid-seventeenth century, the government rejected Christianity and trade with European nations and ruthlessly persecuted Japanese converts and expelled all foreigners, except for a handful of Dutch traders on a small island off the coast of Kyuushuu. Japan was virtually isolated from the rest of the world. The majority of the Portuguese loanwords of ecclesiastical origin eventually disappeared, although a surprisingly large number of other Portuguese loanwords survived.

The Tokugawa government, powerful as it was, was not able to stop change from taking place within Japanese society. Commercial economy continued to grow, and by the eighteenth century the merchants, though nominally at the bottom of the social hierarchy, were making a decisive contribution toward creating a sophisticated urban culture. *Kabuki*, a new dramatic form which depicted the life of the townsfolk as well as historical tales; *Haiku*, the short poem; and woodblock printing were all developed during this period.

There was also a class of intellectuals developing out of the once largely illiterate warrior class. The feudal lords established schools to educate the warriors; and the warriors, along with the Buddhist monks and the Shinto priests, taught the townsmen and peasants at small private academies called "temple schools." It is estimated that by the end of the Tokugawa period, literacy among males was about 45 percent, and among females, 15 percent.

By the early eighteenth century, books on the western sciences became available to a small group of students interested in the West known as students of "Dutch learning." They became versed in fields

TABLE 5.3   *Vocabulary Borrowed from Dutch*

Dutch	Japanese	Meaning
bier	*biiru*	"beer"
blik	*buriki*	"tin plate"
brandpunt	*pinto*	"focus"
flanel	*neru*	"flannel"
glas	*garasu*	"glass"
gom	*gomu*	"rubber"
koffie	*koohii*	"coffee"
mes	*mesu*	"scalpel"
pek	*penki*	"paint"
ransel	*randoseru*	"knapsack used by school children"
rheumatisch	*ryuumachi*	"rheumatism"
spuit	*supoito*	"squirt"

such as gunnery, smelting, shipbuilding, cartography, astronomy, and medicine. They also contributed to introducing a considerable amount of Dutch vocabulary into Japanese. Many of these loanwords were replaced by German, French, and English terminologies in later years, but many others still remain in contemporary Japanese. Table 5.3 gives a few examples of loanwords from Dutch that are still in use.

Political stability, a nationwide commercial economy, widespread literacy, a small but important group of intellectuals who were familiar with the western sciences, and a strong sense of national identity of the late Tokugawa period served to prepare the people of Japan to face their next drastic encounter with the West in the middle of the nineteenth century.

1.3   Modern Times—The Meiji Restoration and the Road to Modernization

In the first half of the nineteenth century, the American whaling vessels and clipper ships crossing the Pacific to China desired permission to enter Japanese ports to replenish water and supplies. In July 1853, Commodore Matthew C. Perry steamed into Tokyo Bay with a letter from the President of the United States demanding the inauguration of trade relations. This sudden intrusion of foreigners produced consternation in the already weakened Tokugawa government.

The nation was split into two factions—conservatives who advocated the expulsion of the foreigners, and realists, the students of "Dutch learning," who saw the inevitable new tide and advocated the opening of Japan. In the winter of 1854, when Perry returned, the Tokugawa government could do nothing but to sign a treaty permitting the opening of two ports: one in Honshuu, near Edo, and another in Hokkaidoo.

The situation thereafter deteriorated rapidly until the Tokugawa regime finally collapsed in January 1868. The imperial family was moved from Kyoto to Edo, to the great castle where the Tokugawas had ruled the nation during the previous two and a half centuries. It was announced that the "restoration" of imperial rule had been accomplished.

From 1868 to the turn of the century, Japan hastened to transform herself into a modern nation. This was accomplished under the rule of Emperor Meiji, but still following the old line of collective leadership by able young politicians who were from the lower strata of the warrior class. The first important task was the abolition of the outward vestiges of feudalism. The new leaders persuaded the large number of autonomous feudal lords to offer their domains to the emperor as tokens of their allegiance, for which they were compensated with large payments in the form of government bonds. In 1871, the government decreed legal equality for all Japanese. In 1873, the government established universal military service—a revolutionary reform diminishing the privileged position of the warrior-administrator class, which at that time constituted about 6 percent of the total population.

The next task was the development of modern political institutions, a new social order, and a new economic system to build a modern industrialized nation. The government hired experts in Western technology, sent Japanese students abroad to study the latest European technology and institutions—to Britain to study the navy and merchant marine, to Germany to study the army and medicine, to France to study local government and legal systems, and to the United States to study business methods. The United States also sent to Japan a large number of Protestant missionaries who provided instruction in English and also founded many pioneering schools.

In 1871, the government embarked on a program of universal education, and by the beginning of the twentieth century there was a six-year compulsory elementary school, followed by a five-year middle school and a three-year high school, with a three-year university at the top of the educational pyramid. Higher education, however, was open only to a handful of students who constituted the leadership elite of modern Japan. On February 11, 1889, a constitution was promulgated that placed absolute power in the emperor. The constitution also created a parliament with an entirely elected House of Representatives and a House of Peers. The electorate, however, was limited to men paying a prescribed amount in direct taxes. They numbered about 6 percent of the adult male population and were largely peasants and landowners.

The new wave of Western influence also meant that a large amount of new vocabulary entered Japanese. Most of the words were from English, both American and British, but many others entered from German, French, and even Italian. Table 5.4 presents a few of the earlier loanwords.

By the beginning of the twentieth century, the Japanese also began to create their own Japanese-English expressions, a practice that continues to be widely exercised in present-day Japan. For instance, *miruku hooru* "milk hall" referred to a coffee shop where milk was the main item served; *teeburu supiichi* "table speech" referred to the after-dinner speech (this is still used); and *moga* and *mobo* denoted the fashionable young men and women who were infatuated by the Western influence in the Roaring Twenties.

Having modernized herself sufficiently to be able to compete with the Western imperialists, Japan startled the Western world by winning significant concessions from Russia in the war of 1904–5; and then she took a series of aggressive actions against China, taking control of Taiwan, Okinawa, and Korea. In World War I, Japan allied herself with Great Britain and gained some of the German colonies in the North Pacific. She also gradually expanded her power in Manchuria. In December 1940, Japan entered an all-out war against the European Allies and fought against them throughout the Pacific region, in addition

TABLE 5.4   *Vocabulary Borrowed from English, French, and German*

Source	Japanese	Meaning
gasoline	*gasorin*	
high collar	*haikara*	"fashionable"
inverness cape	*inbanesu*	
lemonade	*ramune*	
salary	*sararii*	
typewriter	*taipuraitaa*	
white shirt	*waishatsu*	
atelier (Fr)	*atorie*	"artist's studio"
guêtres (Fr)	*geetoru*	"puttee"
mètre (Fr)	*meetoru*	"meter"
Gaze (Ger)	*gaaze*	"surgical gauze"
Karte (Ger)	*karute*	"patient's record"

to a continued invasion of China. Japan's militaristic expansionist era of half a century closed when she unconditionally surrendered to the Allied Forces on August 14, 1945.

The recorded history of Japan prior to modern times can be divided into two periods of roughly six hundred years each. In each of these periods, she underwent a time of active cultural intercourse with the outside world, and then, a period of reflection on and assimilation of the foreign elements into her own tradition. The Japanese language was an integral part of this history. In modern times, Japan has become a highly industrialized and technologized society. She is now fully enmeshed in the global community of nations. The Japanese language, having emerged from a nearly complete boycott of all English words during World War II, seems to be barely able to keep pace with new technological terminologies. The words such as *konpyuutaa* "computer," *masu-komi* "mass communication," *terebi* "television," *suupaa-(maaketto)* "super market," *insutanto fuudo* "instant food," *rasshu awaa* "rush hour," and *purehabu juutaku* "prefabricated house" are just as much part of the household vocabulary in Japan as they are in many other parts of the world.

2   THE STRUCTURE OF JAPANESE

2.1   Sentence Formation in Japanese

Because the cultures of China and Japan have a great deal in common, many people incorrectly assume that their languages are therefore also related. In fact, except for shared vocabulary due to borrowing, they have no more in common than say English and Japanese. Chinese is a branch of the Sino-Tibetan language family. As for Japanese, because of the many similarities with Korean, it is speculated that it may be distantly related to Korean, and, still more distantly, to the Altaic language family, which means it might share common ancestry with Turkish, Mongolian, and Hungarian. Indeed Japanese is far more similar to these languages than to Chinese.

2.1.1   *Japanese—A Verb-final Language*   The basic word order of transitive sentences in Japanese is that of Subject–Object–Verb, with a very rigid constraint that the verb appear at the end of the sentence. As for subject and object, there is considerable freedom in their positions. For instance, we can say (4a) or (4b) (note that subjects are marked by *ga* and objects by *o*):

(4) a.   *Taroo-ga   tegami-o   kakimasu.*
        Subj.   letter-Obj.   write
      Taroo writes a letter/letters.

b. *tegami-o   Taroo-ga   kakimasu.*
    letter-Obj.   Subj.   write

but, we cannot say either (4c) or (4d) (asterisks indicate ungrammaticality):

c. **tegami-o   kakimasu   Taroo-ga.*

d. **kakimasu   Taroo-ga   tegami-o.*

or, any other alternatives in which the verb does not occur at the end.

It should also be noted at this point that in Japanese the noun phrases are often omitted when there is an understanding between the speaker and the hearer as to what they refer. Thus, to talk about what Taroo does, one might just say:

(5) *tegami-o   kakimasu.*
     letter-Obj.   write
     (He) writes letters.

2.1.2 *Japanese Postpositions*   Verb-final languages have a strong tendency to have 'postpositions' instead of 'prepositions'; Japanese follows suit with a great variety of such expressions, some seventy of them. First there are the 'case' markers: we have already seen the subject and object markers *-ga* and *-o*; another is the genitive marker *-no*, like English "-'s": "Taroo's letter" is *Taroo-no tegami*. Look at the following sentence, which uses all three case particles.

(6) *Kazuo-ga   Sooseki-no   shoosetsu-o   yomimashita.*
     Subj.   Gen. novel   -Obj.   read
     Kazuo read Sooseki's novel.

Then there are those comparable to English prepositions. For instance, "to" in:

(7) John goes to school.

will be represented by *-e* as follows:

     Jon-ga gakkoo-e ikimasu.
             school -to   go

Ni represents the location of an entity. It is comparable to "at" in:

(8) John is at school.

In Japanese, sentence (8) would be:

> *Jon-ga   gakkoo-ni   imasu.*
>   school -at   be

But in Japanese, the "at" denoting the place of activity is not *-ni*, but *-de*. For instance:

> (9) *Kazuko-ga   gakkoo-de   eigo-o   naratte   imasu.*
>   school -at   English   learn   be
>   Kazuko is learning English at school.

And, *-de* represents one other meaning, namely "by means of" in English.

> (10) *Kazuko-ga   basu-de   kimasu.*
>   bus -by   come
>   Kazuko comes by bus.

Finally, "to/until" and "from" in English are *-made* and *-kara* in Japanese. The Japanese expressions denote both location and time just as the English ones do.

> (11) *Kazuko-ga   Tokyo-kara   Nagoya-made   ikimasu.*
>   from   to   go
>   Kazuko goes from Tokyo (as far as) to Nagoya.
>
> (12) *Kazuo-ga   ichi   -ji   -kara   san   -ji   -made   imasu.*
>   one   o'clock-from   three o'clock-until   be
>   Kazuo is (here) from one o'clock to three o'clock.

A third group of postpositions are called 'sentence particles.' There are six frequently used ones, *-ne*, *-yo*, *-wa*, *-zo*, *-na*, and *-sa*, which represent the speaker's attitude. *Ne* is comparable to the tag-question in English which represents the speaker's lack of assertiveness.

> (13) *kore-ga   anata-no   hon   desu   ne.*
>   this   you   's   book   be
>   This is your book, isn't it?

Yo represents the speaker's insistence.

> (14) *kore-ga   anata-no   hon   desu   yo.*
>   I'm telling you—this is your book.

2.1.3   *Question Formation*   Questions are signaled by an inter-rogative particle -*ka* at the end of the sentence. For instance:

(15)   *Tokyo-ga   Nihon-no   shuto   desu.*
         Japan   's   capital   be
       Tokyo is the capital of Japan.

is turned into a yes-no question, as follows:

(16)   *Tokyo-ga   Nihon-no   shuto   desu   ka.*
       Is Tokyo the capital of Japan?

So also for information questions, those formed with interrogative words such as "what" and "who." The phrase that represents the thing in question is simply replaced by an appropriate question word. The -*ka* question marker is retained at the end of the sentence. Japanese has the following nine question words:

(a)	*nani/nan*	what
(b)	*dare*	who
(c)	*doko*	where
(d)	*dore*	which one
(e)	*dono* + Noun	which + Noun
(f)	*donna*	what kind
(g)	*doo*	how
(h)	*itsu*	when
(i)	*dooshite*	why

Let us form some WH-questions using sentence (17) below:

(17)   *Masuda-ga   shiai -ni   kachimashita.*
                       match-in   won
       Masuda won a match.

First, the who-question—repace *Masuda* with *dare*:

(18)   ***dare****-ga   shiai-ni   kachimashita   ka.*
       Who won the match?

Second, the what-question—replace *shiai* with *nani*:

(19)   *Masuda-ga   **nani**-ni   kachimashita   ka.*
       What did Masuda win?

Third, the which-question—add *dono* in front of *shiai*:

(20) *Masuda-ga **dono**-shiai-ni kachimashita ka.*
      Which match did Masuda win?

We can combine (18) and (20), and add the *where-* and *when*-questions as well. We will have:

(21) *dare-ga doko-de itsu dono-shiai-ni*
      who   where-at when which-match-at

      kachimashita ka.
      won
      Who won which match, where and when?

and the answer will be:

(22) *Masuda-ga Hakone-de shi-gatsu too-ka -ni*
                  in   four-month ten-day on
      shoogi-no meijin-sen -ni kachimashita.
      chess 's championship-in   won
      Masuda won the Japanese chess championship in Hakone on April 10th.

2.1.4 *Japanese—A Left-branching Language* One of the important characteristics of human language is 'recursion', the way in which sentences, for example, can show up within larger sentences, which in turn can be part of still larger sentences. A consequence of recursion is that there is no such thing as the longest sentence of a language—an already long sentence can be expanded and made still longer. One of the ways that a sentence is expanded and made longer is by what is called 'embedding'. English uses the mechanism known as 'right-branching embedding', e.g., a relative clause that modifies the head-noun comes to the right of it. For instance, take the familiar nursery rhyme "The house that Jack built." The first sentence begins with:

(23) This is the house

which is expanded by a *that*-clause to its right.

(24) This is the house that Jack built.

The very final sentence which begins with:

(25) This is the farmer sowing his corn, that fed the cock that crowed in the morn, that ...

has altogether ten *that*-clauses, each one of which modifies the noun to its left.

In Japanese, branching goes in the opposite direction from English, i.e., to the left of the head-noun. Thus the translation of "The house that Jack built" would begin with:

(26) *kore-ga   uchi   desu.*
      this   house   be

This will be expanded into:

(27) *kore-ga   Jakku-ga   tateta   uchi   desu.*
      this   built   house   be

Note that Japanese has no relative pronoun: *Jakku-ga tateta* "Jack built" simply goes to the left of *uchi* "(the) house." And the final sentence would be something like:

(28) *kore-ga   ...   o-boo-san-o   okoshita   ondori-ni   esa-o*
      this   priest   awakened cock -to food

      yatta   noofu   desu.
      gave   farmer   be
          This is the farmer that fed the cock that awakened the priest . . . .

Each one of the remaining relative clauses with the head-noun would precede the other and would fit in the space left in sentence (28).

    2.1.5 *Backward Gapping*   One final point regarding word order in Japanese is the direction of verb phrase deletion. In English, for instance, there is a process of deleting all but the first one of a series of identical verbs or verb phrases in coordinate sentences. Thus a sentence such as:

(29) a.   John ate an apple, Jack ate a pear, and Bill ate a peach.

can be simplified to:

      b.   John ate an apple, Jack a pear, and Bill a peach.

We call this operation "gapping," and the way it operates in English is "forward gapping."

In Japanese, gapping works in the opposite direction and is called "backward gapping." In other words, all but the last of the identical verbs is deleted. Look at the Japanese version of sentence (29).

(30) a. *Jon-ga   ringo-o   tabemashita,   Jakku-ga   nashi-o*
       John   apple   ate   Jack   pear
      tabemashita,   soshite,   Biru-ga   momo-o   tabemashita.
      ate   and   Bill   peach   ate

can be simplified to:

    b. *Jon-ga   ringo-o,   Jakku-ga   nashi-o,   soshite,   Biru-ga*
       John   apple   Jack   pear   and   Bill
      momo-o   tabemashita.
      peach   ate

The same holds true of the next sentence:

(31) a. *Kyaroru-ga   koohii-o   nomimasu,   Arisu-ga   koocha-o*
       Carol   coffee   drink   Alice   black tea
      nomimasu,   soshite,   Pegii-ga   Nihon-cha-o   nomimasu.
      drink   and   Peggy   Japan-tea   drink

can be simplified to:

    b. *Kyaroru-ga   koohii-o,   Arisu-ga   koocha-o,   soshite,*
       Carol   coffee   Alice   black tea   and
      Pegii-ga   Nihon-cha-o   nomimasu.
      Peggy   Japan -tea   drink
      Carol drinks coffee, Alice black tea, and Peggy
      Japanese tea.

2.1.6 *Temporal Expressions* Japanese has two so-called basic tense markers, namely *-u/ru*, the nonpast, and *-ta/da*, the past. The nonpast marker *-u* is suffixed to the verb stems which end in a consonant, and *-ru* to the ones which end in a vowel. The past marker *-ta* is suffixed to all but the ones which end in a voiced consonant, and those take *-da*. (There are some irregularities which will be explained later.)

When the nonpast marker is added to a verb which represents some kind of activity (an activity or an accomplishment verb), or event which occurs instantaneously (an achievement verb), it represents either habitual or future occurrence. That is:

(32) *Akio-ga   shinbun-o   yomimas-u.*
            newspaper   read   -Nonpast

means, either (a) or (b).

    (a)   Akio reads a/the newspaper(s) (regularly).

    (b)   Akio will read a/the newspaper(s).

and:

(33) *Akiko-ga   kimas-u.*
      come -Nonpast

means, either (a) or (b).

(a) Akiko comes (regularly).

(b) Akiko will come.

On the other hand, when *-u* is part of an expression that describes a location, a quality or a state (a stative verb), it can be used in contexts where in English we would use either the simple present, the present perfect, or the future.

(34) *Jiroo-ga   uchi-ni   imas-u.*
      home-at   be -Nonpast

(a) Jiroo is at home (regularly).

(b) Jiroo is/has been at home.

(c) Jiroo will be at home.

As for *-ta*, when it is added to an activity verb, it corresponds to either the past or the present perfect in English. For instance:

(35) *Akio-ga   repooto-o   yomimashi-ta.*
      report   read   -Past

(a) Akio read the report.

(b) Akio has read the report.

When it is added to an achievement verb, it corresponds to any one of the three readings as shown below.

(36) *Akiko-ga   kimashi-ta.*
      come   -Past

(a) Akiko came.

(b) Akiko has come (on some occasion).

(c) Akiko has come (and is here now).

When it is added to a stative verb, it normally conveys the straightforward past tense reading.

(37) *Jiroo-ga   uchi -ni   imashi-ta.*
             home-at   be -Past
      Jiroo was at home.

Up until now we have been using 'polite' verb forms, with a special morpheme for 'polite'; without this special morpheme, verbs have a neutral or informal stylistic value. The 'polite' morpheme alternates its shape according to tense. The tense endings alternate as well, according to the sound that precedes them. Japanese has two types of regular verbs and a handful of irregular verbs. The first type of regular verbs ends in a vowel *-i* and *-e*, and the second type of verbs ends in a consonant (there are nine different consonants). Table 5.5 is a list of representative examples.

In addition to the tense markers, Japanese has a basic aspectual marker, *-te/de* ('progressive') which works in combination with *i-*, the same verb "be" that we saw in example (34). Its basic meaning is that the activity or state continues at the designated time. (The shape of the stem for this form is the same as the one for 'neutral-past'.)

(38) *Jiroo-ga   tegami-o   kai -te   i -mas -u.*
             letter   write-Prog. be-Polite-Nonpast
      Jiroo is writing/has been writing a letter.

(39) *Jiroo-ga   tegami-o   kai -te   i -mashi-ta.*
             letter   write-Prog. be-Polite-Nonpast
      Jiroo was writing/had been writing a letter.

Notice we have a very similar construction in English except that the order of elements is reversed.

Jiroo **was** at home.
Jiroo **was** write-ing.

Jiroo-ga   uchi-ni   **i-mashi-ta.**
Jiroo-ga   kai-te   **i-mashi-ta.**

The same verb "be" works as the pivot for both a locative and a progressive verb construction, and this same verb carries the tense marking. In Japanese tense-bearing forms always occur at the end of the verb phrase.

2.1.7. *Negation in Japanese* The basic negative sentences in Japanese are formed by adding a negative morpheme *-na/ana* to the stem of the verb in the nonpast, and *-na/ana* plus *-kat* in the past. *Na* follows the verbs that end in a vowel, and *-ana*, the ones that end in a consonant. An interesting feature of negative sentences is that subjects

TABLE 5.5 Neutral and Polite Verb Forms

TYPE I

	Neutral		Polite	
	Nonpast	**Past**	**Nonpast**	**Past**
"see"	mi-ru	mi-ta	mi-mas-u	mi-mashi-ta
"be"	i-ru	i-ta	i-mas-u	i-mashi-ta
"get up"	oki-ru	oki-ta	oki-mas-u	oki-mashi-ta
"sleep"	ne-ru	ne-ta	ne-mas-u	ne-mashi-ta
"eat"	tabe-ru	tabe-ta	tabe-mas-u	tabe-mashi-ta
"leave"	de-ru	de-ta	de-mas-u	de-mashi-ta

TYPE II

	Neutral		Polite	
	Nonpast	**Past**	**Nonpast**	**Past**
"write"	kak-u	kai-ta	kaki-mas-u	kaki-mashi-ta
"swim"	oyog-u	oyoi-da	oyogi-mas-u	oyogi-mashi-ta
"read"	yom-u	yon-da	yomi-mas-u	yomi-mashi-ta
"die"	shin-u	shin-da	shini-mas-u	shini-mashi-ta
"call"	yob-u	yon-da	yobi-mas-u	yobi-mashi-ta
"win"	kats-u	kat-ta	kachi-mas-u	kachi-mashi-ta
"lend"	kas-u	kashi-ta	kashi-mas-u	kashi-mashi-ta
"exist"	ar-u	at-ta	ari-mas-u	ari-mashi-ta
"think"	omo(w)-u	omot-ta	omoi-mas-u	omoi-mashi-ta

TYPE III (Irregular)

	Neutral		Polite	
	Nonpast	**Past**	**Nonpast**	**Past**
"do"	su-ru	shi-ta	shi-mas-u	shi-mashi-ta
"come"	ku-ru	ki-ta	ki-mas-u	ki-mashi-ta
"be" (Copula)	da	dat-ta	des-u	deshi-ta

are normally marked as 'topics', with -*wa* instead of with -*ga*. Knowing when to use -*wa* is one of the central problems in learning to speak Japanese. We will look at negation first with the 'neutral' verb forms.

(40) *Eiji-ga*   *suteeki-o* $\begin{Bmatrix} \text{a.} & \textit{tabe-ru} \\ \text{b.} & \textit{tabe-ta} \end{Bmatrix}$.
                    steak

Eiji $\begin{Bmatrix} \text{a.} & \text{eats} \\ \text{b.} & \text{ate} \end{Bmatrix}$ steak.

changes to:

(41) *Eiji-wa*   *suteeki-o* $\begin{Bmatrix} \text{a.} & \textit{tabe-na-i} \\ \text{b.} & \textit{tabe-na-kat-ta} \end{Bmatrix}$.

Eiji $\begin{Bmatrix} \text{a.} & \text{does not eat} \\ \text{b.} & \text{did not eat} \end{Bmatrix}$ steak.

(42) *Eiko-ga*   *eki -made* $\begin{Bmatrix} \text{a.} & \textit{aruk-u} \\ \text{b.} & \textit{arui-ta} \end{Bmatrix}$.
                    station-to

Eiko $\begin{Bmatrix} \text{a.} & \text{walks} \\ \text{b.} & \text{walked} \end{Bmatrix}$ to the station.

changes to:

(43) *Eiko-wa*   *eki-made* $\begin{Bmatrix} \text{a.} & \textit{aruk-ana-i} \\ \text{b.} & \textit{aruk-ana-kat-ta} \end{Bmatrix}$.

Eiko $\begin{Bmatrix} \text{a.} & \text{does not walk} \\ \text{b.} & \text{did not walk} \end{Bmatrix}$ to the station.

Up until now we have been using 'polite' verb forms, with -*mas-u* for the nonpast, and -*mashi-ta* for the past. These forms take a different inflection for negation. The nonpast -*mas-u* changes to -*mas-en*, and the past -*mashi-ta* changes to -*mas-en deshi-ta*. Therefore, sentence (40) in the -*mas*-form would be:

(44) *Eiji-ga*   *suteeki-o* $\begin{Bmatrix} \text{a.} & \textit{tabe-mas-u} \\ \text{b.} & \textit{tabe-mashi-ta} \end{Bmatrix}$.

Eiji $\begin{Bmatrix} \text{a.} & \text{eats} \\ \text{b.} & \text{ate} \end{Bmatrix}$ steak.

and, its negative counterpart would be:

(45) *Eiji-wa*   *suteeki-o* $\begin{Bmatrix} \text{a.} & \textit{tabe-mas-en} \\ \text{b.} & \textit{tabe-mas-en deshi-ta} \end{Bmatrix}$.

Eiji $\begin{Bmatrix} \text{a.} & \text{does not eat} \\ \text{b.} & \text{did not eat} \end{Bmatrix}$ steak.

Similarly, sentences (42) and (43) in the *-mas-*form would be:

(46)   *Eiko-ga   eki-made* $\begin{Bmatrix} a. & aruki\text{-}mas\text{-}u \\ b. & aruki\text{-}mashi\text{-}ta \end{Bmatrix}$.

Eiko $\begin{Bmatrix} a. & \text{walks} \\ b. & \text{walked} \end{Bmatrix}$ to the station.

(47)   *Eiko-wa   eki-made* $\begin{Bmatrix} a. & aruki\text{-}mas\text{-}en \\ b. & aruki\text{-}mas\text{-}en\ deshi\text{-}ta \end{Bmatrix}$.

Eiko $\begin{Bmatrix} a. & \text{does not walk} \\ b. & \text{did not walk} \end{Bmatrix}$ to the station.

By way of summary, let us look at a short dialogue in Japanese. We present the English sentence with glosses first, so that the reader can try forming sentences without looking at the examples. See how much of the sentence you can construct on your own.

A.   *Who   won   in   the   election?*
     dare-ga   kachi-   -ni   senkyo
     dare-ga senkyo-ni kachi-mashi-ta ka.

B.   *Didn't   you   read   this   morning's   paper?*
     anata-wa   yomi-   kesa   -no   shinbun
     anata-wa kesa-no shinbun-o yomi-mas-en deshi-ta ka.

A.   *No.   I   don't read   the paper   every   morning.*
     iie   watashi-wa   yomi-   shinbun   mai-   asa
     iie. watashi-wa mai-asa shinbun-o yomi-mas-en.

B.   *I'm telling you—Mr. Miki   won.*
           yo   Miki-san-ga   kachi-
     Miki-san-ga kachi-mashi-ta yo.

A.   *Is   that   the Mr. Miki   who   lost   last year?*
     des-   sore-wa   Miki-san   make-   kyonen
     sore-wa kyonen make-ta Miki-san des-u ka.

B.   *Yes.   It   is.*   (translate "(That)   is   so.")
     hai.   des-   soo
     hai. soo des-u.

2.2   Some Japanese Expressions Reflecting the Speaker's Perspective

Language enables the speaker to express his own perspective, i.e., the way he sees the world and understands it. It is not uncommon for two participants in an incident to describe the same event from entirely different points of view.

2.2.1 *How Japanese Marks Topics* The speaker's perspective is reflected, in its most fundamental sense, in what he chooses to talk about. English can mark this by intonation contours. Compare the way the speaker of English might say sentence (48):

(48) John is standing in front of the station.

Context 1: Speakers A and B are talking about John, who, unknown to them, is down the street at the station. Speaker A then notices John, and he utters sentence (48). Now consider how sentence (48) would be pronounced in context 2: Speakers A and B are down the street from the station talking about some distant topic when Speaker A suddenly notices John, their mutual friend, standing in front of the station. Speaker A says sentence (48). In the first context, *John* is the topic of the conversation, and it is the fact that he is standing in front of the station that is new information. The intonation rises just on this new information. "John" is on a low pitch because he doesn't represent new information. In the second context, the entire sentence conveys new information, and so there is a sustained high pitch throughout. What is crucial is what the speaker thinks he can assume to be shared information with the hearer.

In Japanese, this distinction is made not by intonation, but by two syntactic markers, -*wa* and -*ga*. Therefore, the Japanese translation of sentence (48) in context 1 would be (49a) with *Jon* followed by -*wa*, and in context 2 it would be (49b) with *Jon-ga*, as shown below. *Wa* is called the topicalizer, and -*ga*, the subject marker.

(49) {a. *Jon-wa*}   *eki -no mae -ni tat -te*
      {b. *Jon-ga*}   station's   front-in stand-Prog.
                      i -mas -u
                      be-Polite-Nonpast

Look at the next example of a conversation in Japanese where this principle is at work in a more natural way.

(50) Speaker A *tokoro-de,   yuube   Sakai-san* {a. -*ga* }
                 by the way   last night   {b. *-*wa* }
                 asobi-ni   ki -mashi-ta yo.
                 play -to   come-Polite
                      By the way, last night Mr. Sakai came for a visit.

      Speaker B *soo   des-u ka.*   *Sakai-san* {a. *-*ga* }
                 so   be(Polite)   {b. -*wa* }
                 genki   des-u   ka.
                 healthy   be
                      Is that so? Is Mr. Sakai healthy?

Speaker A is reporting the fact that Mr. Sakai came for a visit—it is new information to Speaker B, therefore, *-ga* is being used. In Speaker B's response to A, he is referring to the Mr. Sakai that Speaker A brought up—it is shared information between the two, therefore, *-wa* is used.

The speaker also uses *-wa* when he is talking generically. For instance:

> (51) *kujira-wa   honyuu -rui   des-u.*
>   whale   mammal-kind   be -Nonpast
>   Whales are mammals.

The sentence is about whales in general, which are considered to be in the 'permanent registry' shared by all speakers. When a Japanese goes shopping and asks for something, he also uses *-wa* as in:

> (52) *suihanki-wa   ari -mas -u   ka.*
>   rice cooker   exist-Polite-Nonpast   Ques.
>   Are there rice cookers = Do you have rice cookers?

The person is interested in buying only one rice cooker, but he does not have a particular one in mind; *suihanki* is a generic term for all models of rice cookers.

There is one other case where the distinction is based on the same principle. When Speaker B responds to Speaker A's question such as:

> (53) *dare-ga   mado-o   ake -mashi-ta   ka.*
>   window   open-Polite -Past   Ques.
>   Who opened the window?

he would use *-ga*:

> (54) *Suzuki-san-ga   ake-mashi-ta.*
>   open
>   Mr. Suzuki opened (it).

because the speaker has chosen one person, namely Mr. Suzuki, out of all the possibilities, and it is new information to the hearer. In contrast, when the speaker is comparing two persons, or things, he would use *-wa*. He would say, for instance:

> (55) *Suzuki-san-wa   mai   -asa   roku-ji   -ni   oki*
>   every morning   six o'clock-at   get up
>
>   *-mas   -u.   ga, Satoo-san-wa   hachi-ji-ni   oki-mas-u.*
>   -Polite -Nonpast   but   eight
>
>   Mr. Suzuki gets up at six every morning, but Mr. Satoo gets up at eight.

The Structure of Japanese 269

Lastly, the use of -wa is not restricted to the subject noun phrase. The speaker can talk about anything he wants to talk about; therefore, he can use -wa with any other element in the sentence. For instance:

(56) *Nihon-de-wa Kyuushuu-to Hokkaidoo-kara sekitan-ga*
Japan -in   and   from   coal

tor -e   -mas -u.   *Shikoku-kara-wa*
take-Potential-Polite-Nonpast   from

tor-e-mas-en.
              not

> In Japan, coal can be gotten (can be obtained) from Kyuushuu and Hokkaidoo. Speaking of Shikoku, (coal) cannot be obtained from there.

And, as seen here, the thing that is being talked about does tend to be brought to the front of the sentence.

2.2.2 *How Japanese Represents Psychological Distance* The speaker's perspective can also be described in terms of the psychological distance that he feels exists between himself and the event he talks about.

The Objective-Reportative Sense of the Progressive with -te i-ru A progressive sentence in the nonpast can, in appropriate contexts, have a variety of interpretations, e.g.:

(57) *Masao-ga Hakata-ni it -te   i -ru.*
                         to go-Prog. be-Nonpast

(a) Masao is going to Hakata.

(b) Masao went/has gone to Hakata (and is there now).

(c) Masao will go to Hakata.

But there is a further meaning, for which English does not have a convenient equivalent, possible for sentence (57) or in an example such as the following with the verb *de-* "leave/graduate":

(58) *Naomi-wa   juu-nen mae-ni daigaku-o*
         Topic ten-year ago -in college

a. *de -mashi -ta*
   leave-Polite -Past
b. *de -te   i -mas -u*
   leave-Prog. be-Polite-Nonpast

Naomi graduated from college ten years ago.

Version (a) of the sentence is a straightforward reporting of a past event, while (b) conveys the feeling that the speaker is making the statement from a particularly detached and objective point of view, in this case probably on the basis of recorded evidence. Thus, the next sentence becomes rather awkward.

(59) ?*watashi-mo   juu-nen mae-ni daigaku-o   de -te
       I   -too   year ago-in college   leave-Prog.
       i -mas -u.
       be-Polite-Nonpast
          I, too, graduated from college ten years ago.

It is awkward because a speaker would not ordinarily be detached in talking about his graduation from college and would certainly not need recorded evidence—memory would suffice.

There is a group of exclamatory phrases that express the physical or psychological state of the speaker and do not take the progressive nonpast *-te i-ru*, for example ones involving the expressions *tsukare-* "become tired," *o-naka-ga suk-* "stomach become empty" (with the respectful prefix *o-*, which will be commented on later) and *komar-* "be in trouble":

(60) *aa, tsukare-te i-ru!   Oh, am I tired!

(61) *aa, o-naka-ga sui-te i-ru!   Oh, am I hungry!

(62) *aa, komat-te i-ru!   Oh, am I in trouble!

They take the past *-ta* without the progressive as shown below:

(63) aa, tsukare-ta!

(64) aa, o-naka-ga sui-ta!

(65) aa, komat-ta!

All three sentences express the speaker's physical or psychological state in which he is deeply involved. They are not objective-reportative remarks. It should follow, then, that if the speaker were to make an objective statement about his condition rather than cry out in despair, he should be able to use the progressive *-te i-ru* appropriately. And indeed he will:

(66) kyoo- wa   tsukare-te   i -mas -u   no de,
       today-Topic   tired   -Prog. be-Polite-Nonpast   since
       hayaku   ne -mas -u.
       early go   sleep-Polite-Nonpast
          Since I am tired today, I will go to bed early.

Focus and the Sense of Adversity in Passivization Passivization in Japanese involves the passive morpheme -(*r*)*are*. Since the order of noun phrases is relatively free in Japanese, a passive may, but need not, have the two noun phrases in different positions from those they take in the active, as they do in English. So, for instance:

(67) *Naomi-ga   Seiji-o   ut -ta.*
                            hit -Past
       Naomi hit Seiji.

can be passivized as either (68) or (69):

(68) *Seiji-ga   Naomi-ni   ut -are -ta.*
                    by   hit-Pass.-Past
       Seiji was hit by Naomi.

(69) *Naomi-ni Seiji-ga ut-are-ta.*
       By Naomi, Seiji was hit.

The meanings of sentences (67), (68), and (69) however are not exactly the same. As in English, passivization in Japanese is often used to put a special focus on the element which has been passivized (the new subject); just so, sentence (68) has a focus on Seiji, and it would be appropriate as an answer to a question such as:

(70) Who was hit by Naomi?

But sentence (69) has a focus on Naomi, and it would be appropriate as an answer to a question such as:

(71) Who was it that Seiji was hit by?

This ordinary passive always has the object of a transitive verb promoted to subject, as in examples (67)–(69) where we see *Seiji* take on the subject marker -*ga* instead of the object marker -*o*; Japanese has another construction called the 'adversitive passive' which lacks exactly this characteristic, so much so that it can be used with intransitive verbs where there is no object, or with transitive verbs, in which case objects keep their -*o* case marking. It conveys the sense of someone's being affected (most often adversely) by an event over which he has no control. For instance, take a natural phenomenon such as rain. If the speaker is simply stating the fact, he would say:

(72) *ame-ga   furi-mashi-ta.*
       rain   fall -Polite-Past
          It rained.

But if the speaker were caught in the rain and became drenched, or if he had to cancel a picnic on account of it, he could express his sense of annoyance by saying:

(73) *watashi-wa   ame-ni   fur-are -mashi-ta.*
       I   rain -by fall-Pass.-Polite -Past
       I was subjected to it raining.

Here is another example:

(74) *Kazuko-ga   otooto   -ni   atarashii-kutsu-o*
                   younger brother -by   new   shoes
       yogos-are -te,   komat -te   i -ru.
       dirty Pass.-Gerund distress-Prog. be-Nonpast
             Having been subjected to her younger brother's dirtying
             (her) new shoes, Kazuko is distressed.

The incident itself of Kazuko's brother dirtying her shoes had nothing to do with her directly, but she is inconvenienced by it.

Finally, because of the adversitive reading one gets with the verb "to rain" in the passive, a sentence such as (76) below becomes rather strange, whereas (75) would be quite appropriate.

(75) *ame-ga   fut -te,   yokat-ta!*
       rain   fall-Gerund   good -Past
       It rained and was good = It was good that it rained.

(76) *??ame-ni   fur-are-te,   yokat-ta!*   ("??" before an
                   Pass.   example indicates
                                             questionable
                                             usage.)
       (I) was subjected to it raining, and it was good.

But, sometimes, the speaker would add a phrase such as *kekkyoku* which means "ultimately" and say something like:

(77) *ame-ni   fur-are-te,   kekkyoku   yokat   -ta.*
                   Pass.   ultimately
       (I) was subjected to it raining, (but) it ultimately turned out for the best.

2.2.3 *How Japanese Distinguishes Sensations of Self and Nonself*
Another device for expressing psychological distance between the speaker and the thing which he is talking about is *-gar*, which is suffixed

to words representing the physical and emotional sensations of those other than the speaker himself.

In English, under normal circumstances, when Speaker A says:

(78)　I'm $\begin{Bmatrix} \text{cold} \\ \text{hot} \end{Bmatrix}$.

or:

(79)　I'm $\begin{Bmatrix} \text{sad} \\ \text{lonely} \\ \text{delighted} \end{Bmatrix}$.

Speaker B has no right to say things like:

(80)　How do you know you are?

because Speaker B is not capable of making judgments on the sensations that Speaker A claims to feel. But if Speaker A says:

(81)　Susan is $\begin{Bmatrix} \text{cold} \\ \text{lonely} \\ \text{delighted} \\ \text{etc.} \end{Bmatrix}$.

Speaker B can challenge him by saying:

(82)　How do you know she is $\begin{Bmatrix} \text{cold} \\ \text{lonely} \\ \text{delighted} \\ \text{etc.} \end{Bmatrix}$?

and Speaker A can defend himself by saying something like:

(83)　I know she is because she told me so.

or:

(84)　Susan $\begin{Bmatrix} \text{looks} \\ \text{seems} \end{Bmatrix}$ that way.

In Japanese, when the speaker is expressing his own physical or emotional sensation, he would say:

(85)   *watashi-wa* $\left\{\begin{array}{l} samui \\ atsui \\ sabishii \\ ureshii \\ \text{etc.} \end{array}\right\}$.

I am $\left\{\begin{array}{l} \text{cold} \\ \text{hot} \\ \text{lonely} \\ \text{delighted} \\ \text{etc.} \end{array}\right\}$.

But, when the speaker is talking about someone else's sensation at the time when he is speaking, he must say, using the suffix *gar-* in the progressive (where with the suffix *-te*, *gar-* takes the shape *gat-* by a regular rule), the following:

(86)   *Suuzan-wa* $\left\{\begin{array}{l} samu- \\ atsu- \\ sabishi- \\ ureshi- \\ \text{etc.} \end{array}\right\}$ *gat-te   i -mas -u.*
  Prog.   be-Polite-Nonpast

Susan seems $\left\{\begin{array}{l} \text{cold} \\ \text{hot} \\ \text{lonely} \\ \text{delighted} \\ \text{etc.} \end{array}\right\}$.

The reader will observe that the final *-i* of the adjectives in (85) is not present here; we have *samu* instead of *samui*, *atsu* instead of *atsui*, etc. The final *-i* is in fact the nonpast marker that occurs on adjectives when they are the final word of the clause. Tense is always carried by the final word of the clause, and in (86) we see nonpast realized as *-u*. Note that in (86) the statement could be based either on his observation, or on a message from Susan herself. *Gar-* is an expression that distinguishes the psychological world of the speaker himself and those of others.

2.2.4   *How Japanese Deals with the Notions of 'Existence' and 'Possession'*   Our final example dealing with the speaker's perspective is on the notions of existence and possession, which are probably two of the most important human concepts and which are related epistemologically and linguistically in interesting ways. Languages of the world express these two notions in various ways, for example, an event that is described existentially in one language may be described possessively in another.

Japanese, unlike English, has two existential verbs, namely *i-* which is customarily said to be used for animate entities, and *ar-* which is used for inanimate entities.

(87)   There is $\begin{Bmatrix} \text{a.} & \text{a child} \\ \text{b.} & \text{a tree} \end{Bmatrix}$ in the garden.

$$
\begin{array}{ll}
niwa\ \ \text{-}ni & \left[\begin{array}{lll}
\text{a.} & kodomo\text{-}ga & i\ \ \text{-}ru \\
 & \text{child} & \text{be-Nonpast} \\[4pt]
\text{b.} & ki\text{-}ga & ar\text{-}u \\
 & \text{tree} & \text{be-Nonpast}
\end{array}\right].
\end{array}
$$

garden-in

The word for possession in Japanese is *mots-* ("have"). We find however that many of the *have*-sentences in English are expressed existentially in Japanese and that *i-* and *ar-* behave rather mysteriously. Let us look at some notable examples.

First, in Japanese people are not possessed—they exist alongside the person to whom they belong. Thus, while in English, one would say:

(88)   "Bill has a wife and three children."

in Japanese, the same idea is more likely to be expressed existentially, as given in (89a) rather than possessively, as in (89b).

(89) a.   *Biru(-ni)-wa   tsuma-to   kodomo-ga   san -nin*[2]
                to   wife -and   child   three-Classifier
   i -ru.
   be-Nonpast
       To Bill, there is a wife and three children.

   b.   ?*Biru-wa   tsuma-to   kodomo-o   san -nin*
                wife -and   child   three-Classifier
   mot -te   i -ru.
   have-Prog. be-Nonpast
       Bill has a wife and three children.

Second, pets are never owned, but farm animals can be owned (*kaw-* "raise/keep" is also used for both). Look at the following examples:

(90) a.   *uchi -ni-wa   inu-ga   ni -hiki   i -ru.*
       house-at   dog   two-Class. be-Nonpast
           At (my) house, there are two dogs = I have two dogs.

---

[2]A number of languages in Asia and America, including Japanese, have what is known as the numeral classification system. In counting entities in those languages, one must use classifiers that, in one way or another, characterize the nature of entities. *Nin* used in sentence (89) is the classifier for human beings, except for "one person" and "two persons", which are *hitori* and *futari* respectively. *Hiki* used in (90) is the one for insects, fish, and small animals; and *too* used in (91) is the one for large animals.

    b. **watashi-wa   inu-o   ni -hiki   mot -te*
            I   dog   two-Class. have-Prog.

        i -ru.
        be-Nonpast

        I have two dogs.

(91) a. *Sugi-san-no bokujoo-ni-wa   uma   -ga*
                  ranch -at   horse

        ni-jut-too   -to   ushi-ga jut-too   i -ru.
        twenty-Class.-and cow   ten-Class. be-Nonpast

        At Mr. Sugi's ranch, there are twenty horses and ten
        cows.

    b. *Sugi-san-wa uma-o ni-jut -too   -to   ushi-o*
                   horse twenty-Class.-and cow

        jut -too   mot -te   i -ru.
        ten-Class. have-Prog. be-Nonpast

        Mr. Sugi has twenty horses and ten cows.

Notice, we can now speculate that the farm animals are part of the farmer's property and thus can be owned, whereas pets are considered part of the family—they belong to the family like the rest of its members. So when dogs, for instance, are raised by a dog breeder, one should be able to use both *mots-* and *i-*, and indeed one can:

(92) a. *Kimura-san-no tokoro-ni-wa Akita-ken-ga*
                    's   place -at   dog

        juu-ni -too   i -mas -u.
        ten-two-Class. be-Polite-Nonpast

        At Mr. Kimura's place, there are twelve Akita dogs.
        (Akita dogs are large Japanese dogs)

    b. *Kimura-san-wa Akita-ken-o juu-ni -too.*
                                  ten-two-Class.

        mot -te   i -mas -u.
        have-Prog. be-Polite-Nonpast

        Mr. Kimura has twelve Akita dogs.

Third, inanimate alienable objects can exist alongside the person, or they can be owned. For example:

(93) a. *ano-hito   (-ni)-wa *⎧*kane* ⎫ *-ga ari-mas-u.*
        that-person -to   ⎨*kuruma*⎬
                             ⎩*tochi* ⎭

        To that person, there is ⎧money ⎫
                                 ⎨a car   ⎬.
                                 ⎩property⎭

b. *ano- hito -wa* $\left\{\begin{array}{l}kane\\kuruma\\tochi\end{array}\right\}$ *-o mot-te i-mas-u.*

That person has $\left\{\begin{array}{l}\text{money}\\\text{a car}\\\text{property}\end{array}\right\}$.

Fourth, inanimate inalienable objects exist as part of the other entities but cannot be owned. For example:

(94) a. *kono-heya (-ni)-wa ookii mado-ga ar-u.*
this -room(-in) large window
In this room there is a large window.

b. *?*kono- heya-wa ookii mado-o mot-te i-ru.*
this room large window
This room has a large window.

(95) a. *kono-tsukue(-ni)-wa hikidashi-ga na -i.*
this -desk (-to) drawer not-Nonpast
To this desk, there is no drawer.

b. **kono-tsukue-wa hikidashi-o mot -te*
this-desk drawer have-Prog.
i- na -i.
be-not-Nonpast
This desk does not have a drawer.

And lastly, expressions having to do with illnesses which, in English, normally take the form of the *have*-sentences, take various forms in Japanese. Here are a few of the expressions in English and a common way of saying them in Japanese.

(96) I have $\left\{\begin{array}{ll}\text{a.} & \text{a headache}\\\text{b.} & \text{a cold}\\\text{c.} & \text{a fever}\\\text{d.} & \text{a stomach cancer}\end{array}\right\}$.

(97) a. *watashi-wa atama-ga ita -i.*
head hurt-Nonpast
As for me, (my) head hurts.

b. *watashi-wa kaze-o hii -te i -ru.*
cold catch-Prog. be-Nonpast
I am catching a cold.

c. *watashi-wa netsu-ga ar -u.*
fever exist-Nonpast
As for me, there is a fever.

d. *watashi-wa   i   -gan   da.*
                             stomach-cancer   be(Nonpast)
            As for me, a stomach cancer is.

In addition to what we have seen here, a person learning to speak Japanese has other subtleties to master. For what will have to remain here a mystery, our example (89b) "Bill has a wife and three children" is not nearly so bad to the ears of native speakers as (90b) "I have two dogs." The preferred expression for either family or pets is nevertheless an existential one. This tempts one to think that family is somehow more similar to inanimate objects than pets are. At the same time moreover, the existential expression *ar-*, normally reserved only for inanimate objects, is fully acceptable for family: one can substitute *ar-u* for *i-ru* in example (89a) "To Bill there is a wife and three children," whereas in speaking of pets in (90a) "At my house there are two dogs," only *i-ru* would be acceptable.

These examples remind us that for the expression of certain ideas one sometimes needs more than just an ability to construct sentences and the possession of the necessary vocabulary.

3 JAPANESE AND ITS RELATION TO THE ENVIRONMENT

Language and the style with which it is used reflects its social and natural environment. In this section, we shall discuss the effect on language of a notable psychological characteristic, of social stratification, and of how the Japanese people relate themselves to their natural environment.

3.1 The Psychology of Dependence

It has been said that if one were to point out one fundamental characteristic of the Japanese psychology, it would be dependence. A positive value is placed on dependence, and it encourages individuals to indulge themselves in loving and dependent relationships. Take, for instance, the notion of rendering assistance to others. Let us compare Japanese with members of American society. In America, there is positive value to independence, and there is a strong sense of rendering assistance on a contractual basis. That is, when a friend needs help, one should do one's best to step in and help, but only in the areas where the help has been requested, for each individual has his own territory which must be honored. The person who offers help has the responsibility to discuss the way in which he can help. Each offer is a separate contract.

The Japanese people generally lack this clear sense of contract and

FIGURE 5.3 A Family Meal

the notion of private territory. To a Japanese, helping a friend implies looking after him in an all-inclusive way. It is his responsibility to think of the things he can do to help and to go ahead with them in the manner that he thinks will befit his friend's need. He need not present them to his friend and wait for a decision. When his friend sought his help, he totally entrusted himself to him.

An American seeking help considers it his right to choose the specific sort of help he needs. He may decline the rest, provided he does it gracefully. He has a clear sense of responsibility to look after himself. A Japanese, on the other hand, does not have the freedom to take what he wants and decline the rest; he is obliged to accept all of what is offered to him. He does not have the same sense of having to look after himself, but in fact, he does so by entrusting himself to someone else. Meanwhile, he looks after some other person who is dependent on him. Of course, there are times when a Japanese finds himself in the awkward position of accepting help that he really does not want. On the other hand, he also has the advantage of not having to spell out everything he needs; for him, this would be difficult.

There are some interesting linguistic phenomena that illustrate this difference in the two cultures. First, to take a typical phrase that a person uses at the time of introduction, in American English, a person would say something like "How do you do? I'm pleased to meet you," or simply, "Hello." In Japanese, a typical phrase begins with *hajime-mashite* which means something like "I am meeting you for the first time." It is then followed by *doozo yoroshiku*, which is a shortened version of a phrase that implies something like "Please do whatever you consider fit for me." In other words, an introduction is an invitation, or an extension to the new acquaintance of the right to act for one's benefit. It is an act of entrusting oneself to the other person. To an American, this is clearly a separate step, which might not take place until long after initial greetings.

Let us look at another example of extending—this time not help, but hospitality. In an American home, one often hears the hostess saying to the house guest, "Make yourself at home. And help yourself to whatever you like. There is beer and soft drinks in the refrigerator—please feel free to help yourself at any time." Why? Because it is the responsibility of the hostess to see to it that the guest is offered the best choice that she can offer as well as the freedom to select whatever he would like whenever he would like it. What would a Japanese hostess do in the same situation? She would say the equivalent of "Make yourself at home." But she would not say "Help yourself." Instead, without further ado, she would offer whatever it is that she thinks the guest would most enjoy having at that time.

An American guest in an American home knows that he has been given the freedom to help himself and that it is his responsibility to look after himself. A Japanese guest in a Japanese home knows that he has placed himself in the hands of the hostess, and he accepts the thoughtful offer by the hostess, whatever it may be, unless he has a good reason not to. But what happens to a Japanese guest at an American home? Not being used to looking after himself, he may have a slight sense of being neglected. He would also be very hesitant to open someone else's refrigerator and help himself. What about an American guest at a Japanese home? If the hostess is able to accurately assess his desires, there certainly would be no problem. Otherwise, he may feel a sense of infringement upon his privacy. He might think "I know what I want, and I would appreciate it if you would consult me!"

There are countless stories of agony and laughter occasioned by cross-cultural experiences such as the ones described here. However, it is important for us to remember that they do not indicate that all Japanese people are dependent and behave and speak identically. Far from it. Some Japanese are very independent, vocal, and adamant about their freedom. But the important point is that the psychology of dependence is there as a frame of reference, whether or not a particular individual is independent or dependent.

3.2 Social Stratification and Deferential Language in Japanese

3.2.1 *How Address Forms Work in Japanese*

Proper Names When addressing people by their proper names, there is only one general rule in Japanese: add *-san* either to the family name as in *Suzuki-san*, or to the sequence of the family name and the given name as in *Suzuki Jiroo-san* (note that 'first' and 'last' names come in reverse order in Japanese), regardless of sex, marital, or social status. In one sense, therefore, *-san* is equivalent to all three of the English expressions, Mr., Mrs., and Miss. However, it is significantly different from those English expressions because while the English expressions denote titles representing the social status of the person referred to with or without respect on the part of the speaker, *-san* is strictly an expression of respect. Therefore, while in English one could say "I'm Mrs. Jones," or "This is Mr. Smith speaking," in Japanese one would never say **watashi-wa Mori-san des-u* ("I am Mori-san"). One introduces himself by saying *watashi-wa Mori des-u*, or simply, *Mori des-u*, regardless of one's social status.

In Japanese, the use of the given name is generally limited to the members of one's family, children, and the childhood friends whom one has always called by their given names. In most other cases, people address one another by their family names. They do not switch from calling someone by his family name to calling him by his given name, however long they have known one another. This means that in Japanese one is spared the discomfort, as it happens so often in English, of trying to determine whether to call someone by his first or last name. But it also means that *-san* gives practically no information concerning how one person is regarded by the other in social interaction.

There is one exception to the universal rule of addressing people with *-san*. Teachers and doctors (and innumerable people who are labelled as 'critics' or 'commentators' as well as politicians) are addressed, not by *-san*, but by *-sensei* "teacher," as in *Mori-sensei*. In Japan, a schoolteacher is called *sensei*, not only by his present students, but also by former students and by the public in general. The word *sensei* is a common noun, a respectful title, and it is also a vocative form.

There are variants of *-san* such as *-sama* which is more formal than *-san*, and *-chan* which is an affectionate expression, usually added to children's given names. *Kun* is a casual term used mostly by men to address people who are equal or younger. There also are others such as *-dono* (used mainly in writing) and *-shi*. All of those expressions give far greater information than the primary term, *-san*.

Kinship Terms Table 5.6 lists the major kinship terms in Japanese. Unlike English, Japanese makes a systematic distinction between

TABLE 5.6   *Japanese Kinship Terms*

Persons spoken about	To speak about them to outsiders	To speak about them inside the family
father	*chichi*	*o-too-san*/papa
mother	*haha*	*o-kaa-san*/mama
son	*musuko*	**Name**-(*chan*/*san*) e.g., *Taroo-chan*
daughter	*musume*	**Name**-(*chan*/*san*) e.g., *Yuki-chan*
older brother	*ani*	*o-nii-san*
older sister	*ane*	*o-nee-san*
younger brother	*otooto*	**Name**-(*chan*/*san*)
younger sister	*im ooto*	**Name**-(*chan*/*san*)
grandfather	*sofu*	*o-jii-san*
grandmother	*sobo*	*o-baa-san*
grandchild	*mago*	**Name**-(*chan*/*san*)
uncle	*oji*	*oji-san*
aunt	*oba*	*oba-san*
nephew	*oi*	**Name**-*chan*/*san*
niece	*mei*	**Name**-*chan*/*san*
cousin	*itoko*	**Name**-*san*

the terms used when talking about members of one's own family to people outside or inside the family. To someone not a member of the family, one simply uses the relational terms. However, within the family one normally uses the terms (sometimes different ones) with respectful affixes *o-* and *-san* or the more affectionate *-chan* for older relations, and the name with or without *-san* or *-chan* for younger ones. Generally speaking, the forms that are used to refer to them within the family are also used as vocative forms when speaking directly to them. As one would expect, a complex system of this sort is subject to a good deal of variation from social group to social group, and even from region to region. Within just one style, there are complexities that go beyond what can be represented in a table such as Table 5.6. For example, in the author's experience, it is the case that nephews and nieces will always be named with *-chan* or *-san* when women are speaking, but male speakers will sometimes just say the names.

Notice that the terms for siblings are distinguished by their age in relation to the speaker. There are the neutral terms *kyoodai*, a Sino-Japanese compound "older brother + younger brother" for "brothers," and *shimai* "older sister + younger sister" for "sisters." The former is also used when one talks about how many siblings one has, as in *watashi-wa san-nin kyoodai-ga ari-mas-u* "As for me, there are three siblings = I have three siblings." Neither *kyoodai* nor *shimai* is used in speaking directly to brothers and sisters; in this way they are rather like the English word "sibling."

Personal (Pro)nouns   The pronouns in Japanese that are commonly used today are of two kinds, the general expressions used by both men and women, and those used only by men to address either men or women. Women do not use the second variety, and men use them only in casual or rough situations. The major third-person singular forms are

TABLE 5.7   *Japanese Singular Personal (Pro)nouns*

		I	You	
General	Formal	*watakushi*	
	Normal	*watashi*	*anata*
Male	Casual	*boku*	*kimi*
	Rough	*ore*	*omae*

Third Person

General	Formal	*kono-kata*	*sono-kata*	*ano-kata*	
	Normal	*kono-hito*	*sono-hito*	*ano-hito*	*kare kanojo*
Male	Casual				
	Rough	*koitsu*	*soitsu*	*aitsu*	

compounds with demonstratives *kono-* "this," *sono-* "that," and *ano-* "that over there" plus the word for person, namely *-kata* (formal) or *-hito* (normal). Japanese has a three-way distinction, *ko-*, *so-* and *a-*, which are also used for various other expressions used for indication such as *koko* "here," *soko* "there," and *asoko* "way over there." The rough expressions used only by men, namely *koitsu*, *soitsu*, and *aitsu* also come from *ko-*, *so-*, and *a-* followed by *yatsu*, the shortened version of *yatsuko*, which used to be an affectionate term for a person of lower status or a servant. *Koyatsu*, *soyatsu*, and *ayatsu* changed to *koitsu*, *soitsu*, and *aitsu*; and they now mean something like "this guy," "that guy," and "that guy over there." *Kare* and *kanojo* mean "he" and "she" respectively, and they also have a secondary meaning comparable in English to "boyfriend" and "girlfriend."

There is syntactic evidence that Japanese pronouns are more 'nouns' than 'pronouns', hence the parentheses in the title '(Pro)nouns'. One can say quite freely (and more freely than in English) things like *utsukushii anata* "beautiful you" and *genkina watashi* "healthy me," modifying pronouns in the same way as one would nouns in expressions such as *utsukushii Yoshiko* "beautiful Yoshiko" and *genkina kodomo* "healthy child."

To talk to or about more than one person in Japanese, one would use *-tachi*, a bound morpheme that means "and the others" as in *watashi-tachi* "I and the others." Because of this meaning, when *-tachi* is used with proper nouns and kinship terms as in *Sano-san-tachi* and *o-kaa-san-tachi*, they mean "Mr. or Ms. Sano and the others" and "the mother and the others." There is another suffix *-gata*, a polite form that comes from *-kata* ("person") with voicing in the initial sound. It has a rather restricted use and can appear with only some of the terms that have been discussed so far, e.g., with the respectful kinship terms such as *o-too-san-gata* ("fathers"), *o-kaa-san-gata* ("mothers") and also *sensei-gata* ("teachers") but not with a proper name as in **Mori-san-gata*.

Finally, since ellipsis of the noun phrase is the most common form of referring to people already named, pronouns when they are used convey far more information regarding the interpersonal relations than the pronouns in languages such as English. For instance, under normal circumstances, *anata* "you" is not used when speaking to a person of higher status. One would use the person's name or simply not address him directly. Should one dare to use *anata* in speaking to a person of higher status, it would convey a special message—either of a sense of camaraderie or of indignation and rebellion. *Kare* "he" and *kanojo* "she" convey a familiar and nondeferential sense and are used more often by a young or a middle-aged person in talking about friends and possibly the members of his or her own family. In similar fashion, each of the other expressions requires specific circumstances for them to be appropriate.

3.2.2 *How Nondeferential Expressions Are Used Deferentially*
Languages of the world have two major types of expressions of
deference. The first kind is one that every language appears to have: a
group of grammatical devices and words whose primary function is not
deferential but which nonetheless is used for such a purpose in certain
contexts. Let us look at some examples in English. For instance, a
tag-question is one device that can be used to make a request sound less
demanding, and thus more polite. Instead of:

(98)   Come in.

the speaker would say:

(99)   Come in, won't you?

Another device is a statement in place of a request, particularly, an
impersonal one such as:

(100)   Dinner is served.

instead of:

(101)   Come and eat.

Similarly, a statement with a qualifying expression such as:

(102)   I wonder if you can help me move next week.

sounds more polite than:

(103)   Can you help me move next week?

The same statement in the past tense sounds even more polite.

(104)   I was wondering if you could help me move next week.

Euphemisms, particularly in mentioning unmentionables, is another
way of expressing deference.

(105)   Excuse me, I must go to the little girls' room.

And lastly, hedging is another device. Expressions such as "a little" and
"somewhat" are often used to play down negative feelings in a sentence
such as:

(106)   That's a little unfair, isn't it?

when the speaker thinks that he has been very unfairly treated. On the other hand, expressions such as "terrific" and "tremendous" are used to exaggerate positive feelings.

Japanese has similar devices. As for the forms of request, there is the negative question such as:

(107)   *hairi-mas -en   ka.*
        enter-Polite-not   Ques.
          Won't you come in?

which is often used as a form of invitation, i.e., a polite request. The positive question, on the other hand, is normally a straightforward question. The sentence particle *ne*, which is comparable to the tag-question in English, also serves as a mild request. For instance, one would say:

(108)   *irasshai   -mas -u   ne.*
        come(Honoring)-Polite-Nonpast
        (You) will come, won't you?

The expression *irasshar-* is the honoring form of the verb *ku-* "come," which we shall discuss later, and the sentence can be used as a very polite urging for the hearer to come. The use of an impersonal statement instead of a direct request, too, is common in Japanese in cases such as announcing dinner and inviting people to come to the table.

Hedging with quantitative modifiers such as the ones found in English is also very common. In addition, the Japanese would often use the qualifying phrase *...to omoi-mas-u* "I think...," and thus avoid fully committing himself to his own statement. Euphemisms are as abundant in Japanese as they are in English. For instance, English has "rest room"—itself a euphemism and also "wash room," the "little girls' room," "the little boys' room," and "the powder room" to name a few. Japanese has *tearai*, or *o-tearai*, which means "the place to wash hands," *keshoo-shitsu* "powder room," *toire*, which comes from the English word "toilet," and two other expressions where there is only an indirect connection to literal meaning: *habakari* "awe" or "deference" and *go-fujoo*, which is a compound with the respectful prefix *go-* and the noun *fujoo* meaning "impurity" or "uncleanliness."

Some languages, including Japanese, have a grammatical system the primary function of which is to express deference. In Japanese this set of verbal expressions is called the "honorifics" and is used with the various forms of address we discussed earlier.

3.2.3   *How the System of Honorifics Works in Japanese*   There are three major types of honorifics in Japanese: *sonkei-go* "honoring expressions," *kenjoo-go* "humbling expressions," and *teinei-go* "polite expressions." The honoring and humbling expressions represent the speaker's relationship with the people being discussed and the relationship between those people themselves. The polite expressions, one of which is *-mas*, the polite verb ending that we have been using, represent the speaker's respect toward the hearer(s) and also his estimate of his own position in society.

We shall demonstrate how the system works by taking a sentence and changing parts of it using the honoring, humbling, and polite expressions that would be appropriate for different situations. Look at the straightforward nondeferential sentence:

(109) *Sakai-ga   Suzuki(-no   tame)-ni   chizu-o   kai -ta.*
                              's benefit -for map   write-Past
        Sakai drew a map for Suzuki.

Sentence (109) can be changed in six different ways representing five different situations, and each of the six can be expressed as polite and neutral versions.

First, when the speaker is equal in status to the people about whom he is talking, he simply adds the respectful title *-san* to their names, i.e., he would say *Sakai-san* and *Suzuki-san*. He need not use either the honoring or humbling expressions. The speaker has the choice of using the polite verb ending or not using it, depending on his relationship to the hearer; for example, if the hearer is a good friend, he can be informal and not use it.

(110) *Sakai-san-ga   Suzuki-san-ni   chizu-o*
                                                        map

    a. *kaki -mashi-ta*
        draw-Polite -Past
    b. *kai -ta*
        draw-Past

Second, in talking about his equals, the speaker can also use a compound verb that consists of the main verb plus an honoring verb *age-* "give," which conveys the speaker's sense of affinity with the person who did the drawing of the map.

(111) *Sakai-san-ga   Suzuki-san-ni   chizu-o   kai -te*
                                                        map   draw-Gerund

    a. *age -mashi-ta*
        give-Polite -Past
    b. *age -ta*
        give-Past

    Mr. Sakai gave Mr. Suzuki the drawing of a map.

The expression *kai-te age-mashi-ta* consists of the verb *kak-* "write/draw," which changes to *kai-* before the gerundive ending *-te*, and the verb *age-* "give," which literally means "to raise," which is followed by the polite ending in the past tense *-mashi-ta*. The speaker can also be informal with the hearer and say *kai-te age-ta*.

Third, the speaker would use a different honoring expression, *o-...-ni nar-* when he has considerably lower status than *Sakai*, for instance, if he is much younger than *Sakai*.

(112) *Sakai-san-ga   Suzuki-san-ni   chizu-o   o- kaki -ni*
                                      map   Res.-draw-to

$$\left\{\begin{array}{l} \text{a.} \quad \textit{nari} \quad \textit{-mashi-ta} \\ \quad\quad \text{become-Polite -Past} \\ \text{b.} \quad \textit{nat} \quad\quad \textit{-ta} \\ \quad\quad \text{become-Past} \end{array}\right\}.$$

Mr. Sakai came to draw a map for Mr. Suzuki.
(It came about that Mr. Sakai drew a map for Mr. Suzuki.)

The verb phrase *o-kaki-ni nari-mashi-ta* consists of a respectful prefix *o-* followed by the verb *kak-* "write/draw," which is followed by *-ni nar-*, which literally means "to become" and the polite verb ending in the past tense *-mashi-ta*. The speaker can use the neutral ending if the hearer is someone with whom he can be informal.

Fourth, the speaker would use a humbling expression *o-...su-* when *Sakai*, the person who did the drawing of the map has considerably lower status than *Suzuki* who accepted it.

(113) *Sakai-san-ga   Suzuki-san-ni   chizu-o   o- kaki-*
                                      map   Res.-draw-

$$\left\{\begin{array}{l} \text{a.} \quad \textit{shi-mashi-ta} \\ \quad\quad \text{do -Polite -Past} \\ \text{b.} \quad \textit{shi-ta} \\ \quad\quad \text{do -Past} \end{array}\right\}.$$

The expression *o-kaki-shi-mashi-ta* consists of the respectful prefix *o-*, *kak-* "draw," and the irregular verb *su-* "do," which changes to *shi-* before *mas-* or *-ta*. The speaker is showing respect toward *Suzuki* by humbling *Sakai*, rather than honoring *Suzuki*. The same expression is used when the speaker himself did the drawing of the map for *Suzuki*. He would say:

(114) *watakushi-ga   Suzuki-san-ni   chizu-o*
      I(Formal)   map
      o-kaki -shi-mashi-ta.
      Res.-draw-do -Polite -Past

I did the drawing of a map for Mr. Suzuki.

Notice, the speaker is using the formal first-person pronoun *watakushi* "I" as well as the polite ending *-mashi-ta* to indicate his respect toward the hearer. If the hearer is someone with whom the speaker can be informal, he can simply say:

(115) *watashi-ga Suzuki-san-ni chizu-o o-kaki-shi-ta.*

using the normal form *watashi* and the neutral ending *-shi-ta* instead of *-shi-mashi-ta*.

Finally, the speaker has a choice of two expressions to use, one honoring and the other humbling, when *Suzuki* has lower status than *Sakai* and when the speaker has a sense of affinity with *Suzuki*. They are the compound verbs with one other verb of giving, *kudasar-*, and the verb of receiving *itadak-*, as in *kai-te kudasar-* and *kai-te itadak-*. The former honors *Sakai*, and the latter humbles *Suzuki*.

(116) *Sakai-san-ga   Suzuki-san-ni   chizu-o   kai -te*
  map   draw-Gerund

  a. *kudasai-mashi-ta*
  give   -Polite -Past
  b. *kudasat-ta*
  give   -Past

  Mr. Sakai gave Mr. Suzuki the drawing of a map.

(117) *Sakai-san-ni   Suzuki-san-ga   chizu-o   kai -te*
  from

  a. *itadaki-mashi-ta*
  receive-Polite -Past
  b. *itadai -ta*
  receive-Past

  From Mr. Sakai, Mr. Suzuki received the drawing of a map.

Notice, in sentence (117) *Sakai-san* is followed by particle *-ni* instead of *-ga*, and *Suzuki-san* is followed by *-ga* because of the verb "to receive." These expressions can also be used when the speaker himself is the one who received the map. He would simply replace *Suzuki-san* with *watakushi* or *watashi* ("I") depending on the hearer.

The speakers of Japanese use the respectful prefix *o-* (*go-* for Sino-Japanese words) for objects that are close to their daily life, as well as for the kinship terms and the verbs denoting human activities. For instance, they say *o-cha* instead of *cha* "tea," *o-kashi* instead of *kashi* "candies," *go-han* "cooked rice/meal," *go-chisoo* "feast," and *o-furo* "bath." Moreover, in a very polite conversation, one would prefix *o-* to expressions having to do with the qualities of objects and entities, e.g., *o-shizuka* instead of *shizuka* "quiet" and *o-kirei* instead of *kirei* "beautiful." For instance, the speaker would say something like:

(118) *kono-hen-wa   o- shizuka   des   -u   ne.*
       this -area   Res.-quiet   be(Polite)-Nonpast Tag
       This area is quiet, isn't it?

to compliment the quiet neighborhood in which the hearer lives.

We have so far introduced the honoring expressions *o-* . . . *-ni nar*, *-te age* and *-te kudasar*, the humbling expressions *o-* . . . *su* and *-te itadak*, the polite ending *-mas*, the polite form of copula "be" *des*, and the prefixes *o-* and *go*. These forms are the basic ones that can be used with various other expressions.

3.2.4 *How the Japanese Decide When to Use Which Forms*
Three-quarters of a century after the Meiji Restoration, from late summer 1945 when the country lay in ruins in the wake of World War II until the early fifties, Japan went through another period of drastic social and institutional change. It was called the 'democratization' of Japan, carried out by the American occupation army under the command of General Douglas MacArthur. The new constitution took effect on May 3, 1947. In the first chapter, it proclaimed the emperor of Japan to be the symbol of the State and the unity of the people but without any political powers; and in the second, it renounced war and the maintenance of land, sea, and air forces as well as other war potentials. In the third chapter, it spelled out in great detail the fundamental human rights of all citizens of Japan. Women were assured equal rights with men, which included the right to vote and equal rights in inheritance and marriage. Legislative measures were taken to break up the great concentration of wealth in the hands of the select industrialists; absentee land-ownership too was abolished, and land was distributed to the members of the farming communities.

Today, Japan is unmistakably a country of middle-class citizens. Since 1969, an annual government poll has consistently indicated that 90 percent of the Japanese people consider themselves to belong to the middle class. But just as in any other society in the world regardless of the form of the government, Japanese society has social stratification. The decision-making processes of the Japanese people regarding how to behave, what to say when, and how to say it are based on the way the society is stratified. Some factors are uniquely Japanese, but others are universal in all human societies.

There are two basic types of factors to be considered—interpersonal and personal. The interpersonal ones can be subdivided into situational and relational factors. By situational factors, we mean the various circumstances that provide one person with more power than another.

The relational factors are those that determine the relationship for an extended period of time, such as group affiliation and seniority.

Let us look at a few notable cases where the situational power factor is at work. First, let us examine the customer-salesperson relationship where the former has a decisive power over the latter. The following would be a typical conversation at a department store.

(119) Customer: *kore-(wa)*
                          this

- a. *o- ikura des -u ka*
       Res.-how much be(Pol.)-Nonpast-Q.
- b. *ikura des-u ka*
- c. *ikura*

How much is this?

Salesperson: *sore-wa   ichi-man -en   de gozai -mas-u.*
                    that   ten thousand-yen be(Hum.)-Polite

That is ten thousand yen.

Customer: *todoke-te*
                  deliver-Ger.

- a. *itadak   -e   -mas-u ka*
       receive(Hum.)-Potential-Polite
- b. *kure -mas-u ka*
       receive-Polite
- c. *kure -ru*
       receive-Nonpast

Will you deliver (it)?

Salesperson: *hai.   o -todoke itashi   -mas-u.*
                            Res.-deliver do(Hum.)-Polite

Yes, (we) will delivery (it).

Notice how the difference in power influences language. While the customer has a choice of three styles of speaking—from a very courteous style to a rather rude one, a well-trained salesperson must remain courteous regardless of the customer. Here he is using *o-* ... *itas-* with the humbling form of *su* "do" which is even more humbling than *o-* ... *su*, the form that was introduced earlier. The same principle holds in the relationship between a doctor and a patient, thus the latter will always speak deferentially to the former. The doctor, on the other hand, may speak casually, although he normally does not use the most casual form for personal reasons that we shall discuss later.

The next case is a situation in which a person who has a higher status asks a person of lower status to do a personal favor for him. Instead of saying something like:

(120)   *kono-tegami-o   dashi   -te   kudasa   -i.*
    this -letter   dispatch-Gerund   give(Hon.)-Nonpast
    Please mail this letter. (lit.: "Please give the dispatching of
    this letter.")

which is a polite request, he would put his request in the form of a negative question such as:

(121)   *kono-tegami-o   dashi   -te   kudasai   -mas   -en   ka.*
    this -letter   dispatch-Ger.   give(Hon.)-Polite-not
    Won't you please mail this letter? (lit.: "Won't you
    please give the dispatching of this letter?")

which is even more polite.

The last case has to do with a social relation that has undergone a considerable change of image in postwar Japan: the relationship between government officials and the public. Until the end of the war, Japanese government officials, from the top bureaucrats to the policemen on the beat, were regarded as the keepers of the power and the authority of government. Thus, there was a strong tendency among them to speak down to the citizens of the country. Since the end of the war, the government officials have become public servants. While people speak to them using polite expressions because they receive services, the government officials are also expected to speak courteously in return. They use polite expressions, although they need not use humbling ones.

There are three major categories of relational factors: two are the distinction between ingroup versus outgroup (as with the family) and seniority, i.e., the age and the professional and/or social position that accompanies an advance in age. Sex is the other factor that plays a role.

In respect to the ingroup versus outgroup dimension, note that an adult speaker of Japanese is expected to use the humbling expressions to talk about the members of his family to anyone who is an outsider. Conversely, the same speaker is generally expected to use the honoring expressions to refer to anyone who is a member of someone else's family. This however depends, to a greater or lesser degree, on the age and status of the person to whom or about whom one is speaking. When the two factors, ingroup/outgroup and age, conflict, the former takes precedence. That is, when speaking about the members of one's own family to anyone who is not a member, age is not a factor. For instance, talking about the health of his own father, the speaker would say:

(122)   *chichi-wa   genki-de   ori   -mas-u.*
    father   healthy   be(Hum.)-Polite
    (My) father is healthy.

But in asking about the health of the hearer's father, he would have to say:[3]

(123) *o- too-san-wa   o- genki   des-u ka.*
    Res.-father   Res.-health be(Pol.)

or:

(124) *o-too-san-wa   o-genki-de   irasshai-mas-u ka.*
                      be(Hon.)-Polite
    Is (your) father healthy?

Sentence (123) can be used between two friends, and (124) would be used if the hearer is, for example, the speaker's teacher or supervisor, and/or if the speaker is a very polite person.

It is of great importance, however, to see how the notion 'ingroup' extends beyond one's immediate family. The major groups of significance for language use tend to be the following—blood relatives and in-laws, teachers and their students, university professors and their advisees, and salaried workers, blue-collar as well as white-collar, who work for business and industrial firms of all sizes. A company employee would use the humbling expressions to talk about people in his own company to a person who works for another company. A teacher or a professor would use the humbling expressions to talk about his own students to teachers from other schools or prospective employers while the students are enrolled, although he would tend not to continue humbling them after graduation. The students, on the other hand, at no time use the humbling expressions to refer to their teacher.

This means that, although the groups just mentioned undoubtedly comprise an important sector of Japanese society today, there are many other people engaged in various types of occupations who do not consider themselves as belonging to ingroups, at least regarding the use of their language. For instance, while university professors regard their students as members of their 'group', they do not consider their respective universities as part of their group in the way that employees do their corporations. Physicians who work at hospitals, although they, too, are full-time salaried employees, are not group oriented.

Here is an example of the difference in the language of a group-oriented person and that of a person who is not. Suppose someone calls up from outside and asks for a Mr. Mori, a department head at the corporation. The man or the woman who answers the call would say:

---

[3]The *-de* that combines with the noun "health" in (122) and (124) is a special suffix for forming what are called pseudo-adjectives from nouns in certain constructions.

(125)   ⌠a.   *buchoo-wa* ⌉   *tadaima*   *gaishutsu*   *shi-te*
    ⌊b.   *Mori-wa* ⌟   now   go out   do

    ori   *-mas-u.*
    be(Hum.)-Polite
    ⌠a.   The department head⌉   is out at the moment.
    ⌊b.   (Mr.) Mori   ⌟

Notice, the person does not say *buchoo-san* "Mr. department head," or
Mori-san "Mr. Mori." He would not say it even if he were the most
junior member of the company. Then the person continues with *gaishu-*
tsu shi-te ori-mas-u, again, humbling Mr. Mori and respecting the
person who is on the outside. A university professor who is answering a
similar call from outside the university, in contrast, would say something
like:

(126)   *Mori-sensei-wa*   *gaishutsu*   *shi-te*   *irasshai -mas-u.*
        teacher   go out   do   be(Hon.)-Polite
        Professor Mori is out.

He would call his colleague "Mori-sensei" and use *irasshar-*, the honoring expression, rather than *ir-*, the plain nonhonoring form of "be." He
would not use the humbling expression even if the colleague were a
junior member of the faculty.

One way to describe the ingroup versus outgroup situation in Japan
would be to say that Japanese society places the family at the center of
the society and a whole spectrum of family-like communities in its outer
layers—the corporations lie very close to the center, and the groups of
professional people such as university professors and physicians probably lie the farthest from the center. There are numerous other layers of
groups that lie in between. Those groups would use the humbling,
honoring, and polite expressions to varying degrees depending on how
they view their groups; and the variation is considerable.

We notice in this general definition of the group in Japanese society
that what is considered the "ingroup" is typically hierarchically
organized—it is a pyramid structure. The cohesiveness of such a group is
maintained by strong mutual dependency relationships among its members
horizontally and vertically, but more noticeably vertically. This is where
the second factor, namely seniority in age and rank, comes in.

Earlier, we discussed the change of image of the government
officials in post-war Japan. Seniority, the respect for age and rank, is
another aspect of Japanese society where there has been a considerable
change in the attitudes of the people in the past thirty years, along with
some substantial changes in the family structure itself. Until recently,
traditional Japanese families have had a vertical structure based on the
notion of seniority. A large number of family members have lived

together dependent on each other, with children relating to not only their parents, but also to grandparents and other relatives as well, and with the oldest son being the principal inheritor of family property and therefore being viewed as having a special responsibility to oversee family affairs. Today, only 25 percent of Japanese households live with grandparents and other relatives; over 60 percent are nuclear families. The average size of those nuclear families is between three and four persons and the oldest son no longer has the special privilege or responsibility of being the principal inheritor. It is interesting to note that while corporate structure which is modelled after the family retains a highly vertical structure based, primarily, on seniority, the family itself has lost much of its traditional hierarchy.

The style of speaking adopted by the younger people in speaking to their elders within the family, and to society in general, has become much less deferential and far more egalitarian in recent years. Between husband and wife, too, there is variation, but with the younger generation, they are much more equal.

And this leads to our final point about interpersonal language in Japanese: the difference between men's speech and women's speech. Women have traditionally been trained to speak more politely than men among themselves as well as toward men. However, the picture is complicated by the fact that in Japanese certain forms are used only by men, or only by women, some of which are deferential and some of which are not. Moreover, there is also one other social factor to be considered: in Japan until recently, very few women have held professional positions and positions of authority over men. In the past few years, it has been noted that the few women who are in managerial positions in corporations and government agencies experience little difference in the attitude and behavior of the men and women who work under them. Although there undoubtedly are some men who, at first, are bothered by having female bosses, they eventually show just as much respect, linguistically and otherwise, for them as they do for their male superiors.

In short, the factors that speakers of Japanese take into consideration in deciding how to say things are of two categories—situational and relational. With respect to the former, it is always the person who is seeking help and guidance who uses deferential language. With respect to the latter, the things that matter are group affiliation and seniority. As those factors indicate, deferential language in Japanese does not mark social class in any simplistic way for either the people spoken to, or the people spoken about. Everyone in Japanese society has the chance to use all of the deferential expressions in his daily life, depending on the various circumstances in which he finds himself.

It is interesting to note, however, that deferential language is perceived as a marker of the social class of speakers. Deferential expressions are the linguistic prestige features of the Japanese society in modern times. Japanese people consider the ability to use deferential expressions 'appropriately', i.e., the ability to use them appropriately when they are called for, and not use them when they are not called for, to be the mark of good education and good upbringing. Hence, well-educated intellectuals who, otherwise, are liberal in their outlook are generally more conservative regarding the use of the deferential expressions. They tend to speak in a more polite language regardless of who they are speaking to, more as a reflection of their estimate of their own position in the society than from their respect of others.

There is a strong tendency among the learners of Japanese, and learners of languages in general, to think that all native speakers know how to use deferential expressions and how to speak appropriately. Nothing could be farther from reality. The system of deferential expressions is difficult for native speakers to learn, for those expressions convey complex messages regarding not only the interpersonal relations between the speaker and others, but also much about the speakers themselves. People often make social errors in speaking, and this is at least as much the case with a language like Japanese, which has so much social deference built into the grammar, as with other languages. Each speaker learns, or tries to learn, appropriate ways of speaking that are befitting to each stage of his life. What is more, the way of speaking that is considered appropriate for each stage of an individual's life changes as the society as a whole changes and adjusts itself to the changes in the larger world.

3.3 Some Japanese Expressions Reflecting Love of Nature

It is often said that the natural environment has a direct bearing on the vocabulary of a language. For instance, Eskimo has several words for snow, but English has only one; this is because Eskimos have great need to distinguish different kinds of snow, while most English speakers do not. At first glance, such an explanation seems reasonable. However the relationship between the natural environment and language is far more complex and mysterious. While it may be safe to assume that the speakers of one language would not have a word related to a natural phenomenon that they have never experienced, it is not safe to assume that the converse is also true. Sometimes there are important things for which they do not have names. It is a fascinating fact that among languages of the world that are spoken in similar geographical and climatic environments, each has its own unique set of vocabulary that enables the speakers of the language to describe and pay tribute to the beauty of nature in their own way.

The Japanese language has an unusually rich vocabulary of words and expressions related to the seasons. The traditional Japanese calendar is the lunar one, which divides the four seasons into twenty-four subseasons, each of which is further divided into a beginning, a middle, and an end. For instance, the beginning of the spring is *risshun*, a Sino-Japanese morpheme *ritsu-* meaning "stand" followed by *shun* "spring." It is dated around February 4. The beginning of the summer is *rikka*, dated around May 6, the fall *risshuu*, around August 8, and the winter *rittoo*, around November 8. The beginning of the colder time of the winter is called *shookan* "little cold," the coldest time is *daikan* "big cold." The rainy season, as well as the rain of this season itself, is called either *tsuyu*, a native Japanese expression, or *baiu*, a Sino-Japanese expression. It comes to all of Japan, except for the northernmost regions, for approximately one month beginning the middle of June, at about the time when the plums ripen. The characters for *baiu* are *bai* "plum" and *u* "rain," and the same characters are also read *tsuyu*. The rainy season is followed by a hot and humid summer; the peak of this season from around July 20 to August 10 is called *doyoo*. This is when the surges called *doyoo-nami* "*doyoo* waves" begin to run high along the Pacific coast warning the swimmers that it is the summer's end. Both the rainy season with ample rain and a hot and humid summer are vital to rice growing.

The dates marking the beginning of the four major seasons are approximately one to one and a half months ahead of the beginning of the actual climatic season in most parts of Japan. On these days, however, the people of Japan read about it in the newspapers, hear about it on the radio and television news, and begin to look forward to the arrival of a new season, particularly the fall after a long hot summer and the spring after the snow and biting winds.

Along with the words marking seasons, there are expressions for the characteristic of different times of the year. There are words for different kinds of rain, winds, fair skies, cloudy skies, thunder, summer heat, winter cold, and so on. To name a few, *hana-gumori* ("flower-cloudy") means "cloudy weather with thin clouds covering the sky, which has a light-hearted cheerfulness" and is associated with spring, and *taka-gumori* ("high-cloudy") means "cloudy weather with clouds at an especially high altitude." *Soyo-kaze* means "the winds that blow quietly" and is also associated with the spring, *suzu-kaze* is the cool breeze of the summer, and *kogarashi*, which literally means "tree killing," denotes "the biting winds of the winter." *Harusame* is the spring rain that falls quietly, *shigure* is the sporadic rain that comes in the late fall and early winter, and *yuudachi* is the shower that comes in the early evening and is typical of the summer season. *Yuudachi* consists of *yuu* "evening," and *tachi* "stand" (with voicing in the initial sound), which is the native Japanese word for *ritsu-* of *risshun*, etc., and thus it literally means "the beginning of the evening." One of the dictionaries of seasonal words and expressions lists over eight hundred fifty of them just pertaining to the weather—many are scientific terms, but many more are traditional expressions that people still use in their daily life.

Next, there is a host of seasonally related expressions—flowers, plants, trees, birds and insects, fruit and vegetables, fish, various kinds of household goods, and the markets and festivals held at the Buddhist temples and Shinto shrines in all parts of Japan. For instance, the early spring is symbolized by such things as *ume* "plum blossoms" and *uguisu* "bush warbler," which are followed by *momo* "peach blossoms" and *sakura* "cherry blossoms." The height of summer is symbolized by *hotaru* "fireflies," *asagao* "morning glories," and *doyoo-no unagi* "*doyoo*'s eel," which is marinated in a special sauce and broiled. It is said that eels are good for one to eat on hot summer days when one's appetite generally declines. The arrival of fall is symbolized by *koorogi* "cricket" and *susuki* "Japanese pampus grass"; this is followed by the season of *kiku* "crysanthemum," *momiji* "red maples," and *aki-matsuri* "fall festivals." Finally, the height of the winter is the first of January, New Year's Day, when the entire nation celebrates with special decorations and foods that symbolize longevity, prosperity, and happiness in the new year.

Indeed, when a Japanese thinks of home, he thinks of not only his family, but also of the flowers in bloom in the family garden and the seasonal foods: fruit, vegetables, and fish that he can enjoy when he returns home. And when he writes a letter, it always begins with a remark on the weather and the season. He will say things like "It is already mid-May, and the young foliage is fresh and green...." The Japanese literary arts, particularly Japanese poetry, cannot exist without all those expressions about nature and changes in nature.

In recent years, advancement in technology and increasing urbanization have made the life of the Japanese people far less dependent on seasonal changes than it used to be. They have also done some serious damage to the rich ecological life of the country. Japan now is faced with the problem of accommodating both the need for natural resources demanded by increasing technologization and at the same time the need for conservation of the environment. In 1976, for the first time in thirty years, the percentage of the nuclear families slightly declined. The people, who are faced with the prohibitively high cost of properties, have begun to reassess and return to a modified version of the old way of sharing a house with parents. But modern life styles have brought various adaptations to the construction of their homes. The young people, who once flocked into cities by the millions, are now beginning to turn away from conjested urban centers. This trend, which is called the *yuu-taan genshoo* "U-Turn phenomenon," is slowly rejuvenating the rural areas, which have been on the decline for many years, and helping to decentralize the population. No doubt the Japanese language, with its changes and innovations, is an integral part of the quest of the people of Japan.

SUGGESTIONS FOR FURTHER READING

The original studies are a logical starting point for further reading. Kuno's *The Structure of the Japanese Language* has discussions relevant to "Sentence Formation in Japanese" (2.1), "How Japanese Marks the Topic" (2.2.1), and many other topics. Shibatani's *Syntax and Semantics* has, among others, relevant articles for "Temporal Expressions in Japanese" (2.1.6), "Negation in Japanese" (2.1.7), "The Sense of Adversity in Passivization" (2.2.2., subsection), and "How the System of Honorifics Works in Japanese" (3.2.3). Kyoko Inoue's "Studies in the Perfect" is the basis of "How Japanese Represents Psychological Distance" (2.2.2., subsection), and Kuroda's "Where Epistemology, Style and Grammar Meet" is the basis of "How Japanese Distinguishes Sensations of Self and Nonself" (2.2.3). Lovins' "Loanwords and the Phonological Structure of Japanese" is an analysis of the Western loanwords relevant to "A History of Japan" (1). Li's *Subject and Topic* has several important articles. Alfonso's two volumes are excellent for those who wish to learn Japanese and also as a reference work. Martin's reference grammar is highly recommended. Doi, Miller, Reischauer, and Seward are suggested reading for a general view of Japanese history and culture.

Alfonso, Anthony. *Japanese Language Patterns: A Structural Approach*, 2 vols. Tokyo: Sophia University L. L. Center of Applied Linguistics, 1966.
Doi, Takeo. *The Anatomy of Dependence*, translated by John Bester. Tokyo: Kodansha International Ltd., 1973.
Inoue, Kyoko. "Studies in the Perfect." Ph.D. dissertation, University of Michigan, 1975. Available from University Microfilms, Ann Arbor, Michigan.
Kuno, Susumu. *The Structure of the Japanese Language*. Cambridge, Mass.: MIT Press, 1973.
Kuroda, Shige-Yuki. "Where Epistemology, Style, and Grammar Meet: A Case Study from Japanese." In *Festschrift for Morris Halle*, edited by Stephen R. Anderson and Paul Kiparsky, pp. 377–91. New York: Holt, Rinehart and Winston, 1973.
Li, Charles, ed. *Subject and Topic*. New York: Academic Press, 1976.
Lovins, Julie Beth. *Loanwords and the Phonological Structure of Japanese*. Bloomington: Indiana University Linguistics Club, 1975.
Martin, Samuel E. *A Reference Grammar of Japanese*. New Haven: Yale University Press, 1975.

Miller, Roy Andrew. *The Japanese Language.* Chicago: University of Chicago Press, 1967.

Reischauer, Edwin O. *Japan: The Story of a Nation.* Rev. ed. New York: Alfred A. Knopf, 1974.

Seward, Jack. *Japanese in Action: An Unorthodox Approach to the Spoken Language and the People Who Speak It.* 1st ed. New York: Walker/ Weatherhill, 1969.

Shibatani, Masayoshi, ed. *Syntax and Semantics: Japanese Generative Grammar,* vol. 5. New York: Academic Press, 1976.

I wish to thank Alton L. Becker, John M. Lawler, and Noriko A. McCawley for their encouragement and valuable comments on different versions of this work. My special thanks go to James D. McCawley not only for valuable comments but also for a number of valuable examples which he generously provided. I also wish to express my indebtedness to all other scholars whose work directly or indirectly contributed to my writing of this chapter.

CPSIA information can be obtained at www.ICGtesting.com
Printed in the USA
269716BV00002B/6/A